W9-AEC-214

# A Pageant of Elizabethan Poetry

# A Pageant of Elizabethan Poetry

Arranged by

Arthur Symons

Blackie & Son Limited
London Glasgow Dublin Bombay
1906

In a pageant there is much shining disorder, a happy tumult, which it needs helping sunlight, willing spectators, and a good marching music to link into any semblance of order. In this "Pageant of Elizabethan Poetry" there is indeed a scheme in the arrangement, but a scheme as loose as I could make it, and one which I have done my best to disguise. It begins buoyantly, with music and dancing and some almost wordless singing, the music and banners of the pageant; then follow the praise and celebration of wine, sleep, and content, of spring and the seasons, and then pastoral masquerades and the delight of all lovely natural growths, the triumph of nature; and then the auxiliary chronicles and canticles of fairies, Cupid, and the graces and forces outside nature; and after these some praise of poets who have praised beauty; and then the praise and delineation of beauty, a Renaissance ecstasy, ending with the later, more sophisticated, delight in "beauty's sweetest dress". Then we hear the announcement of love, and a more or less dispassionate considering of love and women, how men would love if they might and how they would have women be; and then the dispraise of love, which is the slave's homage of revolt, and the scornful weighing and valuing of women, which is mostly disappointed hope, and the hate which is itself a form of love; and then love-poems, a multitude, and of all moods, beginning with Sidney, the great love-poet of that age, and ending with Sidney, and within that circle turning as within the limits of an enchantment. The great ritual of the "Epithalamion" leads through bride-songs, dawn-songs, and slumber-songs to a lullaby which becomes sacred; and that brings us by childish and homely ways to some hymns and pious meditations, which merge into men's thoughts about the hazards of life and the meaning of the world, with a great battle coming into the midst of these things, for a moral in action; and then we see old age, and hear laments over change and fate, and because "dust hath closed Helen's eye", and the dirges and epitaphs of death, and no inconsolable conclusion.

# A PAGEANT OF ELIZABETHAN POETRY

## 1

Shake off your heavy trance!
  And leap into a dance
Such as no mortals use to tread:
  Fit only for Apollo
To play to, for the moon to lead,
  And all the stars to follow!

*Francis Beaumont.*

## 2

Orpheus with his lute made trees,
And the mountain-tops that freeze,
  Bow themselves when he did sing:
To his music plants and flowers
Ever sprung; as sun and showers
  There had made a lasting spring.

Everything that heard him play,
Even the billows of the sea,
  Hung their heads, and then lay by.
In sweet music is such art,
Killing care and grief of heart
  Fall asleep, or, hearing, die.

*Fletcher.*

3

Follow your saint, follow with accents sweet!
Haste you, sad notes, fall at her flying feet!
There, wrapped in cloud of sorrow, pity move,
And tell the ravisher of my soul I perish for her
love:
But if she scorns my never-ceasing pain,
Then burst with sighing in her sight and ne'er return
again!

All that I sang still to her praise did tend;
Still she was first, still she my songs did end:
Yet she my love and music both doth fly,
The music that her echo is and beauty's sympathy.
Then let my notes pursue her scornful flight!
It shall suffice that they were breathed and died for
her delight.

*Campion.*

4

Rose-cheeked Laura, come;
Sing thou smoothly with thy beauty's
Silent music, either other
Sweetly gracing.

Lovely forms do flow
From concent divinely framed;
Heaven is music, and thy beauty's
Birth is heavenly.

These dull notes we sing
Discords need for helps to grace them,
Only beauty purely loving
Knows no discord,

But still moves delight,
Like clear springs renewed by flowing,
Ever perfect, ever in them-
selves eternal.

*Campion.*

5

## The Shepherds' Brawl

1. We love, and have our loves rewarded.
2. We love, and are no whit regarded.
1. We find most sweet affection's snare.
2. That sweet, but sour despairful care.
1. Who can despair whom hope doth bear?
2. And who can hope that feels despair?

*All.* As without breath no pipe doth move,
No music kindly without love.

*Sidney.*

6

## A Song to the Maskers

Come down and dance ye in the toil
Of pleasure to a heat;
But if to moisture, let the oil
Of roses be your sweat.

Not only to yourselves assume
These sweets, but let them fly
From this to that, and so perfume
E'en all the standers by;

As goddess Isis when she went
Or glided through the street,
Made all that touched her, with her scent,
And whom she touched, turn sweet.

*Herrick.*

7

Come unto these yellow sands,
And then take hands:
Courtsied when you have and kissed
The wild waves whist,
Foot it featly here and there;
And, sweet sprites, the burthen bear.
Hark, hark!
Bow-wow.

The watch-dogs bark:
Bow-wow.

Hark, hark! I hear
The strain of strutting chanticleer
Cry Cock-a-diddle-dow.

*Shakespeare.*

8

Sing his praises that doth keep
Our flocks from harm,
Pan, the father of our sheep;
And arm in arm
Tread we softly in a round,
Whilst the hollow neighbouring ground
Fills the music with her sound.

Pan, oh, great god Pan, to thee
    Thus do we sing!
Thou that keep'st us chaste and free
    As the young spring;
Ever be thy honour spoke,
From that place the morn is broke,
To that place day doth unyoke!

*Fletcher.*

## 9

How should I your true love know
    From another one?
By his cockle hat and staff,
    And his sandal shoon.

He is dead and gone, lady,
    He is dead and gone;
At his head a grass-green turf,
    At his heels a stone.

*Shakespeare.*

## 10

And will he not come again?
And will he not come again?
    No, no, he is dead:
    Go to thy death-bed:
He never will come again.

His beard was as white as snow,
All flaxen was his poll:
    He is gone, he is gone,
    And we cast away moan:
God ha' mercy on his soul!

*Shakespeare.*

11

# The Mad Maid's Song

Good-morrow to the day so fair,
Good-morning, sir, to you;
Good-morrow to mine own torn hair,
Bedabbled with the dew.

Good-morning to this primrose too,
Good-morrow to each maid
That will with flowers the tomb bestrew
Wherein my love is laid.

Ah! woe is me, woe, woe is me,
Alack and well-a-day!
For pity, sir, find out that bee
Which bore my love away.

I 'll seek him in your bonnet brave,
I 'll seek him in your eyes;
Nay, now I think they 've made his grave
I' the bed of strawberries.

I 'll seek him there; I know ere this
The cold, cold earth doth shake him;
But I will go or send a kiss
By you, sir, to awake him.

Pray, hurt him not though he be dead,
He knows well who do love him,
And who with green turfs rear his head,
And who do rudely move him.

He's soft and tender (pray take heed);
With bands of cowslips bind him,
And bring him home; but 't is decreed
That I shall never find him.

*Herrick.*

## 12

Hey nonny no!
Men are fools that wish to die!
Is 't not fine to dance and sing
When the bells of death do ring?
Is 't not fine to swim in wine,
And turn upon the toe
And sing hey nonny no,
When the winds blow and the seas flow?
Hey nonny no!

*Anonymous.*

## 13

Tell me where is fancy bred,
Or in the heart or in the head?
How begot, how nourished?
Reply, reply.
It is engendered in the eyes,
With gazing fed; and fancy dies
In the cradle where it lies.
Let us all ring fancy's knell:
I 'll begin it,—Ding, dong, bell.
Ding, dong, bell.

*Shakespeare.*

## 14

Sweet Suffolk owl, so trimly dight
With feathers like a lady bright,
Thou sing'st alone, sitting by night,
Te whit, te whoo!
Thy note, that forth so freely rolls,
With shrill command the mouse controls,
And sings a dirge for dying souls,
Te whit, te whoo!

*Anonymous.*

## 15

Ha ha! ha ha! this world doth pass
Most merrily, I 'll be sworn;
For many an honest Indian ass
Goes for an Unicorn.
Farra diddle dino;
This is idle fino.

Ty hye! ty hye! O sweet delight!
He tickles this age that can
Call Tullia's ape a marmosyte
And Leda's goose a swan.
Farra diddle dino;
This is idle fino.

So so! so so! fine English days!
When false play 's no reproach:
For he that doth the coachman praise,
May safely use the coach.
Farra diddle dino;
This is idle fino.

*Anonymous.*

## 16

Jog on, jog on, the foot-path way,
And merrily hent the stile-a:
A merry heart goes all the day,
Your sad tires in a mile-a.

*Shakespeare.*

## 17

Why, let the stricken deer go weep,
The hart ungalled play;
For some must watch, while some must sleep:
So runs the world away.

*Shakespeare.*

## 18

*Œnone.* Fair and fair, and twice so fair,
As fair as any may be;
The fairest shepherd on our green,
A love for any lady.

*Paris.* Fair and fair, and twice so fair,
As fair as any may be;
Thy love is fair for thee alone,
And for no other lady.

*Œnone.* My love is fair, my love is gay,
As fresh as bin the flowers in May,
And of my love my roundelay,
My merry, merry, merry roundelay,
Concludes with Cupid's curse:
They that do change old love for new,
Pray gods they change for worse!

*Ambo Simul.* They that do change old love for new,
Pray gods they change for worse!

*Œnone.* My Love can pipe, my love can sing,
My love can many a pretty thing,
And of his lovely praises ring
My merry, merry roundelays,
Amen to Cupid's curse:
They that do change old love for new,
Pray gods they change for worse!

*Ambo Simul.* They that do change old love for new,
Pray gods they change for worse!

*Peele.*

## 19

Come, thou monarch of the vine,
Plumpy Bacchus with pink eyne!
In thy fats our cares be drowned,
With thy grapes our hairs be crowned:
Cup us, till the world go round,
Cup us, till the world go round!

*Shakespeare.*

## 20

God Lyaeus, ever young,
Ever honoured, ever sung,
Stained with blood of lusty grapes,
In a thousand lusty shapes,
Dance upon the mazer's brim,
In the crimson liquor swim;
From thy plenteous hand divine,
Let a river run with wine:
God of youth, let this day here
Enter neither care nor fear.

*Fletcher.*

## 21

# Anacreontic

Born I was to be old,
And for to die here:
After that, in the mould
Long for to lie here.
But before that day comes
Still I be bousing,
For I know in the tombs
There 's no carousing.

*Herrick.*

## 22

# The Dead Host's Welcome

'Tis late and cold; stir up the fire;
Sit close, and draw the table nigher;
Be merry, and drink wine that 's old,
A hearty medicine 'gainst a cold:
Your beds of wanton down the best,
Where you shall tumble to your rest;
I could wish you wenches too,
But I am dead, and cannot do.
Call for the best the house may ring,
Sack, white, and claret, let them bring,
And drink apace, while breath you have;
You'll find but cold drink in the grave:
Plover, partridge, for your dinner,
And a capon for the sinner,

You shall find ready when you're up,
And your horse shall have his sup:
Welcome, welcome, shall fly round,
And I shall smile, though under ground.

*Fletcher.*

23

## A Round

Now that the Spring hath filled our veins
With kind and active fire,
And made green liveries for the plains,
And every grove a quire:

Sing we a song of merry glee,
And Bacchus fill the bowl.
1. Then here's to thee; 2. And thou to me
And every thirsty soul.

Nor Care nor Sorrow e'er paid debt,
Nor never shall do mine;
I have no cradle going yet,
Not I, by this good wine.

No wife at home to send for me,
No hogs are in my ground,
No suit in law to pay a fee,
Then round, old Jockey, round.

Shear sheep that have them, cry we still,
But see that no man 'scape
To drink of the sherry,
That makes us so merry,
And plump as the lusty grape.

*Browne.*

24

# The Vision

Methought I saw, as I did dream in bed,
A crawling vine about Anacreon's head.
Flushed was his face; his hairs with oil did shine;
And, as he spake, his mouth ran o'er with wine.
Tippled he was, and tippling lisped withal;
And lisping reeled, and reeling like to fall.
A young enchantress close by him did stand,
Tapping his plump thighs with a myrtle wand:
She smiled; he kissed; and kissing, culled her too,
And being cup-shot, more he could not do.
For which, methought, in pretty anger she
Snatched off his crown, and gave the wreath to me;
Since when, methinks, my brains about do swim,
And I am wild and wanton like to him.

*Herrick.*

25

# His Farewell to Sack

Farewell, thou thing, time past so known, so dear
To me as blood to life and spirit; near,
Nay, thou more near than kindred, friend, man, wife,
Male to the female, soul to body; life
To quick action, or the warm soft side
Of the resigning, yet resisting bride.
The kiss of virgins, first fruits of the bed,
Soft speech, smooth touch, the lips, the maidenhead:
These and a thousand sweets could never be
So near or dear as thou wast once to me.

O thou, the drink of gods and angels! wine
That scatter'st spirit and lust, whose purest shine
More radiant than the summer's sunbeam shows;
Each way illustrious, brave, and like to those
Comets we see by night, whose shagged portents
Foretell the coming of some dire events,
Or some full flame which with a pride aspires,
Throwing about his wild and active fires;
'Tis thou, above nectar, O divinest soul!
Eternal in thyself, that can'st control
That which subverts whole nature, grief and care,
Vexation of the mind, and damn'd despair.
'Tis thou alone who, with thy mystic fan,
Work'st more than wisdom, art, or nature can
To rouse the sacred madness and awake
The frost-bound blood and spirits, and to make
Them frantic with thy raptures flashing through
The soul like lightning, and as active too.
'Tis not Apollo can, or those thrice three
Castalian sisters, sing, if wanting thee.
Horace, Anacreon, both had lost their fame,
Had'st thou not filled them with thy fire and flame.
Phoebean splendour! and thou, Thespian spring!
Of which sweet swans must drink before they sing
Their true paced numbers and their holy lays,
Which makes them worthy cedar and the bays.
But why, why longer do I gaze upon
Thee with the eye of admiration?
Since I must leave thee, and enforced must say
To all thy witching beauties, Go away.
But if thy whimpering looks do ask me why,
Then know that nature bids thee go, not I.
'Tis her erroneous self has made a brain
Uncapable of such a sovereign
As is thy powerful self. Prithee not smile,

Or smile more inly, lest thy looks beguile
My vows denounced in zeal, which thus much show
thee
That I have sworn but by thy looks to know thee.
Let others drink thee freely, and desire
Thee and their lips espoused, while I admire
And love thee, but not taste thee. Let my muse
Fail of thy former helps, and only use
Her inadulterate strength: what 's done by me
Hereafter shall smell of the lamp, not thee.

*Herrick*

26

## The Welcome to Sack

So soft streams meet, so springs with gladder smiles
Meet after long divorcement by the isles;
When love, the child of likeness, urgeth on
Their crystal natures to a union:
So meet stolen kisses, when the moony nights
Call forth fierce lovers to their wished delights;
So kings and queens meet when desire convinces
All thoughts but such as aim at getting princes,
As I meet thee. Soul of my life and fame!
Eternal lamp of love! whose radiant flame
Out-glares the heaven's Osiris, and thy gleams
Out-shine the splendour of his mid-day beams.
Welcome, O welcome, my illustrious spouse;
Welcome as are the ends unto my vows;
Ay! far more welcome than the happy soil
The sea-scourged merchant, after all his toil,
Salutes with tears of joy; when fires betray
The smoky chimneys of his Ithaca.

Where hast thou been so long from my embraces,
Poor pitied exile? Tell me, did thy graces
Fly discontented hence, and for a time
Did rather choose to bless another clime?
Or went'st thou to this end, the more to move me,
By thy short absence, to desire and love thee?
Why frowns my sweet? Why won't my saint confer
Favours on me, her fierce idolater?
Why are those looks, those looks the which have been
Time-past so fragrant, sickly now drawn in
Like a dull twilight? Tell me, and the fault
I'll expiate with sulphur, hair and salt;
And, with the crystal humour of the spring,
Purge hence the guilt and kill this quarrelling.
Wo't thou not smile or tell me what's amiss?
Have I been cold to hug thee, too remiss,
Too temperate in embracing? Tell me, has desire
To thee-ward died i' the embers, and no fire
Left in this raked-up ash-heap as a mark
To testify the glowing of a spark?
Have I divorced thee only to combine
In hot adultery with another wine?
True, I confess I left thee, and appeal
'Twas done by me more to confirm my zeal
And double my affection on thee, as do those
Whose love grows more inflamed by being foes.
But to forsake thee ever, could there be
A thought of such-like possibility?
When thou thyself dar'st say thy isles shall lack
Grapes before Herrick leaves Canary sack.
Thou mak'st me airy, active to be borne,
Like Iphiclus, upon the tops of corn.
Thou mak'st me nimble, as the winged hours,
To dance and caper on the heads of flowers,
And ride the sunbeams. Can there be a thing

Under the heavenly Isis that can bring
More love into my life, or can present
My genius with a fuller blandishment?
Illustrious idol! could the Egyptian seek
Help from the garlic, onion, and the leek
And pay no vows to thee, who wast their best
God, and far more transcendent than the rest?
Had Cassius, that weak water-drinker, known
Thee in thy vine, or had but tasted one
Small chalice of thy frantic liquor, he,
As the wise Cato, had approved of thee.
Had not Jove's son, that brave Tirynthian swain,
Invited to the Thesbian banquet, ta'en
Full goblets of thy generous blood, his sprite
Ne'er had kept heat for fifty maids that night.
Come, come and kiss me; love and lust commends
Thee and thy beauties; kiss, we will be friends
Too strong for fate to break us. Look upon
Me with that full pride of complexion
As queens meet queens, or come thou unto me
As Cleopatra came to Antony,
When her high carriage did at once present
To the triumvir love and wonderment.
Swell up my nerves with spirit; let my blood
Run through my veins like to a hasty flood.
Fill each part full of fire, active to do
What thy commanding soul shall put it to;
And till I turn apostate to thy love,
Which here I vow to serve, do not remove
Thy fires from me, but Apollo's curse
Blast these-like actions, or a thing that 's worse,
When these circumstants shall but live to see
The time that I prevaricate from thee.
Call me the son of beer, and then confine
Me to the tap, the toast, the turf; let wine

Ne'er shine upon me; may my numbers all
Run to a sudden death and funeral.
And last, when thee, dear spouse, I disavow,
Ne'er may prophetic Daphne crown my brow.

*Herrick.*

27

## On Himself

I fear no earthly powers,
But care for crowns of flowers;
And love to have my beard
With wine and oil besmeared.
This day I 'll drown all sorrow:
Who knows to live to-morrow?

*Herrick.*

28

Weep you no more, sad fountains;
What need you flow so fast?
Look how the snowy mountains
Heaven's sun doth gently waste!
But my sun's heavenly eyes
View not your weeping,
That now lies sleeping
Softly, now softly lies
Sleeping.

Sleep is a reconciling,
A rest that peace begets;
Doth not the sun rise smiling
When fair at even he sets?

Rest you then, rest, sad eyes!
  Melt not in weeping,
  While she lies sleeping,
Softly, now softly lies
          Sleeping.

*Anonymous.*

## 29

Dear, why should you command me to my rest,
When now the night doth summon all to sleep?
Methinks this time becometh lovers best;
Night was ordained, together friends to keep.
How happy are all other living things,
Which though the day disjoin by several flight,
The quiet evening yet together brings,
And each returns unto his love at night
O thou that art so courteous else to all,
Why shouldst thou, Night, abuse me only thus,
That every creature to his kind dost call,
And yet 't is thou dost only sever us?
  Well could I wish it would be ever day,
  If, when night comes, you bid me go away.

*Drayton.*

## 30

Sleep, Silence' child, sweet father of soft rest,
Prince, whose approach peace to all mortals brings,
Indifferent host to shepherds and to kings,
Sole comforter of minds with grief opprest;
Lo, by thy charming rod all breathing things
Lie slumbering, with forgetfulness possest,
And yet o'er me to spread thy drowsy wings
Thou spares, alas! who cannot be thy guest.

Since I am thine, O come, but with that face
To inward light which thou art wont to show,
With feigned solace ease a true-felt woe;
Or if, deaf god, thou do deny that grace,
Come as thou wilt, and what thou wilt bequeath:
I long to kiss the image of my death.

*Drummond.*

31

## Madrigal

The ivory, coral, gold,
Of breast, of lips, of hair,
So lively Sleep doth show to inward sight,
That wake I think I hold
No shadow, but my fair:
Myself so to deceive,
With long-shut eyes I shun the irksome light.
Such pleasure thus I have,
Delighting in false gleams,
If Death Sleep's brother be,
And souls relieved of sense have so sweet dreams,
That I would wish me thus to dream and die.

*Drummond.*

32

Care-charmer Sleep, son of the sable Night,
Brother to Death, in silent darkness born,
Relieve my languish, and restore the light;
With dark forgetting of my care, return!
And let the day be time enough to mourn
The shipwreck of my ill-adventured youth;
Let waking eyes suffice to wail their scorn,
Without the torment of the night's untruth

Cease, dreams, the images of day-desires,
To model forth the passions of the morrow;
Never let rising sun approve you liars,
To add more grief to aggravate my sorrow.
Still let me sleep, embracing clouds in vain,
And never wake to feel the day's disdain.

*Daniel.*

## 33

Care-charming Sleep, thou easer of all woes,
Brother to Death, sweetly thyself dispose
On this afflicted prince; fall like a cloud,
In gentle showers; give nothing that is loud,
Or painful to his slumbers; easy, light,
And as a purling stream, thou son of Night
Pass by his troubled senses; sing his pain,
Like hollow murmuring wind or silver rain;
Into this prince gently, oh, gently slide,
And kiss him into slumbers like a bride.

*Fletcher.*

## 34

Art thou poor, yet hast thou golden slumbers?
O, sweet content!
Art thou rich, yet is thy mind perplexed?
O, punishment!
Dost thou laugh to see how fools are vexed
To add to golden numbers golden numbers?
O, sweet content! O, sweet, O, sweet content!

Work apace, apace, apace, apace;
Honest labour bears a lovely face;
Then hey nonny, hey nonny, nonny!

Canst drink the waters of the crisped spring?
    O, sweet content!
Swim'st thou in wealth, yet sink'st in thine own tears?
    O, punishment!
Then he that patiently want's burden bears,
No burden bears, but is a king, a king!
    O, sweet content! O, sweet, O, sweet content!

Work apace, apace, apace, apace;
Honest labour bears a lovely face;
Then hey nonny, hey nonny, nonny!

*Dekker.*

## 35

Ah, sweet Content, where is thy mild abode?
Is it with shepherds, and light-hearted swains,
Which sing upon the downs, and pipe abroad,
Tending their flocks and cattle on the plains?
Ah, sweet Content, where dost thou safely rest?
In heaven, with angels? which the praises sing
Of Him that made, and rules at His behest,
The minds and hearts of every living thing.
Ah, sweet Content, where doth thine harbour hold?
Is it in churches, with religious men,
Which please the gods with prayers manifold,
And in their studies meditate it then?
  Whether thou dost in heaven or earth appear,
  Be where thou wilt: thou wilt not harbour here.

*Barnabe Barnes.*

## 36

Sweet are the thoughts that savour of content;
  The quiet mind is richer than a crown;
Sweet are the nights in careless slumber spent;
  The poor estate scorns fortune's angry frown;
Such sweet content, such minds, such sleep, such bliss,
Beggars enjoy, when princes oft do miss.

The homely house that harbours quiet rest,
  The cottage that affords no pride nor care,
The mean that 'grees with country music best,
  The sweet consort of mirth and music's fare,
Obscured life sets down a type of bliss;
A mind content both crown and kingdom is.

*Greene.*

## 37

Spring, the sweet Spring, is the year's pleasant king;
Then blooms each thing, then maids dance in a ring,
Cold doth not sting, the pretty birds do sing,
  Cuckoo, jug-jug, pu-we, to-witta-woo!

The palm and may make country houses gay,
Lambs frisk and play, the shepherds pipe all day,
And we hear aye birds tune this merry lay,
  Cuckoo, jug-jug, pu-we, to-witta-woo!

The fields breathe sweet, the daisies kiss our feet,
Young lovers meet, old wives a-sunning sit,
In every street these tunes our ears do greet,
  Cuckoo, jug-jug, pu-we, to-witta-woo!
    Spring, the sweet Spring!

*Nashe.*

## 38

What bird so sings, yet so does wail?
O! 't is the ravished nightingale.
"Jug, jug, jug, jug, tereu!" she cries,
And still her woes at midnight rise.
Brave prick-song! who is 't now we hear?
None but the lark so shrill and clear;
Now at heaven's gates she claps her wings,
The morn not waking till she sings.
Hark, hark, with what a pretty throat
Poor robin redbreast tunes his note!
Hark how the jolly cuckoos sing,
"Cuckoo", to welcome in the spring!
"Cuckoo", to welcome in the spring!

*Lyly.*

## 39

The earth, late choked with showers,
Is now arrayed in green;
Her bosom springs with flowers,
The air dissolves her teen:
The heavens laugh at her glory,
Yet bide I sad and sorry.

The woods are decked with leaves,
And trees are clothed gay;
And Flora, crowned with sheaves,
With oaken boughs doth play:
Where I am clothed with black,
The token of my wrack.

The birds upon the trees
  Do sing with pleasant voices,
And chant in their degrees
  Their loves and lucky choices:
When I, whilst they are singing,
With sighs mine arms am wringing.

The thrushes seek the shade,
  And I my fatal grave;
Their flight to heaven is made,
  My walk on earth I have:
They free, I thrall; they jolly,
I sad and pensive wholly.

*Lodge.*

## 40

The peaceful western wind
The winter storms hath tamed,
And Nature in each kind
The kind heat hath inflamed:
The forward buds so sweetly breathe
Out of their earthy bowers,
That heaven, which views their pomp beneath,
Would fain be decked with flowers.

See how the morning smiles
On her bright eastern hill,
And with soft steps beguiles
Them that lie slumbering still!
The music-loving birds are come
From cliffs and rocks unknown
To see the trees and briars bloom
That late were overflown.

What Saturn did destroy,
Love's Queen revives again;
And now her naked boy
Doth in the fields remain,
Where he such pleasing change doth view
In every living thing,
As if the world were born anew
To gratify the spring.

If all things life present,
Why die my comforts then?
Why suffers my content?
Am I the worst of men?
O, Beauty, be not thou accused
Too justly in this case!
Unkindly if true love be used,
'T will yield thee little grace.

*Campion.*

41

## To the Virgins, to make much of Time

Gather ye rosebuds while ye may,
Old time is still a-flying:
And this same flower that smiles to-day
To-morrow will be dying.

The glorious lamp of heaven, the sun,
The higher he 's a-getting,
The sooner will his race be run,
And nearer he 's to setting.

That age is best which is the first,
When youth and blood are warmer;
But being spent, the worse, and worst
Times still succeed the former.

Then be not coy, but use your time,
And while ye may go marry:
For having lost but once your prime
You may for ever tarry.

*Herrick.*

42

# A Description of the Spring

And now all nature seemed in love;
The lusty sap began to move;
New juice did stir the embracing vines,
And birds had drawn their valentines;
The jealous trout that now did lie,
Rose at a well-dissembled fly:
There stood my friend with patient skill,
Attending of his trembling quill.
Already were the eaves possessed
With the swift pilgrim's daubed nest:
The groves already did rejoice
In Philomel's triumphing voice.
The showers were short, the weather mild,
The morning fresh, the evening smiled.
Joan takes her neat-rubbed pail and now
She trips to milk the sand-red cow;
Where, for some sturdy football swain,
Joan strokes a sillabub or twain.
The field and gardens were beset
With tulip, crocus, violet;

And now, though late, the modest rose
Did more than half a blush disclose.
Thus all looked gay, all full of cheer,
To welcome the new-liveried year.

*Wotton.*

## 43

O, the month of May, the merry month of May,
So frolic, so gay, and so green, so green, so green!
O, and then did I unto my true love say,
Sweet Peg, thou shalt be my Summer's Queen.

Now the nightingale, the pretty nightingale,
The sweetest singer in all the forest quire,
Entreats thee, sweet Peggy, to hear thy true love's tale:
Lo, yonder she sitteth, her breast against a briar.

But O, I spy the cuckoo, the cuckoo, the cuckoo;
See where she sitteth; come away, my joy:
Come away, I prithee, I do not like the cuckoo
Should sing where my Peggy and I kiss and toy.

O, the month of May, the merry month of May,
So frolic, so gay, and so green, so green, so green;
And then did I unto my true love say,
Sweet Peg, thou shalt be my Summer's Queen.

*Ben Jonson.*

## 44

It was a lover and his lass,
With a hey, and a ho, and a hey nonino,
That o'er the green corn-field did pass
In the spring time, the only pretty ring time,
When birds do sing, hey ding a ding, ding:
Sweet lovers love the spring.

Between the acres of the rye,
  With a hey, and a ho, and a hey nonino,
These pretty country folks would lie,
  In spring time, the only pretty ring time,
When birds do sing, hey ding a ding, ding:
Sweet lovers love the spring.

This carol they began that hour,
  With a hey, and a ho, and a hey nonino,
How that a life was but a flower
  In spring time, the only pretty ring time,
When birds do sing, hey ding a ding, ding:
Sweet lovers love the spring.

And therefore take the present time,
  With a hey, and a ho, and a hey nonino;
For love is crowned with the prime
  In spring time, the only pretty ring time,
When birds do sing, hey ding a ding, ding:
Sweet lovers love the spring.

*Shakespeare.*

45

# The Hamadryad's Song

Pluck the fruit and taste the pleasure,
  Youthful lordings, of delight;
Whilst occasion gives you seizure,
  Feed your fancies and your sight:
After death, when you are gone,
Joy and pleasure is there none.

Here on earth is nothing stable,
  Fortune's changes well are known;

Whilst as youth doth then enable,
  Let your seeds of joy be sown:
After death, when you are gone,
Joy and pleasure is there none

Feast it freely with your lovers,
  Blithe and wanton sports do fade,
Whilst that lovely Cupid hovers
  Round about this lovely shade:
Sport it freely one to one,
After death is pleasure none.

Now the pleasant spring allureth,
  And both place and time invites:
But, alas! what heart endureth
  To disclaim his sweet delights?
After death, when we are gone,
Joy and pleasure is there none.

*Lodge.*

## 46

When daffodils begin to peer,
  With heigh! the doxy over the dale,
Why, then comes in the sweet o' the year;
  For the red blood reigns in the winter's pale.

The white sheet bleaching on the hedge,
  With heigh! the sweet birds, O, how they sing!
Doth set my pugging tooth on edge;
  For a quart of ale is a dish for a king.

The lark, that tirra-lyra chants,
  With heigh! with heigh! the thrush and the jay,
Are summer songs for me and my aunts,
  While we lie tumbling in the hay.

*Shakespeare.*

## 47

Under the greenwood tree
Who loves to lie with me,
And turn his merry note
Unto the sweet bird's throat,
Come hither, come hither, come hither:
Here shall he see
No enemy
But winter and rough weather.

Who doth ambition shun
And loves to live i' the sun,
Seeking the food he eats
And pleased with what he gets,
Come hither, come hither, come hither:
Here shall he see
No enemy
But winter and rough weather.

*Shakespeare.*

## 48

The merry cuckoo, messenger of spring,
His trumpet shrill hath thrice already sounded,
That warns all lovers wait upon their king,
Who now is coming forth with garland crowned.
With noise whereof the choir of birds resounded,
Their anthems sweet, devised of love's praise,
That all the woods their echoes back rebounded,
As if they knew the meaning of their lays.
But 'mongst them all, which did love's honour raise,
No word was heard of her that most it ought;

But she his precept proudly disobeys,
And doth his idle message set at naught.
Therefore, O love, unless she turn to thee
Ere cuckoo end, let her a rebel be!

*Spenser.*

49

New year, forth looking out of Janus' gate,
Doth seem to promise hope of new delight:
And bidding the old adieu, his passed date
Bids all old thoughts to die in dumpish spright:
And, calling forth out of sad winter's night
Fresh Love, that long hath slept in cheerless bower,
Wills him awake, and soon about him dight
His wanton wings and darts of deadly power.
For lusty Spring now in his timely hour
Is ready to come forth, him to receive;
And warns the earth with divers-coloured flower
To deck herself, and her fair mantle weave.
Then you, fair flower, in whom fresh youth doth reign,
Prepare yourself new love to entertain.

*Spenser.*

50

## Corinna's Going A-Maying

Get up, get up for shame, the blooming morn
Upon her wings presents the god unshorn.
See how Aurora throws her fair
Fresh-quilted colours through the air:
Get up, sweet slug-a-bed, and see
The dew bespangling herb and tree.

Each flower has wept and bowed toward the east
Above an hour since: yet you not dressed;
Nay! not so much as out of bed?
When all the birds have matins said
And sung their thankful hymns, 't is sin,
Nay, profanation to keep in,
Whereas a thousand virgins on this day
Spring, sooner than the lark, to fetch in May.

Rise and put on your foliage, and be seen
To come forth, like the spring-time, fresh and green,
And sweet as Flora. Take no care
For jewels for your gown or hair:
Fear not; the leaves will strew
Gems in abundance upon you:
Besides, the childhood of the day has kept,
Against you come, some orient pearls unwept;
Come and receive them while the light
Hangs on the dew-locks of the night:
And Titan on the eastern hill
Retires himself, or else stands still
Till you come forth. Wash, dress, be brief in praying:
Few beads are best when once we go a-Maying.

Come, my Corinna, come; and, coming, mark
How each field turns a street, each street a park
Made green, and trimmed with trees: see how
Devotion gives each house a bough
Or branch: each porch, each door ere this
An ark, a tabernacle is,
Made up of white-thorn neatly interwove;
As if here were those cooler shades of love.
Can such delights be in the street
And open fields and we not see 't?

Come, we 'll abroad; and let 's obey
The proclamation made for May:
And sin no more, as we have done, by staying;
But, my Corinna, come, let 's go a-Maying.

There 's not a budding boy or girl this day
But is got up, and gone to bring in May.
A deal of youth, ere this, is come
Back, and with white-thorn laden, home.
Some have despatched their cakes and cream
Before that we have left to dream:
And some have wept, and wooed, and plighted troth,
And chose their priest, ere we can cast off sloth:
Many a green-gown has been given;
Many a kiss, both odd and even:
Many a glance too has been sent
From out the eye, love's firmament;
Many a jest told of the keys betraying
This night, and locks picked, yet we 're not a-Maying.

Come, let us go while we are in our prime;
And take the harmless folly of the time.
We shall grow old apace, and die
Before we know our liberty.
Our life is short, and our days run
As fast away as does the sun;
And, as a vapour or a drop of rain
Once lost, can ne'er be found again,
So when or you or I are made
A fable, song, or fleeting shade,
All love, all liking, all delight
Lies drowned with us in endless night.
Then while time serves, and we are but decaying,
Come, my Corinna, come, let 's go a-Maying.

*Herrick.*

## 51

### *Spring*

When daisies pied and violets blue
  And lady-smocks all silver-white
And cuckoo-buds of yellow hue
  Do paint the meadows with delight,
The cuckoo then, on every tree,
Mocks married men; for thus sings he,
          Cuckoo;
Cuckoo, cuckoo: O word of fear,
Unpleasing to a married ear!

When shepherds pipe on oaten straws
  And merry larks are ploughmen's clocks,
When turtles tread, and rooks, and daws,
  And maidens bleach their summer smocks,
The cuckoo then, on every tree,
Mocks married men; for thus sings he,
          Cuckoo;
Cuckoo, cuckoo: O word of fear,
Unpleasing to a married ear!

### *Winter*

When icicles hang by the wall
  And Dick the shepherd blows his nail
And Tom bears logs into the hall
  And milk comes frozen home in pail,
When blood is nipped and ways be foul,
Then nightly sings the staring owl,
          Tu-whit;
Tu-who, a merry note,
While greasy Joan doth keel the pot.

When all aloud the wind doth blow
  And coughing drowns the parson's saw
And birds sit brooding in the snow
  And Marian's nose looks red and raw,
When roasted crabs hiss in the bowl,
Then nightly sings the staring owl,
        Tu-whit;
Tu-who, a merry note,
While greasy Joan doth keel the pot.

*Shakespeare.*

## 52

From you have I been absent in the spring,
When proud-pied April dressed in all his trim
Hath put a spirit of youth in everything,
That heavy Saturn laughed and leaped with him.
Yet nor the lays of birds nor the sweet smell
Of different flowers in odour and in hue
Could make me any summer's story tell,
Or from their proud lap pluck them where they grew;
Nor did I wonder at the lily's white,
Nor praise the deep vermilion in the rose;
They were but sweet, but figures of delight,
Drawn after you, you pattern of all those.
  Yet seemed it winter still, and, you away,
  As with your shadow I with these did play.

*Shakespeare.*

## 53

My love is strengthened, though more weak in
seeming;
I love not less, though less the show appear:
That love is merchandized whose rich esteeming
The owner's tongue doth publish everywhere.
Our love was new and then but in the spring
When I was wont to greet it with my lays,
As Philomel in summer's front doth sing
And stops her pipe in growth of riper days:
Not that the summer is less pleasant now
Than when her mournful hymns did hush the night,
But that wild music burthens every bough
And sweets grown common lose their dear delight.
Therefore like her I sometime hold my tongue,
Because I would not dull you with my song.

*Shakespeare.*

## 54

How like a winter hath my absence been
From thee, the pleasure of the fleeting year!
What freezings have I felt, what dark days seen!
What old December's bareness everywhere!
And yet this time removed was summer's time,
The teeming autumn, big with rich increase,
Bearing the wanton burthen of the prime,
Like widowed wombs after their lord's decease:
Yet this abundant issue seemed to me
But hope of orphans and unfathered fruit;
For summer and his pleasures wait on thee,
And, thou away, the very birds are mute;
Or, if they sing, 't is with so dull a cheer
That leaves look pale, dreading the winter's near.

*Shakespeare.*

## 55

Blow, blow, thou winter wind,
Thou art not so unkind
As man's ingratitude;
Thy tooth is not so keen,
Because thou art not seen,
Although thy breath be rude.
Heigh-ho! sing, heigh-ho! unto the green holly:
Most friendship is feigning, most loving mere folly:
Then heigh-ho, the holly!
This life is most jolly.

Freeze, freeze, thou bitter sky,
That dost not bite so nigh
As benefits forgot:
Though thou the waters warp,
Thy sting is not so sharp
As friend remembered not.
Heigh-ho! sing, heigh-ho! unto the green holly:
Most friendship is feigning, most loving mere folly:
Then heigh-ho, the holly!
This life is most jolly.

*Shakespeare.*

## 56

Now winter nights enlarge
The number of their hours;
And clouds their storms discharge
Upon the airy towers.
Let now the chimneys blaze
And cups o'erflow with wine,
Let well-tuned words amaze
With harmony divine!

Now yellow waxen lights
Shall wait on honey love,
While youthful revels, masques, and courtly sights,
Sleep's leaden spells remove.

This time doth well dispense
With lovers' long discourse;
Much speech hath some defence,
Though beauty no remorse.
All do not all things well;
Some measures comely tread,
Some knotted riddles tell,
Some poems smoothly read.
The summer hath his joys,
And winter his delights;
Though love and all his pleasures are but toys,
They shorten tedious nights.

*Campion.*

57

## The Passionate Shepherd to his Love

Come live with me and be my love,
And we will all the pleasures prove
That hills and valleys, dales and fields,
Woods, or steepy mountain yields.

And we will sit upon the rocks,
Seeing the shepherds feed their flocks
By shallow rivers, to whose falls
Melodious birds sing madrigals.

And I will make thee beds of roses,
And a thousand fragrant posies;
A cap of flowers, and a kirtle
Embroidered all with leaves of myrtle;

A gown made of the finest wool
Which from our pretty lambs we pull;
Fair-lined slippers for the cold,
With buckles of the purest gold;

A belt of straw and ivy-buds,
With coral clasps and amber studs;
And if these pleasures may thee move,
Come live with me, and be my love.

The shepherd-swains shall dance and sing
For thy delight each May-morning;
If these delights thy mind may move,
Then live with me, and be my love.

*Marlowe.*

58

## To Phyllis, to Love and Live with Him

Live, live with me, and thou shalt see
The pleasures I'll prepare for thee;
What sweets the country can afford
Shall bless thy bed and bless thy board.
The soft, sweet moss shall be thy bed
With crawling woodbine over-spread;
By which the silver-shedding streams
Shall gently melt thee into dreams.

Thy clothing, next, shall be a gown
Made of the fleece's purest down.
The tongues of kids shall be thy meat,
Their milk thy drink; and thou shalt eat
The paste of filberts for thy bread
With cream of cowslips buttered;
Thy feasting-tables shall be hills
With daisies spread and daffodils,
Where thou shalt sit, and red-breast by,
For meat, shall give thee melody.
I'll give thee chains and carcanets
Of primroses and violets.
A bag and bottle thou shalt have,
That richly wrought, and this as brave;
So that as either shall express
The wearer's no mean shepherdess.
At shearing-times, and yearly wakes,
When Themilis his pastime makes,
There thou shalt be; and be the wit,
Nay, more, the feast, and grace of it.
On holidays, when virgins meet
To dance the heyes with nimble feet,
Thou shalt come forth, and then appear
The queen of roses for that year;
And having danced, 'bove all the best,
Carry the garland from the rest.
In wicker baskets maids shall bring
To thee, my dearest shepherdling,
The blushing apple, bashful pear,
The shame-faced plum, all simpering there.
Walk in the groves, and thou shalt find
The name of Phyllis in the rind
Of every straight and smooth-skin tree;
Where kissing that, I'll twice kiss thee.
To thee a sheep-hook I will send,

Be-pranked with ribands to this end,
This, this alluring hook might be
Less for to catch a sheep than me.
Thou shalt have possets, wassails fine,
Not made of ale, but spiced wine,
To make thy maids and self free mirth,
All sitting near the glittering hearth.
Thou shalt have ribands, roses, rings,
Gloves, garters, stockings, shoes and strings
Of winning colours, that shall move
Others to lust, but me to love.
These, nay, and more, thine own shall be
If thou wilt love, and live with me.

*Herrick.*

59

# The River-God's Song

Do not fear to put thy feet
Naked in the river sweet;
Think not leech, or newt, or toad,
Will bite thy foot, when thou hast trod;
Nor let the water rising high,
As thou wad'st in, make thee cry
And sob; but ever live with me,
And not a wave shall trouble thee!

*Fletcher.*

60

## Daffodil

*Batte*

Gorbo, as thou camest this way,
By yonder little hill,
Or as thou through the fields did stray,
Saw'st thou my Daffodil?

She's in a frock of Lincoln green,
Which colour likes her sight,
And never hath her beauty seen,
But through a veil of white;

Than roses richer to behold,
That trim up lovers' bowers,
The pansy and the marigold,
Though Phoebus' paramours.

*Gorbo*

Thou well describ'st the daffodil;
It is not full an hour,
Since by the spring, near yonder hill,
I saw that lovely flower.

*Batte*

Yet my fair flower thou didst not meet
Nor news of her didst bring,
And yet my Daffodil's more sweet
Than that by yonder spring.

*Gorbo*

I saw a shepherd that doth keep
In yonder field of lilies,
Was making (as he fed his sheep)
A wreath of daffodillies.

*Batte*

Yet, Gorbo, thou delud'st me still,
My flower thou didst not see;
For, know, my pretty Daffodil
Is worn of none but me.

To show itself but near her feet
No lily is so bold,
Except to shade her from the heat,
Or keep her from the cold.

*Gorbo*

Through yonder vale as I did pass,
Descending from the hill,
I met a smirking bonny lass,
They call her Daffodil:

Whose presence, as along she went,
The pretty flowers did greet,
As though their heads they downward bent
With homage to her feet.

And all the shepherds that were nigh,
From top of every hill,
Unto the valleys loud did cry,
There goes sweet Daffodil.

Ay, gentle shepherd, now with joy
  Thou all my flocks dost fill,
That's she alone, kind shepherd boy;
  Let us to Daffodil.

*Drayton.*

61

## Phyllida and Corydon

In the merry month of May,
In a morn by break of day,
Forth I walked by the woodside
Whenas May was in his pride:
There I spied all alone
Phyllida and Corydon.
Much ado there was, God wot!
He would love and she would not.
She said, never man was true;
He said, none was false to you.
He said, he had loved her long;
She said, Love should have no wrong.
Corydon would kiss her then;
She said, maids must kiss no men
Till they did for good and all;
Then she made the shepherd call
All the heavens to witness truth
Never loved a truer youth.
Thus with many a pretty oath,
Yea and nay, and faith and troth,
Such as silly shepherds use
When they will not Love abuse,

Love, which long had been deluded,
Was with kisses sweet concluded;
And Phyllida, with garlands gay,
Was made the Lady of the May.

*Nicholas Breton.*

62

## The Ballad of Dowsabel

Far in the country of Arden,
There wonned a knight, hight Cassamen,
As bold as Isenbras:
Fell was he and eager bent,
In battle and in tournament,
As was the good Sir Topas.

He had, as antique stories tell,
A daughter cleped Dowsabel,
A maiden fair and free:
And for she was her father's heir,
Full well she was yconned the leir
Of mickle courtesy.

The silk well couth she twist and twine,
And make the fine march-pine,
And with the needle work:
And she couth help the priest to say
His matins on a holyday,
And sing a psalm in kirk.

She wore a frock of frolic green,
Might well become a maiden queen,
Which seemly was to see:

A hood to that so neat and fine,
In colour like the columbine,
  Ywrought full featously

Her features all as fresh above,
As is the grass that grows by Dove,
  And lythe as lass of Kent:
Her skin as soft as Lemster wool,
As white as snow on Peakish Hull,
  Or swan that swims in Trent.

This maiden in a morn betime,
Went forth when May was in the prime,
  To get sweet setywall,
The honey-suckle, the harlock,
The lily, and the lady-smock,
  To deck her summer hall.

Thus as she wandered here and there,
And picked of the bloomy briar,
  She chanced to espy
A shepherd sitting on a bank,
Like chanticleer he crowed crank,
  And piped full merrily.

He learned his sheep, as he him list,
When he would whistle in his fist,
  To feed about him round,
Whilst he full many a carol sang,
Until the fields and meadows rang,
  And that the woods did sound.

In favour this same shepherd swain
Was like the bedlam Tamberlane,
  Which held proud kings in awe:

But meek as any lamb mought be,
And innocent of ill as he
  Whom his lewd brother slaw.

This shepherd wore a sheep-gray cloak,
Which was of the finest loke
  That could be cut with sheer.
His mittons were of bauzons' skin,
His cockers were of cordiwin,
  His hood of miniver.

His awl and lingel in a thong,
His tar-box on his broad belt hung,
  His breech of Cointree blue;
Full crisp and curled were his locks,
His brows as white as Albion rocks,
  So like a lover true.

And piping still he spent the day,
So merry as the popinjay,
  Which liked Dowsabel;
That would she ought, or would she nought,
This lad would never from her thought,
  She in love-longing fell.

At length she tucked up her frock,
White as a lily was her smock,
  She drew the shepherd nigh:
But then the shepherd piped a good,
That all his sheep forsook their food,
  To hear his melody.

"Thy sheep," quoth she, "cannot be lean,
That have a jolly shepherd swain,
  The which can pipe so well."

"Yea, but," saith he, "their shepherd may,
If piping thus he pine away,
In love of Dowsabel."

"Of love, fond boy, take thou no keep,"
Quoth she, "look well unto thy sheep,
Lest they should hap to stray."
Quoth he, "So had I done full well,
Had I not seen fair Dowsabel
Come forth to gather May."

With that she 'gan to vail her head,
Her cheeks were like the roses red,
But not a word she said;
With that the shepherd 'gan to frown,
He threw his pretty pipes adown,
And on the ground him laid.

Saith she, "I may not stay till night,
And leave my summer hall undight,
And all for love of thee."
"My cote," saith he, "nor yet my fold,
Shall neither sheep nor shepherd hold,
Except thou favour me."

Saith she, "Yet liever I were dead,
Than I should lose my maidenhead,
And all for love of men."
Saith he, "Yet are you too unkind,
If in your heart you cannot find
To love us now and then.

"And I to thee will be as kind,
As Colin was to Rosalind,
Of courtesy the flower."

"Then will I be as true," quoth she,
"As ever maiden yet might be,
Unto her paramour."

With that she bent her snow-white knee,
Down by the shepherd kneeled she,
And him she sweetly kissed.
With that the shepherd whooped for joy.
Quoth he, "There's never shepherd's boy
That ever was so blist."

*Drayton.*

63

## Doron and Carmela

*Doron.* Sit down, Carmela; here are cobs for kings,
Sloes black as jet or like my Christmas shoes,
Sweet cider which my leathern bottle brings;
Sit down, Carmela, let me kiss thy toes.

*Carmela.* Ah Doron! Ah my heart! thou art as white
As is my mother's calf or brinded cow;
Thine eyes are like the slow-worms in the night;
Thine hairs resemble thickest of the snow.

The lines within thy face are deep and clear
Like to the furrows of my father's wain;
The sweat upon thy face doth oft appear
Like to my mother's fat and kitchen-gain.

# The Third Pastor's Song

Who can live in heart so glad
As the merry country lad?
Who upon a fair green baulk
May at pleasure sit and walk,
And amid the azure skies
See the morning sun arise;
While he hears in every spring
How the birds do chirp and sing;
Or, before the hounds in cry,
See the hare go stealing by;
Or, along the shallow brook
Angling with a baited hook,
See the fishes leap and play
In a blessed sunny day;
Or to hear the partridge call
Till she have her covey all;
Or to see the subtle fox,
How the villain plies the box,
After feeding on his prey
How he closely sneaks away,
Through the hedge and down the furrow
Till he gets into his burrow;
Then the bee to gather honey,
And the little black-haired coney
On a bank for sunny place
With her forefeet wash her face:
Are not these, with thousands moe
Than the courts of kings do know,
The true pleasing spirit's sights,
That may breed true love's delights?

But with all this happiness,
To behold that shepherdess
To whose eyes all shepherds yield
All the fairest of the field,
Fair Aglaia, in whose face
Lives the shepherd's highest grace;
In whose worthy wonder's praise
See what her true shepherd says.
She is neither proud nor fine,
But in spirit more divine;
She can neither lour nor leer,
But a sweeter smiling cheer;
She had never painted face,
But a sweeter smiling grace;
She can never love dissemble,
Truth doth so her thoughts assemble,
That when wisdom guides her will
She is kind and constant still.
All in sum, she is that creature
Of that truest comfort's nature
That doth show (but in exceedings)
How their praises had their breedings.
Let then poets feign their pleasure
In their fictions of love's treasure;
Proud high spirits seek their graces
In their idol painted faces;
My love's spirit's lowliness,
In affection's humbleness,
Under heaven no happiness
Seeks, but in this shepherdess.
For whose sake I say and swear,
By the passions that I bear,
Had I got a kingly grace,
I would leave my kingly place,
And in heart be truly glad

To become a country lad;
Hard to lie, and go full bare,
And to feed on hungry fare;
So I might but live to be,
Where I might but sit to see
Once a day, or all day long,
The sweet subject of my song;
In Aglaia's only eyes
All my worldly Paradise.

*Nicholas Breton.*

## 65

Jack and Joan, they think no ill,
But loving live, and merry still;
Do their week-day's work, and pray
Devoutly on the holy day:
Skip and trip it on the green,
And help to choose the Summer Queen;
Lash out, at a country feast,
Their silver penny with the best.

Well can they judge of nappy ale,
And tell at large a winter tale;
Climb up to the apple loft,
And turn the crabs till they be soft.
Tib is all the father's joy,
And little Tom the mother's boy.
All their pleasure is content;
And care, to pay their yearly rent.

Joan can call by name her cows,
And deck her windows with green boughs;
She can wreaths and tuttyes make,
And trim with plums a bridal cake.

Jack knows what brings gain or loss;
And his long flail can stoutly toss:
Makes the hedge which others break;
And ever thinks what he doth speak.

Now, you courtly dames and knights,
That study only strange delights;
Though you scorn the home-spun gray,
And revel in your rich array:
Though your tongues dissemble deep,
And can your heads from danger keep;
Yet, for all your pomp and train,
Securer lives the silly swain.

*Campion.*

66

# His Grange, or Private Wealth

Though clock,
To tell how night draws hence, I 've none,
A cock
I have to sing how day draws on.
I have
A maid, my Prew, by good luck sent
To save
That little Fates me gave or lent.
A hen
I keep, which, creeking day by day,
Tells when
She goes her long white egg to lay.
A goose
I have, which with a jealous ear
Lets loose
Her tongue to tell that danger 's near.

A lamb
I keep (tame) with my morsels fed,
Whose dam
An orphan left him (lately dead).
A cat
I keep, that plays about my house,
Grown fat
With eating many a miching mouse.
To these
A Tracy I do keep whereby
I please
The more my rural privacy;
Which are
But toys to give my heart some ease;
Where care
None is, slight things do lightly please.

*Herrick.*

67

## To Lar

No more shall I, since I am driven hence,
Devote to thee my grains of frankincense;
No more shall I from mantle-trees hang down,
To honour thee, my little parsley crown;
No more shall I (I fear me) to thee bring
My chives of garlic for an offering;
No more shall I from henceforth hear a choir
Of merry crickets by my country fire.
Go where I will, thou lucky Lar stay here,
Warm by a glittering chimney all the year.

*Herrick.*

# The Shepherd's Wife's Song

Ah, what is Love? It is a pretty thing,
As sweet unto a shepherd as a king;
And sweeter too;
For kings have cares that wait upon a crown,
And cares can make the sweetest love to frown:
Ah then, ah then,
If country loves such sweet desires do gain,
What lady would not love a shepherd swain?

His flocks are folded, he comes home at night,
As merry as a king in his delight;
And merrier too;
For kings bethink then what the state require,
Where shepherds careless carol by the fire:
Ah then, ah then,
If country loves such sweet desires do gain,
What lady would not love a shepherd swain?

He kisseth first, then sits as blithe to eat
His cream and curds as doth a king his meat;
And blither too;
For kings have often fears when they do sup,
Where shepherds dread no poison in their cup:
Ah then, ah then,
If country loves such sweet desires do gain,
What lady would not love a shepherd swain?

To bed he goes, as wanton then, I ween,
As is a king in dalliance with a queen;
More wanton too;
For kings have many griefs affects to move,

Where shepherds have no greater grief than love:
Ah then, ah then,
If country loves such sweet desires do gain,
What lady would not love a shepherd swain?

Upon his couch of straw he sleeps as sound
As doth a king upon his beds of down;
More sounder too;
For cares cause kings full oft their sleep to spill,
Where weary shepherds lie and snort their fill:
Ah then, ah then,
If country loves such sweet desires do gain,
What lady would not love a shepherd swain?

Thus with his wife he spends the year as blithe
As doth the king at every tide or sithe;
And blither too;
For kings have wars and broils to take in hand,
Where shepherds laugh and love upon the land:
Ah then, ah then,
If country loves such sweet desires do gain,
What lady would not love a shepherd swain?

*Greene.*

69

# Perigot and Willy's Roundelay

*Perigot.* It fell upon a holy eve,
*Willy.* (Hey-ho, holy day!)
*Perigot.* When holy fathers wont to shrieve,
*Willy.* (Now 'ginneth this roundelay),
*Perigot.* Sitting upon a hill so high,
*Willy.* (Hey-ho, the high hill!)
*Perigot.* The while my flock did feed thereby,
*Willy.* The while the shepherd's self did spill;

*Perigot.* I saw the bouncing Bellibone,
*Willy.* (Hey-ho, Bonnibell!)
*Perigot.* Tripping over the dale alone;
*Willy.* (She can trip it very well:)
*Perigot.* Well decked in a frock of gray,
*Willy.* (Hey-ho, gray is greet!)
*Perigot.* And in a kirtle of green say
*Willy.* (The green is for maidens meet).
*Perigot.* A chapelet on her head she wore,
*Willy.* (Hey-ho, the chapelet!)
*Perigot.* Of sweet violets therein was store,
*Willy.* She sweeter than the violet.
*Perigot.* My sheep did leave their wonted food,
*Willy.* (Hey-ho, silly sheep!)
*Perigot.* And gazed on her as they were wood,
*Willy.* Wood as he that did them keep.

*Perigot.* As the bonny lass passed by,
*Willy.* (Hey-ho, bonny lass!)
*Perigot.* She roved at me with glancing eye,
*Willy.* As clear as the crystal glass:
*Perigot.* All as the sunny beam so bright
*Willy.* (Hey-ho, the sunbeam!)
*Perigot.* Glanceth from Phoebus' face forthright,
*Willy.* So love into my heart did stream.

*Perigot.* Or as the thunder cleaves the clouds,
*Willy.* (Hey-ho, the thunder!)
*Perigot.* Wherein the lightsome levin shrouds,
*Willy.* So cleaves thy soul asunder;
*Perigot.* Or as Dame Cynthia's silver ray
*Willy.* (Hey-ho, the moonlight!)
*Perigot.* Upon the glittering wave doth play,
*Willy.* Such play is a piteous plight:

*Perigot.* The glance into my heart did glide,
*Willy.* (Hey-ho, the glider!)
*Perigot.* Therewith my soul was sharply gride;
*Willy.* Such wounds soon waxen wider.
*Perigot.* Hasting to wrench the arrow out,
*Willy.* (Hey-ho, Perigot!)
*Perigot.* I left the head in my heart-root.
*Willy.* It was a desperate shot.

*Perigot.* There it rankleth aye more and more,
*Willy.* (Hey-ho, the arrow!)
*Perigot.* Nor can I find salve for my sore:
*Willy.* (Love is a cureless sorrow.)
*Perigot.* And though my bale with death I bought,
*Willy.* (Hey-ho, heavy cheer!)
*Perigot.* Yet should thilk lass not from my thought.
*Willy.* So you may buy gold too dear.

*Perigot.* But whether in painful love I pine,
*Willy.* (Hey-ho, pinching pain!)
*Perigot.* Or thrive in wealth, she shall be mine:
*Willy.* But if thou can her obtain.
*Perigot.* And if for graceless grief I die,
*Willy.* (Hey-ho, graceless grief!)
*Perigot.* Witness, she slew me with her eye.
*Willy.* Let thy folly be the prief.

*Perigot.* And you that saw it, simple sheep,
*Willy.* (Hey-ho, the fair flock!)
*Perigot.* For prief thereof my death shall weep
*Willy.* And moan with many a mock.
*Perigot.* So learned I love on a holy eve,
*Willy.* (Hey-ho, holy day!)
*Perigot.* That ever since my heart did grieve:
*Willy.* Now endeth our roundelay.

*Spenser.*

# The Palmer's Ode

Old Menalcas, on a day,
As in field this shepherd lay,
Tuning of his oaten pipe,
Which he hit with many a stripe,
Said to Corydon that he
Once was young and full of glee.
"Blithe and wanton was I then:
Such desires follow men.
As I lay and kept my sheep,
Came the God that hateth sleep,
Clad in armour all of fire,
Hand in hand with queen Desire,
And with a dart that wounded nigh,
Pierced my heart as I did lie;
That when I woke I 'gan swear
Phyllis beauty's palm did bear.
Up I start, forth went I,
With her face to feed mine eye;
There I saw Desire sit,
That my heart with love had hit,
Laying forth bright beauty's hooks
To entrap my gazing looks.
Love I did, and 'gan to woo,
Pray and sigh; all would not do:
Women, when they take the toy,
Covet to be counted coy.
Coy she was, and I 'gan court;
She thought love was but a sport;
Profound hell was in my thought;
Such a pain Desire had wrought,

That I sued with sighs and tears;
Still ingrate she stopped her ears,
Till my youth I had spent.
Last a passion of repent
Told me flat, that Desire
Was a brand of love's fire,
Which consumeth men in thrall,
Virtue, youth, wit, and all.
At this saw, back I start,
Beat Desire from my heart,
Shook off Love, and made an oath
To be enemy to both.
Old I was when thus I fled
Such fond toys as cloyed my head,
But this I learned at Virtue's gate,
The way to good is never late."

*Greene.*

## 71

The ousel cock so black of hue,
  With orange-tawny bill,
The throstle with his note so true,
  The wren with little quill,

The finch, the sparrow, and the jay,
  The plain-song cuckoo gray,
Whose note full many a man doth mark
  And dares not answer nay.

*Shakespeare.*

72

## Upon a Fly

A golden fly one showed to me,
Closed in a box of ivory,
Where both seemed proud: the fly to have
His burial in an ivory grave;
The ivory took state to hold
A corpse as bright as burnished gold.
One fate hath both, both equal grace;
The buried, and the burying-place.
Not Virgil's gnat, to whom the spring
All flowers sent to 's burying;
Not Martial's bee, which in a bead
Of amber quick was buried;
Nor that fine worm that does inter
Herself i' the silken sepulchre;
Nor my rare Phil, that lately was
With lillies tombed up in a glass;
More honour had than this same fly,
Dead, and closed up in ivory.

*Herrick.*

73

## To Violets

Welcome, maids-of-honour,
You do bring
In the spring,
And wait upon her.

She has virgins many,
Fresh and fair;
Yet you are
More sweet than any.

You 're the maiden posies,
And so graced
To be placed
'Fore damask roses.

Yet, though thus respected,
By and by
Ye do lie,
Poor girls, neglected.

*Herrick.*

74

## To Daffodils

Fair daffodils, we weep to see
You haste away so soon;
As yet the early-rising sun
Has not attained his noon.
Stay, stay,
Until the hasting day
Has run
But to the evensong;
And, having prayed together, we
Will go with you along.

We have short time to stay, as you,
We have as short a spring;
As quick a growth to meet decay,
As you, or anything.

We die,
As your hours do, and dry
Away,
Like to the summer's rain;
Or as the pearls of morning's dew,
Ne'er to be found again.

*Herrick.*

75

## To Blossoms

Fair pledges of a fruitful tree,
Why do ye fall so fast?
Your date is not so past
But you may stay yet here a while,
To blush and gently smile;
And go at last.

What! were ye born to be
An hour or half's delight,
And so to bid good-night?
'Twas pity Nature brought ye forth
Merely to show your worth,
And lose you quite.

But you are lovely leaves, where we
May read how soon things have
Their end, though ne'er so brave:
And after they have shown their pride
Like you a while, they glide
Into the grave.

*Herrick.*

# To Meadows

Ye have been fresh and green,
   Ye have been filled with flowers,
And ye the walks have been
   Where maids have spent their hours.

You have beheld how they
   With wicker arks did come
To kiss and bear away
   The richer cowslips home.

You 've heard them sweetly sing,
   And seen them in a round:
Each virgin like a spring,
   With honeysuckles crowned.

But now we see none here
   Whose silvery feet did tread,
And with dishevelled hair
   Adorned this smoother mead.

Like unthrifts, having spent
   Your stock and needy grown,
You 're left here to lament
   Your poor estates, alone.

*Herrick.*

77

# To Primroses Filled with Morning Dew

Why do ye weep, sweet babes? can tears
Speak grief in you,
Who were but born
Just as the modest morn
Teemed her refreshing dew?
Alas! you have not known that shower
That mars a flower,
Nor felt the unkind
Breath of a blasting wind,
Nor are ye worn with years,
Or warped as we,
Who think it strange to see
Such pretty flowers, like to orphans young,
To speak by tears before ye have a tongue.

Speak, whimpering younglings, and make known
The reason why
Ye droop and weep;
Is it for want of sleep?
Or childish lullaby?
Or that ye have not seen as yet
The violet?
Or brought a kiss
From that sweetheart to this?
No, no, this sorrow shown
By your tears shed
Would have this lecture read:
That things of greatest, so of meanest worth,
Conceived with grief are, and with tears brought forth.

*Herrick.*

78

## The Primrose

Ask me why I send you here
This sweet Infanta of the year?
Ask me why I send to you
This primrose, thus bepearled with dew?,
I will whisper to your ears:
The sweets of love are mixed with tears.

Ask me why this flower does show
So yellow-green, and sickly too?
Ask me why the stalk is weak
And bending (yet it does not break)?
I will answer: These discover
What fainting hopes are in a lover.

*Herrick.*

79

## To the Nightingale

Dear quirister, who from those shadows sends,
Ere that the blushing dawn dare show her light,
Such sad lamenting strains, that night attends
(Become all ear), stars stay to hear thy plight;
If one whose grief even reach of thought transcends,
Who ne'er (not in a dream) did taste delight,
May thee importune who like case pretends,
And seems to joy in woe, in woe's despite;
Tell me (so may thou fortune milder try,
And long, long sing) for what thou thus complains,

Sith, winter gone, the sun in dappled sky
Now smiles on meadows, mountains, woods, and
plains?
The bird, as if my questions did her move,
With trembling wings sobbed forth, I love, I love!

*Drummond.*

80

Phoebus, arise,
And paint the sable skies
With azure, white, and red;
Rouse Memnon's mother from her Tithon's bed,
That she thy career may with roses spread;
The nightingales thy coming each where sing;
Make an eternal spring,
Give life to this dark world which lieth dead;
Spread forth thy golden hair
In larger locks than thou was wont before,
And, emperor-like, decore
With diadem of pearl thy temples fair:
Chase hence the ugly night,
Which serves but to make dear thy glorious light.
This is that happy morn,
That day, long-wished day,
Of all my life so dark
(If cruel stars have not my ruin sworn,
And fates not hope betray),
Which, only white, deserves
A diamond for ever should it mark:
This is the morn should bring unto this grove
My love, to hear and recompense my love.
Fair king, who all preserves,
But show thy blushing beams,
And thou two sweeter eyes

Shalt see, than those which by Peneus' streams
Did once thy heart surprise;
Nay, suns, which shine as clear
As thou when two thou did to Rome appear.
Now, Flora, deck thyself in fairest guise;
If that ye, winds, would hear
A voice surpassing far Amphion's lyre,
Your stormy chiding stay;
Let zephyr only breathe,
And with her tresses play,
Kissing sometimes those purple ports of death.
The winds all silent are,
And Phoebus in his chair,
Ensaffroning sea and air,
Makes vanish every star:
Night like a drunkard reels
Beyond the hills to shun his flaming wheels;
The fields with flowers are decked in every hue,
The clouds bespangle with bright gold their blue:
Here is the pleasant place,
And every thing, save her, who all should grace.

*Drummond.*

## 81

I walked along a stream, for pureness rare,
Brighter than sunshine; for it did acquaint
The dullest sight with all the glorious prey
That in the pebble-paved channel lay.

No molten crystal, but a richer mine,
Even Nature's rarest alchemy ran there;
Diamonds resolved, and substance more divine,
Through whose bright gliding current might appear

A thousand naked nymphs, whose ivory shine,
Enamelling the banks, made them more dear
Than ever was that glorious Palace gate
Where the day-shining Sun in triumph sate.

Upon this brim the eglantine and rose,
The tamarisk, olive, and the almond tree,
As kind companions, in one union grows,
Folding their twining arms, as oft we see
Turtle-taught lovers, either other close,
Lending to dullness feeling sympathy;
And as a costly vallance o'er a bed,
So did their garland tops the brook o'erspread.

Their leaves, that differed both in shape and show,
Though all were green, yet difference such in green,
Like to the checkered bent of Iris' bow,
Prided the running main, as it had been. . . .

*Marlowe.*

82

# The Funeral Rites of the Rose

The rose was sick, and smiling died;
And, being to be sanctified,
About the bed there sighing stood
The sweet and flowery sisterhood.
Some hung the head, while some did bring,
To wash her, water from the spring.
Some laid her forth, while other wept,
But all a solemn fast there kept.
The holy sisters, some among,
The sacred dirge and trentall sung.

But ah! what sweets smelt everywhere,
As heaven had spent all perfumes there.
At last, when prayers for the dead
And rites were all accomplished,
They, weeping, spread a lawny loom
And closed her up, as in a tomb.

*Herrick.*

## 83

A rose, as fair as ever saw the North,
Grew in a little garden all alone;
A sweeter flower did Nature ne'er put forth,
Nor fairer garden yet was ever known;
The maidens danced about it morn and noon,
And learned bards of it their ditties made;
The nimble fairies by the pale-faced moon
Watered the root and kissed her pretty shade.
But well-a-day, the gardener careless grew,
The maids and fairies both were kept away,
And in a drought the caterpillars threw
Themselves upon the bud and every spray.
God shield the stock! if heaven send no supplies,
The fairest blossom of the garden dies.

*Browne.*

84

# Nymphidia

## The Court of Fairy

Old Chaucer doth of Topas tell,
Mad Rabelais of Pantagruel,
A later third of Dowsabel,
    With such poor trifles playing;
Others the like have laboured at,
Some of this thing and some of that,
And many of they know not what,
    But that they must be saying.

Another sort there be, that will
Be talking of the Fairies still,
Nor never can they have their fill,
    As they were wedded to them;
No tales of them their thirst can slake,
So much delight therein they take,
And some strange thing they fain would make,
    Knew they the way to do them.

Then since no Muse hath been so bold,
Or of the later, or the old,
Those elvish secrets to unfold,
    Which lie from others' reading,
My active Muse to light shall bring
The Court of that proud Fairy King,
And tell there of the revelling:
    Jove prosper my proceeding!

And thou, Nymphidia, gentle Fay,
Which, meeting me upon the way,
These secrets didst to me bewray,
    Which now I am in telling;
My pretty, light, fantastic maid,
I here invoke thee to my aid,
That I may speak what thou hast said,
    In numbers smoothly swelling.

This palace standeth in the air,
By necromancy placed there,
That it no tempests needs to fear,
    Which way soe'er it blow it;
And somewhat southward toward the noon,
Whence lies a way up to the moon,
And thence the Fairy can as soon
    Pass to the earth below it.

The walls of spiders' legs are made
Well mortised and finely laid;
He was the master of his trade
    It curiously that builded;
The windows of the eyes of cats,
And for the roof, instead of slats,
Is covered with the skins of bats,
    With moonshine that are gilded.

Hence Oberon him sport to make,
Their rest when weary mortals take,
And none but only fairies wake,
    Descendeth for his pleasure;
And Mab, his merry Queen, by night
Bestrides young folks that lie upright
(In elder times, the mare that hight),
    Which plagues them out of measure.

Hence shadows, seeming idle shapes,
Of little frisking elves and apes
To earth do make their wanton scapes,
As hope of pastime hastes them;
Which maids think on the hearth they see
When fires well-near consumed be,
There dancing hays by two and three,
Just as their fancy casts them.

These make our girls their sluttery rue,
By pinching them both black and blue,
And put a penny in their shoe
The house for cleanly sweeping;
And in their courses make that round
In meadows and in marshes found,
Of them so called the Fairy Ground,
Of which they have the keeping.

These when a child haps to be got
Which after proves an idiot
When folk perceive it thriveth not,
The fault therein to smother,
Some silly, doting, brainless calf
That understands things by the half,
Say that the Fairy left this aulfe
And took away the other.

But listen, and I shall you tell
A chance in Fairy that befell,
Which certainly may please some well
In love and arms delighting,
Of Oberon that jealous grew
Of one of his own Fairy crew,
Too well, he feared, his Queen that knew
His love but ill requiting.

Pigwiggen was this Fairy Knight,
One wondrous gracious in the sight
Of fair Queen Mab, which day and night
He amorously observed;
Which made King Oberon suspect
His service took too good effect,
His sauciness and often checkt,
And could have wished him starved

Pigwiggen gladly would commend
Some token to Queen Mab to send,
If sea or land could ought him lend
Were worthy of her wearing;
At length this lover doth devise
A bracelet made of emmets' eyes,
A thing he thought that she would prize,
No whit her state impairing.

And to the Queen a letter writes,
Which he most curiously indites,
Conjuring her by all the rites
Of love, she would be pleased
To meet him, her true servant, where
They might, without suspect or fear,
Themselves to one another clear
And have their poor hearts eased.

" At midnight the appointed hour,
And for the Queen a fitting bower,"
Quoth he, " is that fair cowslip flower
On Hipcut hill that bloweth:
In all your train there 's not a fay
That ever went to gather may
But she hath made it, in her way;
The tallest there that groweth."

When by Tom Thumb, a Fairy Page,
He sent it, and doth him engage
By promise of a mighty wage
    It secretly to carry;
Which done, the Queen her maids doth call,
And bids them to be ready all:
She would go see her summer hall,
    She could no longer tarry.

Her chariot ready straight is made,
Each thing therein is fitting laid,
That she by nothing might be stayed,
    For nought must her be letting;
Four nimble gnats the horses were,
Their harnesses of gossamer,
Fly Cranion her charioteer
    Upon the coach-box getting.

Her chariot of a snail's fine shell,
Which for the colours did excel,
The fair Queen Mab becoming well,
    So lively was the limning;
The seat the soft wool of the bee,
The cover, gallantly to see,
The wing of a pied butterflee;
    I trow 't was simple trimming.

The wheels composed of crickets' bones,
And daintily made for the nonce,
For fear of rattling on the stones
    With thistle-down they shod it;
For all her maidens much did fear
If Oberon had chanced to hear
That Mab his Queen should have been there,
    He would not have abode it.

She mounts her chariot with a trice,
Nor would she stay, for no advice,
Until her maids that were so nice
To wait on her were fitted;
But ran herself away alone,
Which when they heard, there was not one
But hasted after to be gone,
As she had been diswitted.

Hop and Mop and Drop so clear,
Pip and Trip and Skip that were
To Mab, their sovereign, ever dear,
Her special maids of honour;
Fib and Tib and Pink and Pin,
Tick and Quick and Jill and Jin,
Tit and Nit and Wap and Win,
The train that wait upon her.

Upon a grasshopper they got
And, what with amble and with trot,
For hedge nor ditch they spared not,
But after her they hie them;
A cobweb over them they throw,
To shield the wind if it should blow,
Themselves they wisely could bestow
Lest any should espy them.

But let us leave Queen Mab awhile
(Through many a gate, o'er many a stile,
That now had gotten by this wile),
Her dear Pigwiggen kissing;
And tell how Oberon doth fare,
Who grew as mad as any hare
When he had sought each place with care
And found his Queen was missing.

By grisly Pluto he doth swear,
He rent his clothes and tore his hair,
And as he runneth here and there
    An acorn cup he greeteth,
Which soon he taketh by the stalk,
About his head he lets it walk,
Nor doth he any creature balk,
    But lays on all he meeteth.

The Tuscan poet doth advance
The frantic Paladin of France,
And those more ancient do enhance
    Alcides in his fury,
And others Ajax Telamon,
But to this time there hath been none
So bedlam as our Oberon,
    Of which I dare assure ye.

And first encountering with a Wasp,
He in his arms the fly doth clasp
As though his breath he forth would grasp
    Him for Pigwiggen taking:
"Where is my wife, thou rogue?" quoth he;
"Pigwiggen, she is come to thee;
Restore her, or thou diest by me!"
    Whereat the poor Wasp quaking,

Cries, "Oberon, great Fairy King,
Content thee, I am no such thing:
I am a Wasp, behold my sting!"
    At which the Fairy started;
When soon away the Wasp doth go,
Poor wretch, was never frighted so;
He thought his wings were much too slow,
    O'erjoyed they so were parted.

He next upon a Glow-worm light
(You must suppose it now was night),
Which, for her hinder part was bright,
He took to be a devil,
And furiously doth her assail
For carrying fire in her tail;
He thrashed her rough coat with his flail;
The mad King feared no evil.

"Oh!" quoth the Glow-worm, "hold thy hand,
Thou puissant King of Fairy-land!
Thy mighty strokes who may withstand?
Hold, or of life despair I!"
Together then herself doth roll,
And tumbling down into a hole,
She seemed as black as any coal;
Which vext away the Fairy.

From thence he ran into a hive:
Amongst the bees he letteth drive,
And down their combs begins to rive,
All likely to have spoiled,
Which with their wax his face besmeared,
And with their honey daubed his beard:
It would have made a man afeared
To see how he was moiled.

A new adventure him betides;
He met an Ant, which he bestrides,
And post thereon away he rides,
Which with his haste doth stumble,
And came full over on her snout;
Her heels so threw the dirt about,
For she by no means could get out,
But over him doth tumble.

And being in this piteous case,
And all be-slurred head and face,
On runs he in this wild-goose chase,
As here and there he rambles;
Half blind, against a molehole hit,
And for a mountain taking it,
For all he was out of his wit
Yet to the top he scrambles.

And being gotten to the top,
Yet there himself he could not stop,
But down on the other side doth chop,
And to the foot came rumbling;
So that the grubs, therein that bred,
Hearing such turmoil overhead,
Thought surely they had all been dead;
So fearful was the jumbling.

And falling down into a lake,
Which him up to the neck doth take,
His fury somewhat it doth slake;
He calleth for a ferry;
Where you may some recovery note,
What was his club he made his boat,
And in his oaken cup doth float,
As safe as in a wherry.

Men talk of the adventures strange
Of Don Quishott, and of their change,
Through which he armed oft did range,
Of Sancha Pancha's travel;
But should a man tell everything
Done by this frantic Fairy King,
And them in lofty numbers sing,
It well his wits might gravel.

Scarce set on shore, but therewithal
He meeteth Puck, which most men call
Hobgoblin, and on him doth fall
With words from frenzy spoken:
"Ho, ho," quoth Hob, "God save thy grace!
Who drest thee in this piteous case?
He thus that spoiled my sovereign's face,
I would his neck were broken!"

This Puck seems but a dreaming dolt,
Still walking like a ragged colt,
And oft out of a bush doth bolt,
Of purpose to deceive us;
And leading us makes us to stray,
Long winter's nights, out of the way;
And when we stick in mire and clay,
Hob doth with laughter leave us.

"Dear Puck," quoth he, "my wife is gone:
As e'er thou lov'st King Oberon,
Let everything but this alone,
With vengeance and pursue her;
Bring her to me alive or dead,
Or that vile thief Pigwiggen's head;
That villain hath defiled my bed,
He to this folly drew her."

Quoth Puck, "My liege, I'll never lin,
But I will thorough thick and thin,
Until at length I bring her in;
My dearest lord, ne'er doubt it.
Thorough brake, thorough briar,
Thorough muck, thorough mire,
Thorough water, thorough fire;
And thus goes Puck about it."

This thing Nymphidia overheard,
That on this mad King had a guard,
Not doubting of a great reward
    For first this business broaching;
And through the air away doth go,
Swift as an arrow from the bow,
To let her sovereign Mab to know
    What peril was approaching.

The Queen bound with Love's powerful'st charm
Sate with Pigwiggen arm in arm;
Her merry maids, that thought no harm,
    About the room were skipping;
A humble-bee, their minstrel, played,
Upon his hautboy, every maid
Fit for this revel was arrayed,
    The hornpipe neatly tripping.

In comes Nymphidia, and doth cry,
"My sovereign, for your safety fly,
For there is danger but too nigh;
    I posted to forewarn you:
The King hath sent Hobgoblin out,
To seek you all the fields about,
And of your safety you may doubt
    If he but once discern you."

When, like an uproar in a town,
Before them everything went down;
Some tore a ruff, and some a gown,
    'Gainst one another justling;
They flew about like chaff i' the wind;
For haste some left their masks behind;
Some could not stay their gloves to find;
    There never was such bustling.

Forth ran they, by a secret way,
Into a brake that near them lay;
Yet much they doubted there to stay,
    Lest Hob should hap to find them;
He had a sharp and piercing sight,
All one to him the day and night;
And therefore were resolved by flight
    To leave this place behind them.

At length one chanced to find a nut,
In the end of which a hole was cut,
Which lay upon a hazel root,
    There scattered by a squirrel
Which out the kernel gotten had;
When quoth this Fay, "Dear Queen, be glad;
Let Oberon be ne'er so mad,
    I'll set you safe from peril.

"Come all into this nut," quoth she,
"Come closely in; be ruled by me;
Each one may here a chooser be,
    For room ye need not wrastle:
Nor need ye be together heapt;"
So one by one therein they crept,
And lying down they soundly slept,
    And safe as in a castle.

Nymphidia, that this while doth watch,
Perceived if Puck the Queen should catch
That he should be her over-match,
    Of which she well bethought her;
Found it must be some powerful charm,
The Queen against him that must arm,
Or surely he would do her harm,
    For throughly he had sought her.

And listening if she aught could hear,
That her might hinder, or might fear,
But finding still the coast was clear,
Nor creature had descried her;
Each circumstance and having scanned,
She came thereby to understand,
Puck would be with them out of hand;
When to her charms she hied her.

And first her fern-seed doth bestow,
The kernel of the mistletoe;
And here and there as Puck should go,
With terror to affright him,
She nightshade straws to work him ill,
Therewith her vervain and her dill,
That hindereth witches of their will,
Of purpose to despite him.

Then sprinkles she the juice of rue,
That groweth underneath the yew;
With nine drops of the midnight dew,
From lunary distilling:
The molewarp's brain mixed therewithal;
And with the same the pismire's gall:
For she in nothing short would fall,
The Fairy was so willing.

Then thrice under a briar doth creep,
Which at both ends was rooted deep,
And over it three times she leap,
Her magic much availing:
Then on Proserpina doth call,
And so upon her spell doth fall,
Which here to you repeat I shall,
Not in one tittle failing.

"By the croaking of the frog,
By the howling of the dog,
By the crying of the hog
  Against the storm arising;
By the evening curfew bell,
By the doleful dying knell,
O let this my direful spell,
  Hob, hinder thy surprising!

"By the mandrake's dreadful groans,
By the lubrican's sad moans,
By the noise of dead men's bones
  In charnel-houses rattling;
By the hissing of the snake,
The rustling of the fire-drake,
I charge thee thou this place forsake,
  Nor of Queen Mab be prattling!

"By the whirlwind's hollow sound,
By the thunder's dreadful stound,
Yells of spirits underground,
  I charge thee not to fear us;
By the screech-owl's dismal note,
By the black night-raven's throat,
I charge thee, Hob, to tear thy coat
  With thorns, if thou come near us!"

Her spell thus spoke, she stept aside,
And in a chink herself doth hide,
To see thereof what would betide,
  For she doth only mind him:
When presently she Puck espies,
And well she marked his gloating eyes,
How under every leaf he pries,
  In seeking still to find them.

But once the circle got within,
The charms to work do straight begin,
And he was caught as in a gin;
    For as he thus was busy,
A pain he in his head-piece feels,
Against a stubbed tree he reels,
And up went poor Hobgoblin's heels;
    Alas! his brain was dizzy!

At length upon his feet he gets,
Hobgoblin fumes, Hobgoblin frets;
And as again he forward sets,
    And through the bushes scrambles,
A stump doth trip him in his pace;
Down comes poor Hob upon his face,
And lamentably tore his case,
    Amongst the briars and brambles.

" A plague upon Queen Mab!" quoth he,
" And all her maids where'er they be:
I think the devil guided me,
    To seek her so provoked!"
When stumbling at a piece of wood,
He fell into a ditch of mud,
Where to the very chin he stood,
    In danger to be choked.

Now worse than e'er he was before,
Poor Puck doth yell, poor Puck doth roar,
That waked Queen Mab, who doubted sore
    Some treason had been wrought her:
Until Nymphidia told the Queen,
What she had done, what she had seen,
Who then had well-near cracked her spleen
    With very extreme laughter.

But leave we Hob to clamber out,
Queen Mab and all her Fairy rout,
And come again to have a bout
    With Oberon yet madding:
And with Pigwiggen now distraught,
Who much was troubled in his thought,
That he so long the Queen had sought,
    And through the fields was gadding.

And as he runs he still doth cry,
"King Oberon, I thee defy,
And dare thee here in arms to try,
    For my dear lady's honour:
For that she is a Queen right good,
In whose defence I'll shed my blood,
And that thou in this jealous mood
    Hast laid this slander on her."

And quickly arms him for the field,
A little cockle-shell his shield,
Which he could very bravely wield,
    Yet could it not be pierced:
His spear a bent both stiff and strong,
And well-near of two inches long:
The pile was of a horse-fly's tongue,
    Whose sharpness nought reversed.

And puts him on a coat of mail,
Which was of a fish's scale,
That when his foe should him assail,
    No point should be prevailing:
His rapier was a hornet's sting;
It was a very dangerous thing,
For if he chanced to hurt the King,
    It would be long in healing.

His helmet was a beetle's head,
Most horrible and full of dread,
That able was to strike one dead,
    Yet did it well become him;
And for a plume a horse's hair
Which, being tossed with the air,
Had force to strike his foe with fear,
    And turn his weapon from him.

Himself he on an earwig set,
Yet scarce he on his back could get,
So oft and high he did curvet,
    Ere he himself could settle:
He made him turn, and stop, and bound,
To gallop and to trot the round,
He scarce could stand on any ground,
    He was so full of mettle.

When soon he met with Tomalin,
One that a valiant knight had been,
And to King Oberon of kin;
    Quoth he, "Thou manly Fairy,
Tell Oberon I come prepared,
Then bid him stand upon his guard;
This hand his baseness shall reward,
    Let him be ne'er so wary.

"Say to him thus, that I defy
His slanders and his infamy,
And as a mortal enemy
    Do publicly proclaim him:
Withal that if I had mine own,
He should not wear the Fairy crown,
But with a vengeance should come down,
    Nor we a king should name him."

This Tomalin could not abide
To hear his sovereign vilified;
But to the Fairy Court him hied
(Full furiously he posted),
With everything Pigwiggen said:
How title to the crown he laid,
And in what arms he was arrayed,
As how himself he boasted.

'Twixt head and foot, from point to point,
He told the arming of each joint,
In every piece how neat and quaint,
For Tomalin could do it:
How fair he sat, how sure he rid,
As of the courser he bestrid,
How managed, and how well he did;
The King which listened to it,

Quoth he, "Go, Tomalin, with speed,
Provide me arms, provide my steed,
And everything that I shall need;
By thee I will be guided;
To straight account call thou thy wit;
See there be wanting not a whit,
In everything see thou me fit,
Just as my foe 's provided."

Soon flew this news through Fairy-land,
Which gave Queen Mab to understand
The combat that was then in hand
Betwixt those men so mighty:
Which greatly she began to rue,
Perceiving that all Fairy knew,
The first occasion from her grew
Of these affairs so weighty.

Wherefore attended with her maids,
Through fogs, and mists, and damps she wades,
To Proserpine the Queen of Shades,
    To treat, that it would please her
The cause into her hands to take,
For ancient love and friendship's sake,
And soon thereof an end to make,
    Which of much care would ease her.

A while there let we Mab alone,
And come we to King Oberon,
Who, armed to meet his foe, is gone,
    For proud Pigwiggen crying:
Who sought the Fairy King as fast,
And had so well his journeys cast,
That he arrived at the last,
    His puissant foe espying.

Stout Tomalin came with the King,
Tom Thumb doth on Pigwiggen bring,
That perfect were in everything
    To single fights belonging:
And therefore they themselves engage
To see them exercise their rage
With fair and comely equipage,
    Not one the other wronging.

So like in arms these champions were,
As they had been a very pair,
So that a man would almost swear
    That either had been either;
Their furious steeds began to neigh,
That they were heard a mighty way;
Their staves upon their rests they lay;
    Yet, ere they flew together,

Their seconds minister an oath,
Which was indifferent to them both,
That on their knightly faith and troth
No magic them supplied;
And sought them that they had no charms
Wherewith to work each other's harms,
But came with simple open arms
To have their causes tried.

Together furiously they ran,
That to the ground came horse and man,
The blood out of their helmets span,
So sharp were their encounters;
And though they to the earth were thrown,
Yet quickly they regained their own,
Such nimbleness was never shown,
They were two gallant mounters.

When in a second course again,
They forward came with might and main,
Yet which had better of the twain,
The seconds could not judge yet;
Their shields were into pieces cleft,
Their helmets from their heads were reft,
And to defend them nothing left,
These champions would not budge yet.

Away from them their staves they threw,
Their cruel swords they quickly drew,
And freshly they the fight renew,
They every stroke redoubled;
Which made Proserpina take heed,
And make to them the greater speed,
For fear lest they too much should bleed,
Which wondrously her troubled.

When to the infernal Styx she goes,
She takes the fogs from thence that rose,
And in a bag doth them enclose,
When well she had them blended.
She hies her then to Lethe spring,
A bottle and thereof doth bring,
Wherewith she meant to work the thing
Which only she intended.

Now Proserpine with Mab is gone
Unto the place where Oberon
And proud Pigwiggen, one to one,
Both to be slain were likely:
And there themselves they closely hide,
Because they would not be espied;
For Proserpine meant to decide
The matter very quickly.

And suddenly unties the poke,
Which out of it sent such a smoke,
As ready was them all to choke,
So grievous was the pother;
So that the knights each other lost,
And stood as still as any post;
Tom Thumb nor Tomalin could boast
Themselves of any other.

But when the mist 'gan somewhat cease
Proserpina commandeth peace;
And that a while they should release
Each other of their peril;
"Which here," quoth she, "I do proclaim
To all in dreadful Pluto's name,
That as ye will eschew his blame,
You let me hear the quarrel:

"But here yourselves you must engage
Somewhat to cool your spleenish rage;
Your grievous thirst and to assuage
That first you drink this liquor,
Which shall your understanding clear,
As plainly shall to you appear;
Those things from me that you shall hear
Conceiving much the quicker."

This Lethe water, you must know,
The memory destroyeth so,
That of our weal, or of our woe,
Is all remembrance blotted;
Of it nor can you ever think;
For they no sooner took this drink,
But nought into their brains could sink
Of what had them besotted.

King Oberon forgotten had
That he for jealousy ran mad,
But of his Queen was wondrous glad,
And asked how they came thither:
Pigwiggen likewise doth forget
That he Queen Mab had ever met,
Or that they were so hard beset,
When they were found together.

Nor neither of them both had thought
That e'er they had each other sought,
Much less that they a combat fought,
But such a dream were loathing:
Tom Thumb had got a little sup,
And Tomalin scarce kissed the cup,
Yet had their brains so sure locked up,
That they remembered nothing.

Queen Mab and her light maids, the while,
Amongst themselves do closely smile,
To see the King caught with this wile,
With one another jesting:
And to the Fairy Court they went
With mickle joy and merriment,
Which thing was done with good intent,
And thus I left them feasting.

*Drayton.*

## 85

Over hill, over dale,
Thorough bush, thorough brier,
Over park, over pale,
Thorough flood, thorough fire,
I do wander every where,
Swifter than the moon's sphere;
And I serve the fairy queen,
To dew her orbs upon the green.
The cowslips tall her pensioners be:
In their gold coats spots you see;
Those be rubies, fairy favours,
In those freckles live their savours:
I must go seek some dewdrops here
And hang a pearl in every cowslip's ear.
Farewell, thou lob of spirits; I'll be gone:
Our queen and all her elves come here anon.

*Shakespeare.*

## 86

Now the hungry lion roars,
  And the wolf behowls the moon;
Whilst the heavy ploughman snores,
  All with weary task fordone.
Now the wasted brands do glow,
  Whilst the screech-owl, screeching loud,
Puts the wretch that lies in woe
  In remembrance of a shroud.
Now it is the time of night
  That the graves all gaping wide,
Every one lets forth his sprite,
  In the church-way paths to glide:
And we fairies, that do run
  By the triple Hecate's team,
From the presence of the sun,
  Following darkness like a dream,
Now are frolic: not a mouse
Shall disturb this hallowed house:
I am sent with broom before,
To sweep the dust behind the door.

*Shakespeare.*

## 87

Where the bee sucks there suck I:
In a cowslip's bell I lie;
There I couch when owls do cry.
On the bat's back I do fly,
After summer merrily.
Merrily, merrily shall I live now
Under the blossom that hangs on the bough.

*Shakespeare.*

## 88

Buzz! quoth the Blue-Fly,
    Hum! quoth the Bee;
Buzz and hum! they cry,
    And so do we.
In his ear! in his nose!
    Thus,—do you see?
He eats the Dormouse—
    Else it was he.

*Ben Jonson.*

## 89

# Song of the Cyclops

Brave iron, brave hammer, from your sound
The art of music has her ground;
On the anvil thou keep'st time,
Thy knick-a-knock is a smith's best chime.
    Yet thwick-a-thwack, thwick, thwack-a-thwack,
        thwack,
    Make our brawny sinews crack:
    Then pit-a-pat, pat, pit-a-pat, pat,
    Till thickest bars be beaten flat.

We shoe the horses of the sun,
Harness the dragons of the moon;
Forge Cupid's quiver, bow, and arrows,
And our dame's coach that 's drawn with sparrows.
    Till thwick-a-thwack, &c.

Jove's roaring cannons and his rammers
We beat out with our Lemnian hammers;
Mars his gauntlet, helm, and spear,
And Gorgon shield are all made here.
   Till thwick-a-thwack, &c.

The grate which, shut, the day outbars,
Those golden studs, which nail the stars,
The globe's case and the axle-tree,
Who can hammer these but we?
   Till thwick-a-thwack, &c.

A warming-pan to heat earth's bed,
Lying i' the frozen zone half-dead;
Hob-nails to serve the man i' the moon,
And sparrowbills to clout Pan's shoon
   Whose work but ours?
   Till thwick-a-thwack, &c.

Venus' kettles, pots, and pans
We make, or else she brawls and bans;
Tongs, shovels, and irons have their places,
Else she scratches all our faces.
   Till thwick-a-thwack, &c.

*Dekker.*

90

## The Witches' Sabbath

### 1. *Charm*

Dame, dame! the watch is set:
Quickly come, we all are met.
From the lakes and from the fens,
From the rocks and from the dens,
From the woods and from the caves,
From the churchyards, from the graves,
From the dungeon, from the tree
That they die on, here are we!
(Comes she not yet?
Strike another heat!)

### 2. *Charm*

The weather is fair, the wind is good:
Up, dame, on your horse of wood!
Or else tuck up your gray frock,
And saddle your goat on your green cock,
And make his bridle a bottom of thread
To roll up how many miles you have rid.
Quickly come away,
For we all stay.
(Nor yet? nay then
We'll try her again.)

### 3. *Charm*

The owl is abroad, the bat and the toad,
And so is the cat-a-mountain;
The ant and the mole sit both in a hole,
And the frog peeps out o' the fountain.

The dogs they do bay, and the timbrels play,
  The spindle is now a-turning;
The moon it is red, and the stars are fled,
  But all the sky is a-burning:
The ditch is made, and our nails the spade,
With pictures full, of wax and of wool:
Their livers I stick with needles quick;
There lacks but the blood to make up the flood.
Quickly, dame, then bring your part in!
Spur, spur upon little Martin!
Merrily, merrily, make him sail,
A worm in his mouth and a thorn in his tail,
Fire above, and fire below,
With a whip in your hand to make him go!
    (O now she 's come!
    Let all be dumb.)

*Ben Jonson.*

91

# The Fay's Marriage

MERTILLA, CLAIA, CLORIS

*A Nymph is married to a Fay,*
*Great preparations for the day;*
*All rites of nuptials they recite you,*
*To the bridal and invite you.*

*Mertilla*

But will our Tita wed this Fay?

*Claia*

Yea, and to-morrow is the day.

*Mertilla*

But why should she bestow herself
Upon this dwarfish fairy elf?

*Claia*

Why, by her smallness you may find
That she is of the fairy kind,
And therefore apt to choose her make
Whence she did her beginning take:
Besides he 's deft and wondrous airy,
And of the noblest of the Fairy,
Chief of the Crickets of much fame,
In Fairy a most ancient name.
But to be brief, 't is clearly done,
The pretty wench is wooed and won.

*Cloris*

If this be so, let us provide
The ornaments to fit our bride;
For they knowing she doth come
From us in Elysium,
Queen Mab will look she should be drest
In those attires we think our best;
Therefore some curious things let 's give her,
Ere to her spouse we her deliver.

*Mertilla*

I'll have a jewel for her ear
(Which for my sake I'll have her wear),
'T shall be a dew-drop, and therein
Of Cupids I will have a twin,

Which struggling, with their wings shall break
The bubble, out of which shall leak
So sweet a liquor, as shall move
Each thing that smells to be in love.

*Claia*

Believe me, girl, this will be fine,
And, to this pendent, then take mine:
A cup in fashion of a fly,
Of the lynx's piercing eye,
Wherein there sticks a sunny ray,
Shot in through the clearest day,
Whose brightness Venus' self did move
Therein to put her drink of love,
Which for more strength she did distil,
The limbeck was a phoenix' quill;
At this cup's delicious brink,
A fly approaching but to drink,
Like amber, or some precious gum,
It transparent doth become.

*Cloris*

For jewels for her ears she 's sped;
But for a dressing for her head
I think for her I'll have a tire
That all Fairies shall admire:
The yellows in the full-blown rose,
Which in the top it doth inclose,
Like drops of gold ore shall be hung
Upon her tresses, and among
Those scattered seeds (the eye to please)
The wings of the cantharides:

With some o' the rainbow that doth rail
Those moons in, in the peacock's tail:
Whose dainty colours, being mixed
With the other beauties, and so fixed,
Her lovely tresses shall appear
As though upon a flame they were.
And, to be sure she shall be gay,
We'll take those feathers from the jay;
About her eyes in circlets set,
To be our Tita's coronet.

*Mertilla*

Then, dainty girls, I make no doubt,
But we shall neatly send her out:
But let's amongst ourselves agree
Of what her wedding gown shall be.

*Claia*

Of pansy, pink, and primrose leaves,
Most curiously laid on in threaves:
And, all embroidery to supply,
Powdered with flowers of rosemary;
A trail about the skirt shall run,
The silk-worm's finest, newly spun;
And every seam the nymphs shall sew
With the smallest of the spinner's clue:
And having done their work, again
These to the church shall bear her train:
Which for our Tita we will make
Of the cast slough of a snake,
Which, quivering as the wind doth blow,
The sun shall it like tinsel show.

*Cloris*

And being led to meet her mate,
To make sure that she want no state,
Moons from the peacock's tail we'll shred,
With feathers from the pheasant's head:
Mixed with the plume of, so high price,
The precious bird of paradise;
Which to make up our nymphs shall ply
Into a curious canopy,
Borne o'er her head, by our enquiry,
By elfs, the fittest of the Fairy.

*Mertilla*

But all this while we have forgot
Her buskins, neighbours, have we not?

*Claia*

We had, for those I'll fit her now,
They shall be of the lady-cow:
The dainty shell upon her back
Of crimson strewed with spots of black;
Which as she holds a stately pace,
Her leg will wonderfully grace.

*Cloris*

But then for music of the best,
This must be thought on for the feast.

*Mertilla*

The nightingale of birds most choice
To do her best shall strain her voice;

And to this bird to make a set,
The mavis, merle, and robinet,
The lark, the linnet, and the thrush,
That make a choir of every bush.
But for still music, we will keep
The wren, and titmouse, which to sleep
Shall sing the bride, when she's alone,
The rest into their chambers gone.
And, like those upon ropes that walk,
On gossamer, from stalk to stalk,
The tripping fairy tricks shall play
The evening of the wedding-day.

*Claia*

But, for the bride-bed, what were fit,
That hath not yet been talked of yet.

*Cloris*

Of leaves of roses white and red,
Shall be the covering of her bed:
The curtains, valence, tester, all,
Shall be the flower imperial:
And for the fringe, it all along
With azure harebells shall be hung:
Of lilies shall the pillows be,
With down stuffed of the butterfly.

*Mertilla*

Thus far we handsomely have gone,
Now for our prothalamion,
Or marriage-song, of all the rest
A thing that much must grace our feast.

Let us practise, then, to sing it
Ere we before the assembly bring it;
We in dialogue must do it;
Then, my dainty girls, set to it.

*Claia*

This day must Tita married be,
Come, nymphs, this nuptial let us see.

*Mertilla*

But is it certain that ye say?
Will she wed the noble Fay?

*Cloris*

Sprinkle the dainty flowers with dews,
Such as the gods at banquets use:
Let herbs and weeds turn all to roses,
And make proud the posts with posies:
Shoot your sweets into the air,
Charge the morning to be fair.

*Claia and Mertilla*

For our Tita is this day
To be married to a Fay.

*Claia*

By whom, then, shall our bride be led
To the temple to be wed?

*Mertilla*

Only by yourself and I;
Who that roomth should else supply?

*Cloris*

Come, bright girls, come all together,
And bring all your offerings hither,
Ye most brave and buxom bevy,
All your goodly graces levy,
Come in majesty and state
Our bridal here to celebrate.

*Mertilla and Claia*

For our Tita is this day
Married to a noble Fay.

*Claia*

Whose lot will 't be the way to strow,
On which to church our bride must go?

*Mertilla*

That I think as fit'st of all,
To lively Lelipa must fall.

*Cloris*

Summon all the sweets that are,
To this nuptial to repair;
Till with their throngs themselves they smother,
Strongly stifling one another;
And at last they all consume,
And vanish in one rich perfume.

*Mertilla and Claia*

For our Tita is this day
Married to a noble Fay.

*Mertilla*

By whom must Tita married be?
'T is fit we all to that should see.

*Claia*

The priest he purposely doth come,
The Arch-Flamen of Elysium.

*Cloris*

With tapers let the temples shine,
Sing to Hymen hymns divine;
Load the altars till there rise
Clouds from the burnt sacrifice;
With your censers sling aloof
Their smells, till they ascend the roof

*Mertilla and Claia*

For our Tita is this day
Married to a noble Fay.

*Mertilla*

But coming back when she is wed,
Who breaks the cake above her head?

*Claia*

That shall Mertilla, for she 's tallest,
And our Tita is the smallest.

*Cloris*

Violins, strike up aloud,
Ply the gittern, scour the crowd,
Let the nimble hand belabour
The whistling pipe, and drumbling tabor:
To the full the bagpipe rack,
Till the swelling leather crack.

*Mertilla and Claia*

For our Tita is this day
Married to a noble Fay.

*Claia*

But when to dine she takes her seat,
What shall be our Tita's meat?

*Mertilla*

The gods this feast, as to begin,
Have sent of their ambrosia in.

*Cloris*

Then serve we up the straw's rich berry,
The respas, and Elysian cherry;
The virgin honey from the flowers
In Hybla, wrought in Flora's bowers;
Full bowls of nectar, and no girl
Carouse but in dissolved pearl.

*Mertilla and Claia*

For our Tita is this day
Married to a noble Fay.

*Claia*

But when night comes, and she must go
To bed, dear nymphs, what must we do?

*Mertilla*

In the posset must be brought,
And points be from the bridegroom caught.

*Cloris*

In masks, in dances, and delight,
And rare banquets spent the night;
Then about the room we ramble,
Scatter nuts, and for them scramble;
Over stools and tables tumble,
Never think of noise nor rumble.

*Mertilla and Claia*

For our Tita is this day
Married to a noble Fay.

*Drayton.*

## 92

Hark, all you ladies that do sleep!
  The fairy-queen Proserpina
Bids you awake and pity them that weep:
  You may do in the dark
    What the day doth forbid;
  Fear not the dogs that bark,
    Night will have all hid.

But if you let your lovers moan,
 The fairy-queen Proserpina
Will send abroad her fairies every one,
 That shall pinch black and blue
  Your white hands and fair arms
 That did not kindly rue
  Your paramours' harms.

In myrtle arbours on the downs
 The fairy-queen Proserpina,
This night by moonshine leading merry rounds,
 Holds a watch with sweet love,
  Down the dale, up the hill;
 No plaints nor groans may move
  Their holy vigil.

All you that will hold watch with love,
 The fairy-queen Proserpina
Will make you fairer than Dione's dove;
 Roses red, lilies white,
  And the clear damask hue,
 Shall on your cheeks alight:
  Love will adorn you.

All you that love or loved before,
 The fairy-queen Proserpina
Bids you increase that loving humour more:
 They that have not fed
  On delight amorous,
 She vows that they shall lead
  Apes in Avernus.

*Campion.*

93

## Hymn to Diana

Queen and huntress, chaste and fair,
Now the sun is laid to sleep,
Seated in thy silver chair,
State in wonted manner keep;
Hesperus entreats thy light,
Goddess excellently bright.

Earth, let not thy envious shade
Dare itself to interpose;
Cynthia's shining orb was made
Heaven to clear when day did close:
Bless us then with wished sight,
Goddess excellently bright.

Lay thy bow of pearl apart,
And thy crystal shining quiver;
Give unto the flying hart
Space to breathe, how short soever:
Thou that mak'st a day of night,
Goddess excellently bright.

*Ben Jonson.*

94

## The Song of the Sirens

Steer hither, steer your winged pines,
All beaten mariners,
Here lie Love's undiscovered mines,
A prey to passengers;

Perfumes far sweeter than the best
Which make the Phoenix' urn and nest.
Fear not your ships,
Nor any to oppose you save our lips,
But come on shore,
Where no joy dies till love hath gotten more.

For swelling waves our panting breasts,
Where never storms arise,
Exchange; and be awhile our guests:
For stars gaze on our eyes.
The compass love shall hourly sing,
And as he goes about the ring,
We will not miss
To tell each point he nameth with a kiss.

*Browne.*

## 95

## The Shepherd's Song of Venus and Adonis

Venus fair did ride,
Silver doves they drew her
By the pleasant lawns,
Ere the sun did rise;
Vesta's beauty rich
Opened wide to view her,
Philomel records
Pleasing harmonies.
Every bird of spring
Cheerfully did sing,
Paphos' goddess they salute.

Now Love's Queen so fair
Had of mirth no care;
For her son had made her mute.
In her breast so tender
He a shaft did enter,
When her eyes beheld a boy:
Adonis he was named,
By his mother shamed;
Yet he now is Venus' joy!

Him alone she met,
Ready bound for hunting;
Him she kindly greets,
And his journey stays;
Him she seeks to kiss,
No devices wanting;
Him her eyes still woo,
Him her tongue still prays.
He with blushing red,
Hangeth down the head;
Not a kiss can he afford;
His face is turned away,
Silence said her nay,
Still she wooed him for a word.
"Speak," she said, "thou fairest;
Beauty thou impairest;
See me, I am pale and wan:
Lovers all adore me,
I for love implore thee;"
Crystal tears with that down ran.

Him herewith she forced
To come sit down by her,
She his neck embraced,
Gazing in his face.

He, like one transformed,
Stirred no look to eye her;
Every herb did woo him,
Growing in that place.
Each bird with a ditty
Prayed him for pity,
In behalf of Beauty's Queen.
Water's gentle murmur
Craved him to love her;
Yet no liking could be seen.
"Boy," she said, "look on me,
Still I gaze upon thee,
Speak, I pray thee, my delight."
Coldly he replied,
And in brief denied
To bestow on her a sight.

"I am now too young
To be won by beauty,
Tender are my years,
I am yet a bud."
"Fair thou art," she said,
"Then it is thy duty,
Wert thou but a blossom,
To effect my good.
Every beauteous flower
Boasteth in my power,
Birds and beasts my laws effect;
Myrrha, thy fair mother,
Most of any other,
Did my lovely hests respect.
Be with me delighted,
Thou shalt be requited,
Every nymph on thee shall tend;
All the gods shall love thee,

Man shall not reprove thee;
Love himself shall be thy friend."

"Wend thee from me, Venus,
I am not disposed;
Thou wring'st me too hard,
Prithee let me go;
Fie! what a pain it is,
Thus to be enclosed!
If love begin with labour,
It will end in woe."
"Kiss me, I will leave."
"Here, a kiss receive."
"A short kiss I do it find:
Wilt thou leave me so?
Yet thou shalt not go;
Breathe once more thy balmy wind
It smelleth of the myrrh-tree,
That to the world did bring thee;
Never was perfume so sweet."
When she had thus spoken,
She gave him a token,
And their naked bosoms meet.

"Now," he said, "let's go,
Hark, the hounds are crying,
Grisly boar is up,
Huntsmen follow fast."
At the name of boar,
Venus seemed dying,
Deadly coloured, pale,
Roses overcast.
"Speak," said she, "no more
Of following the boar,
Thou, unfit for such a chase;

Course the fearful hare,
Venison do not spare.
If thou wilt yield Venus grace,
Shun the boar, I pray thee,
Else I still will stay thee."
Herein, he vowed to please her mind;
Then her arms enlarged,
Loth she him discharged:
Forth he went as swift as wind.

Thetis Phoebus' steeds
In the west retained,
Hunting sport was past;
Love her love did seek.
Sight of him too soon,
Gentle queen, she gained;
On the ground he lay,
Blood had left his cheek.
For an orped swine
Smit him in the groin,
Deadly wound his death did bring;
Which, when Venus found,
She fell in a swound,
And, awaked, her hands did wring.
Nymphs and satyrs skipping,
Came together tripping,
Echo every cry expressed;
Venus by her power
Turned him to a flower,
Which she weareth in her crest.

*Constable.*

96

## To Cupid

Maidens, why spare ye?
Or whether not dare ye
  Correct the blind shooter?
Because wanton Venus,
So oft that doth pain us,
  Is her son's tutor!

Now in the Spring
He proveth his wing,
  The field is his bower;
And as the small bee,
About flyeth he
  From flower to flower.

And wantonly roves
Abroad in the groves,
  And in the air hovers;
Which when it him deweth,
His feathers he meweth
  In sighs of true lovers.

And since doomed by Fate
(That well knew his hate)
  That he should be blind,
For very despite,
Our eyes be his white,
  So wayward his kind.

If his shafts losing
(Ill his mark choosing)
  Or his bow broken,

The moan Venus maketh,
And care that she taketh,
Cannot be spoken.

To Vulcan commending
Her love, and straight sending
Her doves and her sparrows,
With kisses, unto him,
And all but to woo him
To make her son arrows.

Telling what he hath done,
Saith she, "Right mine own son!"
In her arms him she closes,
Sweets on him fans,
Laid in down of her swans,
His sheets, leaves of roses.

And feeds him with kisses;
Which oft when he misses
He ever is froward:
The mother's o'erjoying
Makes by much coying
The child so untoward.

Yet in a fine net,
That a spider set,
The maidens had caught him;
Had she not been near him,
And chanced to hear him,
More good they had taught him.

*Drayton.*

97

Cupid and my Campaspe played
At cards for kisses, Cupid paid:
He stakes his quiver, bow, and arrows,
His mother's doves, and team of sparrows;
Loses them too; then down he throws
The coral of his lip, the rose
Growing on 's cheek (but none knows how);
With these, the crystal of his brow,
And then the dimple of his chin:
All these did my Campaspe win.
At last he set her both his eyes;
She won, and Cupid blind did rise.
O Love! has she done this for thee?
What shall, alas! become of me?

*Lyly.*

98

# The Bag of the Bee

About the sweet bag of a bee
  Two cupids fell at odds,
And whose the pretty prize should be
  They vowed to ask the gods.

Which Venus hearing, thither came,
  And for their boldness stripped them,
And, taking thence from each his flame,
  With rods of myrtle whipped them.

Which done, to still their wanton cries,
  When quiet grown she 'd seen them,
She kissed, and wiped their dove-like eyes,
  And gave the bag between them.

*Herrick.*

99

## The Shower of Blossoms

Love in a shower of blossoms came
Down, and half drowned me with the same:
The blooms that fell were white and red;
But with such sweets commingled,
As whether, this, I cannot tell
My sight was pleased more, or my smell:
But true it was, as I rolled there,
Without a thought of hurt or fear,
Love turned himself into a bee,
And with his javelin wounded me:
From which mishap thus use I make,
Where most sweets are, there lies a snake;
Kisses and favours are sweet things;
But those have thorns and these have stings.

*Herrick.*

100

## Charon and Philomel; A Dialogue Sung

*Philomel.* Charon! O gentle Charon! let me woo thee
By tears and pity now to come unto me.
*Charon.* What voice so sweet and charming do I hear?
Say what thou art.
*Philomel.* I prithee first draw near.
*Charon.* A sound I hear, but nothing yet can see;
Speak, where thou art.

*Philomel.* O Charon, pity me!
I am a bird, and though no name I tell,
My warbling note will say I 'm Philomel.

*Charon.* What's that to me? I waft not fish nor fowls,
Nor beasts (fond thing), but only human souls.

*Philomel.* Alas for me!

*Charon.* Shame on thy witching note
That made me thus hoist sail and bring my boat:
But I'll return; what mischief brought thee hither?

*Philomel.* A deal of love and much, much grief together.

*Charon.* What's thy request?

*Philomel.* That since she's now beneath
Who fed my life, I'll follow her in death.

*Charon.* And is that all? I'm gone.

*Philomel.* By love I pray thee.

*Charon.* Talk not of love; all pray, but few souls pay me.

*Philomel.* I'll give thee vows and tears.

*Charon.* Can tears pay scores
For mending sails, for patching boat and oars?

*Philomel.* I'll beg a penny, or I'll sing so long
Till thou shalt say I've paid thee with a song.

*Charon.* Why then begin; and all the while we make
Our slothful passage o'er the Stygian Lake,
Thou and I'll sing to make these dull shades merry,
Who else with tears would doubtless drown my ferry.

*Herrick.*

101

## The Argument of his Book

I sing of brooks, of blossoms, birds, and bowers,
Of April, May, of June, and July-flowers;
I sing of May-poles, hock-carts, wassails, wakes,
Of bridegrooms, brides, and of their bridal-cakes;
I write of youth, of love, and have access
By these to sing of cleanly wantonness;
I sing of dews, of rains, and piece by piece
Of balm, of oil, of spice, and ambergris;
I sing of times trans-shifting, and I write
How roses first came red and lilies white;
I write of groves, of twilights, and I sing
The Court of Mab, and of the fairy king;
I write of hell; I sing (and ever shall)
Of heaven, and hope to have it after all.

*Herrick*

102

## His Prayer to Ben Jonson

When I a verse shall make,
Know I have prayed thee,
For old religion's sake,
Saint Ben, to aid me.

Make the way smooth for me,
When I, thy Herrick,
Honouring thee, on my knee
Offer my lyric.

Candles I'll give to thee,
And a new altar,
And thou, Saint Ben, shalt be
Writ in my Psalter.

*Herrick.*

## 103

# To the Memory of my beloved Master, William Shakespeare, and what he hath left us

To draw no envy, Shakespeare, on thy name,
Am I thus ample to thy book and fame;
While I confess thy writing to be such,
As neither man nor Muse can praise too much.
'T is true, and all men's suffrage. But these ways
Were not the paths I meant unto thy praise;
For silliest ignorance on these may light,
Which, when it sounds at best, but echoes right;
Of blind affection, which doth ne'er advance
The truth, but gropes, and urgeth all by chance;
Or crafty malice might pretend this praise,
And think to ruin, where it seemed to raise.
These are, as some infamous bawd, or whore,
Should praise a matron; what would hurt her more?
But thou art proof against them, and, indeed,
Above the ill-fortune of them, or the need.
I, therefore, will begin: Soul of the age!
The applause! delight! and wonder of our stage!
My Shakespeare, rise! I will not lodge thee by
Chaucer, or Spenser, or bid Beaumont lie

A little farther off, to make thee room:
Thou art a monument without a tomb,
And art alive still, while thy book doth live
And we have wits to read, and praise to give.
That I not mix thee so, my brain excuses,
I mean with great, but disproportioned Muses;
For if I thought my judgment were of years,
I should commit thee surely with thy peers,
And tell how far thou didst our Lily outshine,
Or sporting Kyd, or Marlowe's mighty line.
And though thou hadst small Latin and less Greek,
From thence to honour thee, I will not seek
For names: but call forth thundering Eschylus,
Euripides, and Sophocles to us,
Pacuvius, Accius, him of Cordoua dead,
To live again, to hear thy buskin tread,
And shake a stage; or, when thy socks were on,
Leave thee alone for the comparison
Of all that insolent Greece, or haughty Rome
Sent forth, or since did from their ashes come.
Triumph, my Britain, thou hast one to show,
To whom all scenes of Europe homage owe.
He was not of an age, but for all time!
And all the Muses still were in their prime,
When, like Apollo, he came forth to warm
Our ears, or like a Mercury to charm!
Nature herself was proud of his designs,
And joyed to wear the dressing of his lines!
Which were so richly spun, and woven so fit,
As, since, she will vouchsafe no other wit.
The merry Greek, tart Aristophanes,
Neat Terence, witty Plautus, now not please;
But antiquated and deserted lie,
As they were not of nature's family.
Yet must I not give nature all; thy art,

My gentle Shakespeare, must enjoy a part:
For though the poet's matter nature be,
His art doth give the fashion: and, that he
Who casts to write a living line, must sweat
(Such as thine are), and strike the second heat
Upon the Muse's anvil; turn the same,
And himself with it, that he thinks to frame;
Or for the laurel, he may gain a scorn;
For a good poet's made, as well as born.
And such wert thou! Look how the father's face
Lives in his issue, even so the race
Of Shakespeare's mind and manners brightly shines
In his well turned, and true filed lines;
In each of which he seems to shake a lance,
As brandished at the eyes of ignorance.
Sweet Swan of Avon, what a sight it were
To see thee in our water yet appear,
And make those flights upon the banks of Thames,
That so did take Eliza, and our James!
But stay, I see thee in the hemisphere
Advanced, and made a constellation there!
Shine forth, thou star of poets, and with rage,
Or influence, chide, or cheer the drooping stage,
Which, since thy flight from hence, hath mourned
like night,
And despairs day, but for thy volume's light.

*Ben Jonson.*

## 104

# To Live Merrily and to Trust to Good Verses

Now is the time for mirth,
  Nor cheek or tongue be dumb;
For, with the flowery earth,
  The golden pomp is come.

The golden pomp is come;
  For now each tree does wear,
Made of her pap and gum,
  Rich beads of amber here.

Now reigns the rose, and now
  The Arabian dew besmears
My uncontrolled brow
  And my retorted hairs.

Homer, this health to thee,
  In sack of such a kind
That it would make thee see
  Though thou wert ne'er so blind.

Next, Virgil I'll call forth
  To pledge this second health
In wine, whose each cup's worth
  An Indian commonwealth.

A goblet next I'll drink
  To Ovid, and suppose,
Made he the pledge, he'd think
  The world had all one nose.

Then this immensive cup
  Of aromatic wine,
Catullus, I quaff up
  To that terse muse of thine.

Wild I am now with heat:
  O Bacchus, cool thy rays!
Or, frantic, I shall eat
  Thy thyrse and bite the bays.

Round, round the roof does run,
  And, being ravished thus,
Come, I will drink a tun
  To my Propertius.

Now, to Tibullus, next
  This flood I drink to thee:
But stay, I see a text
  That this presents to me.

Behold, Tibullus lies
  Here burnt, whose small return
Of ashes scarce suffice
  To fill a little urn.

Trust to good verses then;
  They only will inspire
When pyramids, as men,
  Are lost i' the funeral fire.

And when all bodies meet
  In Lethe to be drowned,
Then only numbers sweet
  With endless life are crowned.

*Herrick.*

## 105

Thou leaden brain, which censur'st what I write,
And sayst my lines be dull, and do not move,
I marvel not thou feelst not my delight,
Which never felt'st my fiery touch of love.
But thou, whose pen hath like a pack-horse served,
Whose stomach unto gall hath turned thy food,
Whose senses, like poor prisoners, hunger-starved,
Whose grief hath parched thy body, dried thy blood:
Thou which hath scorned life, and hated death,
And, in a moment, mad, sober, glad, and sorry;
Thou which hast banned thy thoughts, and cursed thy birth,
With thousand plagues more than in purgatory:
Thou, thus whose spirit Love in his fire refines,
Come thou and read, admire, applaud my lines.

*Drayton.*

## 106

In pride of wit, when high desire of fame
Gave life and courage to my labouring pen,
And first the sound and virtue of my name
Won grace and credit in the ears of men;
With those, the thronged theatres that press,
I in the circuit for the laurel strove,
Where the full praise, I freely must confess,
In heat of blood, a modest mind might move.
With shouts and claps at every little pause,
When the proud round on every side hath rung,
Sadly I sit, unmoved with the applause,
As though to me it nothing did belong.
No public glory vainly I pursue,
All that I seek is to eternize you.

*Drayton.*

## 107

Whilst thus my pen strives to eternize thee,
Age rules my lines with wrinkles in my face,
Where, in the map of all my misery,
Is modelled out the world of my disgrace:
Whilst in despite of tyrannizing times,
Medea-like, I make thee young again,
Proudly thou scorn'st my world-outwearing rhymes,
And murderest virtue with thy coy disdain.
And though in youth my youth untimely perish,
To keep thee from oblivion and the grave,
Ensuing ages yet my rhymes shall cherish,
Where I entombed my better part shall save;
  And though this earthly body fade and die.
  My name shall mount upon eternity.

*Drayton.* ?

## 108

How many paltry foolish painted things,
That now in coaches trouble every street,
Shall be forgotten, whom no poet sings,
Ere they be well wrapped in their winding-sheet!
Where I to thee eternity shall give,
When nothing else remaineth of these days,
And queens hereafter shall be glad to live
Upon the alms of thy superfluous praise.
Virgins and matrons, reading these my rhymes,
Shall be so much delighted with thy story,
That they shall grieve they lived not in these times,
To have seen thee, their sex's only glory:
  So shalt thou fly above the vulgar throng,
  Still to survive in my immortal song.

*Drayton.*

## 109

When in the chronicle of wasted time
I see descriptions of the fairest wights,
And beauty making beautiful old rhyme
In praise of ladies dead and lovely knights,
Then, in the blazon of sweet beauty's best,
Of hand, of foot, of lip, of eye, of brow,
I see their antique pen would have expressed
Even such a beauty as you master now.
So all their praises are but prophecies
Of this our time, all you prefiguring;
And, for they looked but with divining eyes,
They had not skill enough your worth to sing:
For we, which now behold these present days,
Have eyes to wonder, but lack tongues to praise.

*Shakespeare.*

## 110

Give beauty all her right,
She's not to one form tied;
Each shape yields fair delight,
Where her perfections 'bide.
Helen, I grant, might pleasing be;
And Rosamond was as sweet as she.

Some the quick eye commends;
Some swelling lips and red;
Pale looks have many friends,
Through sacred sweetness bred.
Meadows have flowers that pleasure move,
Though roses are the flowers of love.

Free beauty is not bound
To one unmoved clime:
She visits every ground,
And favours every time.
Let the old loves with mine compare,
My Sovereign is as sweet and fair.

*Campion.*

## 111

Beauty sat bathing by a spring,
Where fairest shades did hide her,
The winds blew calm, the birds did sing,
The cool streams ran beside her.
My wanton thoughts enticed mine eye
To see what was forbidden:
But better memory said Fie,
So vain desire was chidden.
Hey nonny, nonny, &c.

Into a slumber then I fell,
And fond imagination
Seemed to see, but could not tell
Her feature or her fashion.
But even as babes in dreams do smile
And sometimes fall a-weeping,
So I awaked as wise that while
As when I fell a-sleeping.
Hey nonny, nonny, &c.

*Anthony Munday.*

112

# Rosaline

Like to the clear in highest sphere
  Where all imperial glory shines,
Of selfsame colour is her hair
  Whether unfolded or in twines:
    Heigh-ho, fair Rosaline!
Her eyes are sapphires set in snow,
  Repining heaven by every wink;
The gods do fear whenas they glow,
  And I do tremble when I think:
    Heigh-ho, would she were mine!

Her cheeks are like the blushing cloud
  That beautifies Aurora's face,
Or like the silver crimson shroud
  That Phoebus' smiling looks doth grace:
    Heigh-ho, fair Rosaline!
Her lips are like two budded roses
  Whom ranks of lilies neighbour nigh,
Within whose bounds she balm encloses
  Apt to entice a deity:
    Heigh-ho, would she were mine!

Her neck like to a stately tower
  Where Love himself imprisoned lies,
To watch for glances every hour
  From her divine and sacred eyes:
    Heigh-ho, fair Rosaline!
Her paps are centres of delight,
  Her breasts are orbs of heavenly frame,
Where Nature moulds the dew of light

To feed perfection with the same:
Heigh-ho, would she were mine!

With orient pearl, with ruby red,
With marble white, with sapphire blue,
Her body every way is fed,
Yet soft in touch and sweet in view:
Heigh-ho, fair Rosaline!
Nature herself her shape admires;
The gods are wounded in her sight;
And Love forsakes his heavenly fires
And at her eyes his brand doth light:
Heigh-ho, would she were mine!

Then muse not, Nymphs, though I bemoan
The absence of fair Rosaline,
Since for her fair there's fairer none,
Nor for her virtues so divine:
Heigh-ho, fair Rosaline!
Heigh-ho, my heart! would God that she were mine!

*Lodge.*

113

## Samela

Like to Diana in her summer weed,
Girt with a crimson robe of brightest dye,
Goes fair Samela.
Whiter than be the flocks that straggling feed
When washed by Arethusa fount they lie,
Is fair Samela.

As fair Aurora in her morning gray,
Decked with the ruddy glister of her love
Is fair Samela.
Like lovely Thetis on a calmed day
Whenas her brightness Neptune's fancy move,
Shines fair Samela.
Her tresses gold, her eyes like glassy streams,
Her teeth are pearl, the breasts are ivory
Of fair Samela.
Her cheeks like rose and lily yield forth gleams;
Her brows bright arches framed of ebony:
Thus fair Samela
Passeth fair Venus in her bravest hue,
And Juno in the show of majesty:
For she's Samela.
Pallas in wit, all three, if you will view,
For beauty, wit, and matchless dignity,
Yield to Samela.

*Greene.*

114

## Madrigal

Like the Idalian queen,
Her hair about her eyne,
With neck and breast's ripe apples to be seen,
At first glance of the morn,
In Cyprus' gardens gathering those fair flowers
Which of her blood were born,
I saw, but fainting saw, my paramours.
The Graces naked danced about the place,
The winds and trees amazed
With silence on her gazed;

The flowers did smile, like those upon her face,
And as their aspen stalks those fingers band,
That she might read my case,
A hyacinth I wished me in her hand.

*Drummond.*

115

# To Julia, in Her Dawn, or Daybreak

By the next kindling of the day,
My Julia, thou shalt see,
Ere Ave-Mary thou canst say
I'll come and visit thee.

Yet ere thou counsel'st with thy glass,
Appear thou to mine eyes
As smooth, and nak'd, as she that was
The prime of paradise.

If blush thou must, then blush thou through
A lawn, that thou mayst look
As purest pearls, or pebbles do
When peeping through a brook.

As lilies shrined in crystal, so
Do thou to me appear;
Or damask roses when they grow
To sweet acquaintance there.

*Herrick.*

116

## Upon Julia's Hair Filled with Dew

Dew sat on Julia's hair
 And spangled too,
Like leaves that laden are
 With trembling dew:

Or glittered to my sight,
 As when the beams
Have their reflected light
 Danced by the streams.

*Herrick.*

117

## Upon Her Feet

Her pretty feet
Like snails did creep
A little out, and then,
As if they played at Bo-Peep,
Did soon draw in again.

*Herrick.*

118

## Upon Her Eyes

Clear are her eyes,
Like purest skies,
Discovering from thence
A baby there
That turns each sphere
Like an Intelligence.

*Herrick.*

119

You little stars that live in skies
And glory in Apollo's glory,
In whose aspects conjoined lies
The heaven's will and nature's story,
Joy to be likened to those eyes,
Which eyes make all eyes glad or sorry;
For, when you force thoughts from above,
These over-rule your force by Love.

And thou, O Love, which in these eyes
Hast married reason with affection,
And made them saints of beauty's skies,
Where joys are shadows of perfection,
Lend me thy wings that I may rise
Up not by worth but by election;
For I have vowed, in strangest fashion,
To love and never seek compassion.

*Fulke Greville, Lord Brooke.*

## 120

So saith my fair and beautiful Lycoris,
When now and then she talketh
With me of Love:
"Love is a sprite that walketh,
That soars and flies,
And none alive can hold him,
Nor touch him, nor behold him."
Yet when her eye she turneth,
I spy where he sojourneth:
In her eyes there he flies,
But none can catch him
Till from her lips he fetch him.

*Anonymous.*

## 121

Those eyes that set my fancy on a fire,
Those crisped hairs that hold my heart in chains,
Those dainty hands which conquered my desire,
That wit which of my thoughts doth hold the reins:
Then, Love, be judge, what heart may therewith stand
Such eyes, such head, such wit, and such a hand?
Those eyes for clearness doth the stars surpass,
Those hairs obscure the brightness of the sun,
Those hands more white than ever ivory was,
That wit even to the skies hath glory won.
O eyes that pierce our hearts without remorse!
O hairs of right that wear a royal crown!
O hands that conquer more than Caesar's force!
O wit that turns huge kingdoms upside down!

*Anonymous.*

## 122

I saw my Lady weep,
And Sorrow proud to be advanced so
In those fair eyes where all perfections keep.
Her face was full of woe,
But such a woe (believe me) as wins more hearts
Than Mirth can do with her enticing parts.

Sorrow was there made fair,
And Passion wise; Tears a delightful thing;
Silence beyond all speech, a wisdom rare;
She made her sighs to sing,
And all things with so sweet a sadness move
As made my heart at once both grieve and love.

O fairer than aught else
The world can show, leave off in time to grieve.
Enough, enough: your joyful look excels:
Tears kill the heart, believe.
O strive not to be excellent in woe,
Which only breeds your beauty's overthrow.

*Anonymous.*

## 123

Brown is my Love, but graceful:
And each renowned whiteness
Matched with thy lovely brown loseth its brightness

Fair is my Love, but scornful:
Yet have I seen despised
Dainty white lilies, and sad flowers well prized.

*Anonymous.*

124

## On His Mistress, the Queen of Bohemia

You meaner beauties of the night,
That poorly satisfy our eyes
More by your number than your light,
You common people of the skies;
What are you when the moon shall rise?

You curious chanters of the wood,
That warble forth Dame Nature's lays,
Thinking your passions understood
By your weak accents; what's your praise,
When Philomel her voice shall raise?

You violets that first appear,
By your pure purple mantles known
Like the proud virgins of the year
As if the spring were all your own;
What are you when the rose is blown?

So when my mistress shall be seen
In form and beauty of her mind,
By virtue first, then choice, a Queen,
Tell me if she were not designed
The eclipse and glory of her kind?

*Wotton.*

125

# The Triumph

See the chariot at hand here of Love
  Wherein my lady rideth!
Each that draws is a swan or a dove,
  And well the car Love guideth.
As she goes, all hearts do duty
    Unto her beauty;
And, enamoured, do wish, so they might
    But enjoy such a sight,
That they still were to run by her side,
Through swords, through seas, whither she would ride.

Do but look on her eyes, they do light
  All that Love's world compriseth!
Do but look on her hair, it is bright
  As Love's star when it riseth!
Do but mark, her forehead 's smoother
    Than words that soothe her!
And from her arched brows, such a grace
    Sheds itself through the face,
As alone there triumphs to the life
All the gain, all the good, of the elements' strife.

Have you seen but a bright lily grow,
  Before rude hands have touched it?
Have you marked but the fall o' the snow
  Before the soil hath smutched it?
Have you felt the wool of beaver?
    Or swan's down ever?

Or have smelt o' the bud o' the briar?
Or the nard in the fire?
Or have tasted the bag of the bee?
O so white! O so soft! O so sweet is she!

*Ben Jonson.*

## 126

Awake, thou spring of speaking grace! mute rest becomes not thee!
The fairest women, while they sleep, and pictures, equal be.
O come and dwell in love's discourses,
Old renewing, new creating!
The words which thy rich tongue discourses,
Are not of the common rating.

Thy voice is as an echo clear which Music doth beget,
Thy speech is as an oracle which none can counterfeit:
For thou alone, without offending,
Hast obtained power of enchanting;
And I could hear thee without ending,
Other comforts never wanting.

Some little reason brutish lives with human glory share;
But language is our proper grace, from which they severed are.
As brutes in reason man surpasses,
Men in speech excel each other:
If speech be then the best of graces,
Do it not in slumber smother!

*Campion.*

## 127

# Damelus' Song of his Diaphenia

Diaphenia, like the daffadowndilly,
White as the sun, fair as the lily,
  Heigh-ho, how I do love thee!
I do love thee as my lambs
Are beloved of their dams:
  How blest were I if thou wouldst prove me!

Diaphenia, like the spreading roses,
That in thy sweets all sweets encloses,
  Fair sweet, how I do love thee!
I do love thee as each flower
Loves the sun's life-giving power;
  For dead, thy breath to life might move me.

Diaphenia like to all things blessed
When all thy praises are expressed,
  Dear joy, how I do love thee!
As the birds do love the spring,
Or the bees their careful king:
  Then in requite, sweet virgin, love me!

*Constable.*

## 128

Love me not for comely grace,
For my pleasing eye or face,
Nor for any outward part:
No, nor for a constant heart!
For these may fail or turn to ill:
  So thou and I shall sever.

Keep therefore a true woman's eye,
And love me still, but know not why!
So hast thou the same reason still
To doat upon me ever.

*Anonymous.*

## 129

Why presumes thy pride on that that must so private be,
Scarce that it can good be called, though it seems best to thee,
Best of all that Nature framed or curious eye can see?

'T is thy beauty, foolish Maid, that like a blossom grows;
Which who views no more enjoys than on a bush a rose,
That, by many's handling, fades: and thou art one of those.

If to one thou shalt prove true, and all beside reject,
Then art thou but one man's good, which yields a poor effect:
For the commonest good by far deserves the best respect.

But if for this goodness thou thyself wilt common make,
Thou art then not good at all: so thou canst no way take
But to prove the meanest good or else all good forsake.

Be not then of beauty proud, but so her colours bear
That they prove not stains to her, that them for grace should wear:
So shalt thou to all more fair than thou wert born appear.

*Campion.*

## 130

Do not, O do not prize thy beauty at too high a rate,
Love to be loved whilst thou art lovely, lest thou love too late;
Frowns print wrinkles in thy brows,
At which spiteful age doth smile;
Women in their froward vows
Glorying to beguile.

Wert thou the only world's admired thou canst love but one,
And many have before been loved, thou art not loved alone:
Couldst thou speak with heavenly grace,
Sappho might with thee compare;
Blush the roses in thy face,
Rosamond was as fair.

Pride is the canker that consumeth beauty in her prime,
They that delight in long debating feel the curse of time:
All things with the time do change,
That will not the time obey;
Some even to themselves seem strange
Thorough their own delay.

*Anonymous.*

## 131

Since brass, nor stône, nor earth, nor boundless sea,
But sad mortality o'er-sways their power,
How with this rage shall beauty hold a plea,
Whose action is no stronger than a flower?
O, how shall summer's honey breath hold out
Against the wreckful siege of battering days,
When rocks impregnable are not so stout,
Nor gates of steel so strong, but Time decays?
O fearful meditation! where, alack,
Shall Time's best jewel from Time's chest lie hid?
Or what strong hand can hold his swift foot back?
Or who his spoil of beauty can forbid?
  O, none, unless this miracle have might,
  That in black ink my love may still shine bright.

*Shakespeare.*

## 132

Like as the waves make towards the pebbled shore,
So do our minutes hasten to their end;
Each changing place with that which goes before,
In sequent toil all forwards do contend.
Nativity, once in the main of light,
Crawls to maturity, wherewith being crowned,
Crooked eclipses 'gainst his glory fight,
And Time that gave doth now his gift confound.
Time doth transfix the flourish set on youth
And delves the parallels in beauty's brow,
Feeds on the rarities of nature's truth,
And nothing stands but for his scythe to mow:
  And yet to times in hope my verse shall stand,
  Praising thy worth, despite his cruel hand.

*Shakespeare.*

## 133

To me, fair friend, you never can be old,
For as you were when first your eye I eyed,
Such seems your beauty still. Three winters' cold
Have from the forests shook three summers' pride,
Three beauteous springs to yellow autumn turned
In process of the seasons have I seen,
Three April perfumes in three hot Junes burned,
Since first I saw you fresh, which yet are green.
Ah! yet doth beauty, like a dial-hand,
Steal from his figure and no pace perceived;
So your sweet hue, which methinks still doth stand,
Hath motion and mine eye may be deceived:
  For fear of which, hear this, thou age unbred;
  Ere you were born was beauty's summer dead.

*Shakespeare.*

## 134

Where are all thy beauties now, all hearts enchaining?
Whither are thy flatterers gone with all their feigning?
All fled! and thou alone still here remaining!

Thy rich state of twisted gold to bays is turned!
Cold, as thou art, are thy loves, that so much burned!
Who die in flatterers' arms are seldom mourned.

Yet, in spite of envy, this be still proclaimed,
That none worthier than thyself thy worth hath
    blamed;
When their poor names are lost, thou shalt live
    famed.

When thy story, long time hence, shall be perused,
Let the blemish of thy rule be thus excused,
" None ever lived more just, none more abused".

*Campion.*

## 135

Beauty, sweet love, is like the morning dew,
Whose short refresh upon the tender green
Cheers for a time, but till the sun doth show,
And straight 't is gone, as it had never been.
Soon doth it fade that makes the fairest flourish,
Short is the glory of the blushing rose,
The hue which thou so carefully dost nourish,
Yet which, at length, thou must be forced to lose,
When thou, surcharged with burthen of thy years,
Shall bend thy wrinkles homeward to the earth,
And that in Beauty's lease, expired, appears
The date of age, the kalends of our death:
But, ah! no more, this must not be foretold,
For women grieve to think they must be old.

*Daniel.*

## 136

Lawn as white as driven snow;
Cyprus black as e'er was crow;
Gloves as sweet as damask roses;
Masks for faces and for noses;
Bugle bracelet, necklace amber,
Perfume for a lady's chamber;
Golden quoifs and stomachers,
For my lads to give their dears:

Pins and poking-sticks of steel,
What maids lack from head to heel:
Come buy of me, come; come buy, come buy;
Buy, lads, or else your lasses cry:
Come buy.

*Shakespeare.*

## 137

Still to be neat, still to be drest,
As you were going to a feast;
Still to be powdered, still perfumed:
Lady, it is to be presumed,
Though art's hid causes are not found,
All is not sweet, all is not sound.

Give me a look, give me a face
That makes simplicity a grace;
Robes loosely flowing, hair as free:
Such sweet neglect more taketh me
Than all the adulteries of art;
They strike mine eyes, but not my heart.

*Ben Jonson.*

## 138

# Delight in Disorder

A sweet disorder in the dress
Kindles in clothes a wantonness:
A lawn about the shoulders thrown
Into a fine distraction:
An erring lace which here and there
Enthrals the crimson stomacher:

A cuff neglectful, and thereby
Ribbons to flow confusedly:
A winning wave, deserving note,
In the tempestuous petticoat:
A careless shoe-string, in whose tie
I see a wild civility:
Do more bewitch me than when art
Is too precise in every part.

*Herrick.*

139

## Art above Nature: To Julia

When I behold a forest spread
With silken trees upon thy head,
And when I see that other dress
Of flowers set in comeliness;
When I behold another grace
In the ascent of curious lace,
Which like a pinnacle doth show
The top, and the top-gallant too:
Then, when I see thy tresses bound
Into an oval, square, or round,
And knit in knots far more than I
Can tell by tongue, or true-love tie;
Next, when those lawny films I see
Play with a wild civility,
And all those airy silks to flow,
Alluring me, and tempting so:
I must confess mine eye and heart
Dotes less on Nature than on Art.

*Herrick.*

## 140

My Love in her attire doth show her wit,
  It doth so well become her;
For every season she hath dressings fit,
  For Winter, Spring, and Summer.
    No beauty she doth miss
      When all her robes are on:
    But Beauty's self she is
      When all her robes are gone.

*Anonymous.*

## 141

# Upon Julia's Clothes

Whenas in silks my Julia goes,
Then, then, methinks, how sweetly flows
The liquefaction of her clothes.

Next, when I cast mine eyes and see
That brave vibration each way free;
O how that glittering taketh me!

*Herrick.*

## 142

# The Transfiguration

Immortal clothing I put on
So soon as, Julia, I am gone
To mine eternal mansion.

Thou, thou art here, to human sight
Clothed all with incorrupted light;
But yet how more admiredly bright

Wilt thou appear, when thou art set
In thy refulgent thronelet,
That shin'st thus in thy counterfeit!

*Herrick.*

143

O mistress mine, where are you roaming?
O, stay and hear; your true love's coming,
That can sing both high and low:
Trip no further, pretty sweeting;
Journeys end in lovers meeting,
Every wise man's son doth know.

What is love? 'Tis not hereafter;
Present mirth hath present laughter;
What's to come is still unsure:
In delay there lies no plenty;
Then come kiss me, sweet and twenty,
Youth's a stuff will not endure.

*Shakespeare.*

144

## The Night-Piece: To Julia

Her eyes the glow-worm lend thee,
The shooting-stars attend thee;
And the elves also,
Whose little eyes glow
Like the sparks of fire, befriend thee.

No Will-o'-the-Wisp mislight thee,
Nor snake or slow-worm bite thee;
    But on, on thy way
    Not making a stay,
Since ghost there's none to affright thee.

Let not the dark thee cumber:
What though the moon does slumber?
    The stars of the night
    Will lend thee their light
Like tapers clear without number.

Then, Julia, let me woo thee,
Thus, thus to come unto me;
    And when I shall meet
    Thy silvery feet
My soul I'll pour into thee.

*Herrick.*

## 145

Love's god is a boy,
    None but cowherds regard him,
His dart is a toy,
    Great opinion hath marred him;
The fear of the wag
Hath made him so brag;
Chide him, he'll fly thee
And not come nigh thee.
Little boy, pretty knave, shoot not at random,
For if you hit me, slave, I'll tell your grandam.

Fond love is a child
    And his compass is narrow,
Young fools are beguiled
    With the fame of his arrow;

He dareth not strike
If his stroke mislike:
Cupid, do you hear me?
Come not too near me.
Little boy, pretty knave, hence I beseech you,
For if you hit me, knave, in faith I'll breech you.

The ape loves to meddle
When he finds a man idle,
Else is he a-flirting
Where his mark is a-courting;
When women grow true
Come teach me to sue,
Then I'll come to thee,
Pray thee, and woo thee.
Little boy, pretty knave, make me not stagger,
For if you hit me, knave, I'll call thee beggar.

*Anonymous.*

146

Tell me, dearest, what is love?
'Tis a lightning from above;
'Tis an arrow, 'tis a fire,
'Tis a boy they call Desire.
'Tis a grave,
Gapes to have
Those poor fools that long to prove.

Tell me more, are women true?
Yes, some are, and some as you.
Some are willing, some are strange,
Since you men first taught to change.
And till troth
Be in both,
All shall love, to love anew.

Tell me more yet, can they grieve?
Yes, and sicken sore, but live,
And be wise, and delay,
When you men are as wise as they
Then I see,
Faith will be,
Never till they both believe.

*Fletcher.*

## 147

What then is love but mourning?
What desire, but a self-burning?
Till she, that hates, doth love return,
Thus will I mourn, thus will I sing,
"Come away! come away, my darling!"

Beauty is but a blooming,
Youth in his glory entombing;
Time hath a while, which none can stay:
Then come away, while thus I sing,
"Come away! come away, my darling!"

Summer in winter fadeth;
Gloomy night heavenly light shadeth:
Like to the morn, are Venus' flowers;
Such are her hours: then will I sing,
"Come away! come away, my darling!"

*Campion.*

148

Turn all thy thoughts to eyes,
Turn all thy hairs to ears,
Change all thy friends to spies,
And all thy joys to fears:
True love will yet be free,
In spite of jealousy.

Turn darkness into day,
Conjectures into truth,
Believe what the envious say,
Let age interpret youth:
True love will yet be free,
In spite of jealousy.

Wrest every word and look,
Rack every hidden thought,
Or fish with golden hook;
True love cannot be caught.
For that will still be free,
In spite of jealousy.

*Campion.*

149

✓

Turn I my looks unto the skies,
Love with his arrows wounds mine eyes;
If so I gaze upon the ground,
Love then in every flower is found;
Search I the shade to fly the pain,
He meets me in the shade again;
Wend I to walk in sacred grove,
Even there I meet with sacred Love;

If so I bain me in the spring,
Even on the bank I hear him sing;
If so I meditate alone,
He will be partner of my moan;
If so I mourn, he weeps with me,
And where I am there he will be.
Whenas I talk of Rosalind
The god from coyness waxeth kind,
And seems in self-same flames to fry
Because he loves as well as I.
Sweet Rosalind, for pity rue,
For why than Love I am more true:
He, if he speed, will quickly fly,
But in thy love I live and die.

*Lodge.*

## 150

Love winged my hopes and taught me how to fly
Far from base earth, but not to mount too high:
For true pleasure
Lives in measure,
Which if men forsake,
Blinded they into folly run and grief for pleasure take.

But my vain hopes, proud of their new-taught flight,
Enamoured sought to woo the sun's fair light,
Whose rich brightness
Moved their lightness
To aspire so high
That all scorched and consumed with fire now drown'd in woe they lie.

And none but Love their woeful hap did rue,
For Love did know that their desires were true;
Though Fate frowned
And now drowned
They in sorrow dwell,
It was the purest light of heaven for whose fair love they fell.

*Anonymous.*

## 151

Love guards the roses of thy lips
And flies about them like a bee;
If I approach he forward skips,
And if I kiss he stingeth me.

Love in thine eyes doth build his bower,
And sleeps within his pretty shrine;
And if I look the boy will lower,
And from their orbs shoot shafts divine.

Love works thy heart within his fire,
And in my tears doth firm the same;
And if I tempt it will retire,
And of my plaints doth make a game.

Love, let me cull her choicest flowers:
And pity me, and calm her eye;
Make soft her heart, dissolve her lowers;
Then will I praise thy deity.

But if thou do not, Love, I'll truly serve her
In spite of thee, and by firm faith deserve her.

*Lodge.*

## 152

# Montanus' Sonnet

Phoebe sat,
Sweet she sat,
Sweet sat Phoebe when I saw her,
White her brow,
Coy her eye;
Brow and eye how much you please me!
Words I spent,
Sighs I sent;
Sighs and words could never draw her.
Oh my love,
Thou art lost
Since no sight could ever ease thee.

Phoebe sat
By a fount,
Sitting by a fount I spied her:
Sweet her touch,
Rare her voice;
Touch and voice what may distain you?
As she sang,
I did sigh,
And by sighs whilst that I tried her,
Oh mine eyes!
You did lose
Her first sight, whose want did pain you.

Phoebe's flocks
White as wool,
Yet were Phoebe's locks more whiter.

Phoebe's eyes
Dove-like, mild,
Dove-like eyes, both mild and cruel;
Montan swears,
In your lamps
He will die for to delight her.
Phoebe, yield,
Or I die:
Shall true hearts be fancy's fuel?

*Lodge.*

## 153

Who is Sylvia? what is she,
That all our swains commend her?
Holy, fair and wise is she;
The heaven such grace did lend her,
That she might admired be.

Is she kind as she is fair?
For beauty lives with kindness.
Love doth to her eyes repair,
To help him of his blindness,
And, being helped, inhabits there.

Then to Sylvia let us sing,
That Sylvia is excelling:
She excels each mortal thing
Upon the dull earth dwelling:
To her let us garlands bring.

*Shakespeare.*

154

Love in my bosom, like a bee,
  Doth suck his sweet:
Now with his wings he plays with me,
  Now with his feet.
Within mine eyes he makes his nest,
His bed amidst my tender breast;
My kisses are his daily feast,
And yet he robs me of my rest:
  Ah! wanton, will ye?

And if I sleep, then percheth he
  With pretty flight,
And makes his pillow of my knee
  The livelong night.
Strike I my lute, he tunes the string;
His music plays if so I sing;
He lends me every lovely thing,
Yet cruel he my heart doth sting:
  Whist, wanton, still ye!

Else I with roses every day
  Will whip you hence,
And bind you, when you long to play,
  For your offence.
I 'll shut mine eyes to keep you in;
I 'll make you fast it for your sin;
I 'll count your power not worth a pin.
Alas! what hereby shall I win,
  If he gainsay me?

What if I beat the wanton boy
  With many a rod?

He will repay me with annoy,
Because a god.
Then sit thou safely on my knee;
Then let thy bower my bosom be;
Lurk in mine eyes, I like of thee;
O Cupid, so thou pity me,
Spare not, but play thee!

*Lodge.*

## 155

On a day—alack the day!—
Love, whose month is ever May,
Spied a blossom passing fair
Playing in the wanton air:
Through the velvet leaves the wind,
All unseen, can passage find;
That the lover, sick to death,
Wish himself the heaven's breath.
Air, quoth he, thy cheeks may blow:
Air, would I might triumph so!
But, alack, my hand is sworn
Ne'er to pluck thee from thy thorn:
Vow, alack, for youth unmeet,
Youth so apt to pluck a sweet!
Do not call it sin in me,
That I am forsworn to thee;
Thou for whom Jove would swear
Juno but an Ethiope were;
And deny himself for Jove,
Turning mortal for thy love.

*Shakespeare.*

## 156

" Maids are simple," some men say,
" They, forsooth, will trust no men."
But should they men's wills obey,
Maids are very simple then.

Truth, a rare flower now is grown,
Few men wear it in their hearts;
Lovers are more easily known
By their follies than deserts.

Safer may we credit give
To a faithless wandering Jew
Than a young man's vows believe
When he swears his love is true.

Love they make a poor blind child,
But let none trust such as he:
Rather than to be beguiled,
Ever let me simple be. *Campion.*

## 157

" Art thou that she than whom no fairer is?
Art thou that she desire so strives to kiss?"
" Say I am: how then?
Maids may not kiss
Such wanton-humoured men."

" Art thou that she the world commends for wit?
Art thou so wise and makest no use of it?"
" Say I am: how then?
My wit doth teach me shun
Such foolish, foolish men." *Anonymous.*

## 158

" Open the door! Who 's there within?
The fairest of thy mother's kin,
O come, come, come abroad
And hear the shrill birds sing,
The air with tunes that load!
It is too soon to go to rest,
The sun 's not midway yet to west:
The day doth miss thee
And will not part until it kiss thee."

" Were I as fair as you pretend,
Yet to an unknown, seld-seen friend
I dare not ope the door:
To hear the sweet birds sing
Oft proves a dangerous thing.
The sun may run his wonted race
And yet not gaze on my poor face;
The day may miss me:
Therefore depart, you shall not kiss me."

*Anonymous.*

## 159

Lo! as a careful housewife runs to catch
One of her feathered creatures broke away,
Sets down her babe and makes all swift dispatch
In pursuit of the thing she would have stay,
Whilst her neglected child holds her in chase,
Cries to catch her whose busy care is bent
To follow that which flies before her face,
Not prizing her poor infant's discontent;
So runn'st thou after that which flies from thee,
Whilst I thy babe chase thee afar behind;

But if thou catch thy hope, turn back to me,
And play the mother's part, kiss me, be kind:
  So will I pray that thou mayst have thy "Will",
  If thou turn back, and my loud crying still.

*Shakespeare.*

## 160

To nothing fitter can I thee compare
Than to the son of some rich penny-father,
Who, having now brought on his end with care,
Leaves to his son all he had heaped together.
This new rich novice, lavish of his chest,
To one man gives, doth on another spend,
Then here he riots, yet, amongst the rest,
Haps to lend some to one true honest friend.
Thy gifts thou in obscurity doth waste,
False friends thy kindness, born but to deceive thee;
Thy love that is on the unworthy placed;
Time hath thy beauty, which with age will leave thee;
  Only that little which to me was lent,
  I give thee back when all the rest is spent.

*Drayton.*

## 161

If I hope, I pine; if I fear, I faint and die;
So, between hope and fear, I desperate lie,
Looking for joy to heaven, whence it should come:
But hope is blind; joy, deaf; and I am dumb.
Yet I speak and cry; but, alas, with words of woe:
And joy conceives not them that murmur so.
He that the ears of joy will ever pierce,
Must sing glad notes, or speak in happier verse.

*Campion.*

## 162

Thrice toss these oaken ashes in the air,
Thrice sit thou mute in this enchanted chair,
And thrice three times tie up this true love's knot,
And murmur soft "She will, or she will not."

Go burn these poisonous weeds in yon blue fire,
These screech-owl's feathers and this prickling briar,
This cypress gathered at a dead man's grave,
That all thy fears and cares an end may have.

Then come, you Fairies, dance with me a round,
Melt her hard heart with your melodious sound.
In vain are all the charms I can devise:
She hath an art to break them with her eyes.

*Campion.*

## 163

Marvel not, Love, though I thy power admire,
Ravished a world beyond the farthest thought,
And knowing more than ever hath been taught,
That I am only starved in my desire:
Marvel not, Love, though I thy power admire,
Aiming at things exceeding all perfection,
To wisdom's self to minister direction,
That I am only starved in my desire:
Marvel not, Love, though I thy power admire,
Though my conceit I further seem to bend
Than possibly invention can extend,
And yet am only starved in my desire:
If thou wilt wonder, here's the wonder, Love,
That this to me doth yet no wonder prove.

*Drayton.*

## 164

Behold a wonder here!
  Love hath received his sight,
Which many hundred year
  Hath not beheld the light.

Such beams infused be
  By Cynthia in his eyes,
As first have made him see
  And then have made him wise.

Love now no more will weep
  For them that laugh the while,
Nor wake for them that sleep,
  Nor sigh for them that smile.

So powerful is the Beauty
  That Love doth now behold,
As love is turned to Duty
  That's neither blind nor bold.

Thus Beauty shows her might
  To be of double kind;
In giving Love his sight
  And striking Folly blind.

*Anonymous.*

## 165

My Love bound me with a kiss
  That I should no longer stay;
When I felt so sweet a bliss
  I had less power to part away:
Alas! that women do not know
Kisses make men loath to go.

Yes, she knows it but too well,
For I heard when Venus' dove
In her ear did softly tell
That kisses were the seals of love:
O muse not then though it be so,
Kisses make men loath to go.

Wherefore did she thus inflame
My desires, heat my blood,
Instantly to quench the same
And starve whom she had given food?
Ay, ay, the common sense can show,
Kisses make men loath to go.

Had she bid me go at first
It would ne'er have grieved my heart
Hope delayed had been the worst;
But ah to kiss and then to part!
How deep it struck, speak, gods! you know
Kisses make men loath to go.

*Anonymous.*

## 166

A woman's looks
Are barbed hooks,
That catch by art
The strongest heart
When yet they spend no breath;
But let them speak,
And sighing break
Forth into tears,
Their words are spears
That wound our souls to death.

The rarest wit
Is made forget,
And like a child
Is oft beguiled
With love's sweet-seeming bait;
Love with his rod
So like a god
Commands the mind;
We cannot find,
Fair shows hide foul deceit.

Time, that all things
In order brings,
Hath taught me how
To be more slow
In giving faith to speech,
Since women's words
No truth affords,
And when they kiss
They think by this
Us men to over-reach.

*Anonymous.*

## 167

Her fair inflaming eyes,
Chief authors of my cares,
I prayed in humblest wise
With grace to view my tears:
They beheld me broad awake,
But, alas, no ruth would take.

Her lips with kisses rich,
And words of fair delight,

I fairly did beseech,
  To pity my sad plight:
    But a voice from them brake forth
    As a whirlwind from the north.

Then to her hands I fled,
  That can give heart and all;
To them I long did plead,
  And loud for pity call:
    But, alas, they put me off,
    With a touch worse than a scoff.

So back I straight returned,
  And at her breast I knocked;
Where long in vain I mourned,
  Her heart so fast was locked:
    Not a word could passage find,
    For a rock enclosed her mind.

Then down my prayers made way
  To those most comely parts,
That make her fly or stay,
  As they affect deserts:
    But her angry feet, thus moved,
    Fled with all the parts I loved.

Yet fled they not so fast,
  As her enraged mind:
Still did I after haste,
  Still was I left behind;
    Till I found 'twas to no end
    With a Spirit to contend.

*Campion.*

## 168

" Say, Love, if ever thou didst find
A woman with a constant mind."
"None but one."
" And what should that rare mirror be?"
" Some goddess or some queen is She."
She, She, She, and only She,
She only queen of love and beauty.

" But could thy fiery poisoned dart
At no time touch her spotless heart,
Nor come near?"
" She is not subject to Love's bow:
Her eye commands, her heart saith 'No'."
No, no, no, and only No,
One No another still doth follow.

" How might I that fair wonder know
That mocks desire with endless 'No'?"
" See the moon
That ever in one change doth grow,
Yet still the same: and She is so."
So, so, so, and only So!
From heaven her virtues she doth borrow

" To her, then, yield thy shafts and bow
That can command affection so."
" Love is free:
So are her thoughts that vanquish thee.
There is no queen of Love but She."
She, She, She, and only She,
She only queen of love and beauty.

*Anonymous.*

## 169

Welcome, welcome, do I sing,
Far more welcome than the spring;
He that parteth from you never
Shall enjoy a spring for ever.

He that to the voice is near
  Breaking from your ivory pale,
Need not walk abroad to hear
  The delightful nightingale.

Welcome, welcome, then I sing,
Far more welcome than the spring;
He that parteth from you never
Shall enjoy a spring for ever.

He that looks still on your eyes,
  Though the winter have begun
To benumb our arteries,
  Shall not want the summer's sun.
    Welcome, welcome, &c.

He that still may see your cheeks,
  Where all rareness still reposes,
Is a fool, if e'er he seeks
  Other lilies, other roses.
    Welcome, welcome, &c.

He to whom your soft lip yields,
  And perceives your breath is kissing,
All the odours of the fields
  Never, never shall be missing.
    Welcome, welcome, &c.

He that question would anew
  What fair Eden was of old,
Let him rightly study you,
  And a brief of that behold.
    Welcome, welcome, &c.

*Browne.*

## 170

The sea hath many thousand sands,
  The sun hath motes as many;
The sky is full of stars, and love
  As full of woes as any:
Believe me, that do know the elf,
And make no trial by thyself.

It is in truth a pretty toy
  For babes to play withal;
But O the honies of our youth
  Are oft our age's gall!
Self-proof in time will make thee know
He was a prophet told thee so:

A prophet that, Cassandra-like,
  Tells truth without belief;
For headstrong youth will run his race,
  Although his goal be grief:
Love's martyr, when his heat is past,
Proves Care's confessor at the last.

*Anonymous.*

## 171

If fathers knew but how to leave
  Their children wit as they do wealth,
And could constrain them to receive
  That physic which brings perfect health,
The world would not admiring stand
A woman's face and woman's hand.

Women confess they must obey,
  We men will needs be servants still;
We kiss their hands, and what they say
  We must commend, be't ne'er so ill:
Thus we, like fools, admiring stand
Her pretty foot and pretty hand.

We blame their pride, which we increase
  By making mountains of a mouse;
We praise because we know we please;
  Poor women are too credulous
To think that we admiring stand
Or foot, or face, or foolish hand.

*Anonymous.*

## 172

Silly boy, 'tis full moon yet, thy night as day shines clearly;
Had thy youth but wit to fear, thou couldst not love so dearly.
Shortly wilt thou mourn when all thy pleasures are bereaved;
Little knows he how to love that never was deceived.

This is thy first maiden flame, that triumphs yet unstained;
All is artless now you speak, not one word, yet, is feigned;
All is heaven that you behold, and all your thoughts are blessed;
But no spring can want his fall, each Troilus hath his Cressid.

Thy well-ordered locks ere long shall rudely hang neglected;
And thy lively pleasant cheer read grief on earth dejected.
Much then wilt thou blame thy Saint, that made thy heart so holy,
And with sighs confess, in love that too much faith is folly.

Yet be just and constant still! Love may beget a wonder,
Not unlike a summer's frost, or winter's fatal thunder.
He that holds his sweetheart true, unto his day of dying,
Lives, of all that ever breathed, most worthy the envying.

*Campion.*

## 173

If thou long'st so much to learn, sweet boy, what 'tis to love,
Do but fix thy thought on me and thou shalt quickly prove.

Little suit, at first, shall win,
Way to thy abashed desire,
But then will I hedge thee in
Salamander-like with fire!

With thee dance I will, and sing, and thy fond dalliance bear;
We the grovy hills will climb, and play the wantons there;
Other whiles we'll gather flowers,
Lying dallying on the grass;
And thus our delightful hours
Full of waking dreams shall pass.

When thy joys were thus at height, my love should turn from thee;
Old acquaintance then should grow as strange as strange might be;
Twenty rivals thou shouldst find,
Breaking all their hearts for me,
While to all I 'll prove more kind
And more forward than to thee.

Thus, thy silly youth, enraged, would soon my love defy;
But, alas, poor soul, too late! clipt wings can never fly.
Those sweet hours which we had past,
Called to mind, thy heart would burn;
And couldst thou fly ne'er so fast,
They would make thee straight return.

*Campion.*

## 174

Break now, my heart, and die! O no, she may relent.
Let my despair prevail! O stay, hope is not spent.
Should she now fix one smile on thee, where were despair?
The loss is but easy, which smiles can repair.
A stranger would please thee, if she were as fair.

Her must I love or none, so sweet none breathes as she;
The more is my despair, alas, she loves not me!
But cannot time make way for love through ribs of steel?
The Grecian, enchanted all parts but the heel,
At last a shaft daunted, which his heart did feel.

*Campion.*

## 175

Blame not my cheeks, though pale with love they be;
The kindly heat unto my heart is flown,
To cherish it that is dismayed by thee,
Who art so cruel and unsteadfast grown:
For Nature, called for by distressed hearts,
Neglects and quite forsakes the outward parts.

But they whose cheeks with careless blood are stained,
Nurse not one spark of love within their hearts;

And, when they woo, they speak with passion feigned,
For their fat love lies in their outward parts:
But in their breasts, where Love his court should hold,
Poor Cupid sits and blows his nails for cold.

*Campion.*

## 176

Never love unless you can
Bear with all the faults of man:
Men sometimes will jealous be,
Though but little cause they see;
And hang the head, as discontent,
And speak what straight they will repent.

Men that but one saint adore,
Make a show of love to more:
Beauty must be scorned in none,
Though but truly served in one:
For what is courtship, but disguise?
True hearts may have dissembling eyes.

Men, when their affairs require,
Must a while themselves retire,
Sometimes hunt, and sometimes hawk,
And not ever sit and talk.
If these and such like you can bear,
Then like, and love, and never fear!

*Campion.*

## 177

Thus I resolve, and time hath taught me so,
  Since she is fair and ever kind to me,
Though she be wild and wanton-like in show,
  Those little stains in youth I will not see.
That she be constant, heaven I oft implore:
If prayers prevail not, I can do no more.

Palm-tree the more you press, the more it grows;
  Leave it alone it will not much exceed.
Free beauty if you strive to yoke, you lose:
  And for affection, strange distaste you breed.
What Nature hath not taught, no Art can frame:
Wild born be wild still, though by force you tame.

*Campion.*

## 178

When love on time and measure makes his ground,
  Time that must end, though love can never die,
'T is love betwixt a shadow and a sound,
  A love not in the heart but in the eye;
A love that ebbs and flows, now up, now down,
A morning's favour and an evening's frown.

Sweet looks show love, yet they are but as beams;
  Fair words seem true, yet they are but as wind;
Eyes shed their tears, yet are but outward streams;
  Sighs paint a shadow in the falsest mind.
Looks, words, tears, sighs show love when love they
    leave;
False hearts can weep, sigh, swear, and yet deceive.

*Anonymous.*

179

For her gait if she be walking,
Be she sitting I desire her
For her state's sake, and admire her
For her wit if she be talking.
Gait and state and wit approve her;
For which all and each I love her.

Be she sullen, I commend her
For a modest. Be she merry,
For a kind one her prefer I.
Briefly everything doth lend her
So much grace and so approve her,
That for everything I love her.

*Browne.*

180

## The Sun Rising

Busy old fool, unruly Sun,
Why dost thou thus,
Through windows, and through curtains, call on us?
Must to thy motions lovers' seasons run?
Saucy pedantic wretch, go chide
Late school-boys and sour prentices,
Go tell court-huntsmen that the king will ride,
Call country ants to harvest offices;
Love, all alike, no season knows nor clime,
Nor hours, days, months, which are the rags of time.

Thy beams so reverend and strong
Why shouldst thou think?
I could eclipse and cloud them with a wink,
But that I would not lose her sight so long.
If her eyes have not blinded thine,
Look, and to-morrow late tell me,
Whether both the Indias of spice and mine
Be where thou left'st them, or lie here with me.
Ask for those kings whom thou saw'st yesterday,
And thou shalt hear, "All here in one bed lay".

She's all states, and all princes I;
Nothing else is;
Princes do but play us; compared to this,
All honour's mimic, all wealth alchemy.
Thou, Sun, art half as happy as we,
In that the world's contracted thus;
Thine age asks ease, and since thy duties be
To warm the world, that's done in warming us.
Shine here to us, and thou art everywhere;
This bed thy centre is, these walls thy sphere.

*Donne.*

## 181

Rudely thou wrongest my dear heart's desire,
In finding fault with her too portly pride:
The thing which I do most in her admire,
Is of the world unworthy most envied:
For in those lofty looks is close implied
Scorn of base things, and 'sdain of foul dishonour,
Threatening rash eyes which gaze on her so wide,
That loosely they ne dare to look upon her.

Such pride is praise, such portliness is honour,
That boldened innocence bears in her eyes;
And her fair countenance, like a goodly banner,
Spreads in defiance of all enemies.
Was never in this world aught worthy tried,
Without some spark of such self-pleasing pride.

*Spenser.*

182

In that proud port, which her so goodly graceth,
Whiles her fair face she rears up to the sky,
And to the ground her eyelids low embaseth,
Most goodly temperature ye may descry;
Mild humbless, mixed with awful majesty.
For, looking on the earth whence she was born,
Her mind remembereth her mortality,
Whatso is fairest shall to earth return.
But that same lofty countenance seems to scorn
Base thing, and think how she to heaven may climb;
Treading down earth as loathsome and forlorn,
That hinders heavenly thoughts with drossy slime.
Yet lowly still vouchsafe to look on me;
Such lowliness shall make you lofty be.

*Spenser.*

183

The glorious portrait of that Angel's face,
Made to amaze weak men's confused skill,
And this world's worthless glory to embase,
What pen, what pencil, can express her fill?

For, though he colours could devise at will,
And eke his learned hand at pleasure guide,
Lest, trembling, it his workmanship should spill;
Yet many wondrous things there are beside:
The sweet eye-glances, that like arrows glide,
The charming smiles, that rob sense from the heart,
The lovely pleasance, and the lofty pride,
Cannot expressed be by any art.
  A greater craftsman's hand thereto doth need,
  That can express the life of things indeed.

*Spenser.*

## 184

Was it the work of nature or of art,
Which tempered so the feature of her face,
That pride and meekness, mixed by equal part,
Do both appear to adorn her beauty's grace?
For with mild pleasance, which doth pride displace,
She to her love doth lookers' eyes allure;
And, with stern countenance, back again doth chase
Their looser looks that stir up lusts impure;
With such strange terms her eyes she doth inure,
That with one look she doth my life dismay,
And with another doth it straight recure;
Her smile me draws; her frown me drives away.
  Thus doth she train and teach me with her looks;
  Such art of eyes I never read in books.

*Spenser.*

## 185

Thrice happy she, that is so well assured
Unto herself, and settled so in heart,
That neither will for better be allured,
Ne feared with worse to any chance to start;
But, like a steady ship, doth strongly part
The raging waves, and keeps her course aright;
Ne aught for tempest doth from it depart,
Ne aught for fairer weather's false delight.
Such self-assurance need not fear the spite
Of grudging foes, ne favour seek of friends:
But, in the stay of her own steadfast might,
Neither to one herself nor other bends.
Most happy she, that most assured doth rest;
But he most happy, who such one loves best.

*Spenser.*

## 186

Away with these self-loving lads
Whom Cupid's arrow never glads;
Away, poor souls, that sigh and weep
In love of those that lie asleep;
For Cupid is a meadow-god,
And forceth none to kiss the rod.

Sweet Cupid's shafts, like Destiny,
Do causeless good or ill decree:
Desert is born out of his bow,
Reward upon his wing doth go:
What fools are they that have not known
That Love likes no laws but his own.

My songs they be of Cynthia's praise,
I wear her rings on holy-days,
In every tree I write her name,
And every day I read the same.
Where honour Cupid's rival is,
There miracles are seen of his.

If Cynthia crave her ring of me,
I blot her name out of the tree;
If doubt do darken things held dear,
Then well fare nothing once a year;
For many run, but one must win:
Fools only hedge the cuckoo in.

The worth that worthiness should move
Is love, that is the bow of Love;
And love as well the foster can
As can the mighty nobleman.
Sweet saint, 'tis true, you worthy be,
Yet without love nought worth to me.

*Fulke Greville, Lord Brooke.*

## 187

Love is a sickness full of woes,
All remedies refusing;
A plant that with most cutting grows,
Most barren with best using.
Why so?
More we enjoy it, more it dies;
If not enjoyed, it sighing cries,
Heigh-ho!

Love is a torment of the mind,
  A tempest everlasting;
And Jove hath made it of a kind
  Not well, nor full nor fasting.
                    Why so?
More we enjoy it, more it dies;
If not enjoyed, it sighing cries,
                    Heigh-ho!

*Daniel.*

188

## Florimel's Ditty

How in my thoughts shall I contrive
  The image I am framing,
Which is so far superlative,
  As 'tis beyond all naming?
I would Jove of my counsel make,
  And have his judgment in it,
But that I doubt he would mistake
  How rightly to begin it.
It must be builded in the air,
  And 'tis my thoughts must do it,
And only they must be the stair
  From earth to mount me to it.
For of my sex I frame my lay,
  Each hour ourselves forsaking,
How should I then find out the way,
  To this my undertaking,
When our weak fancies working still,
  Yet changing every minute,
Will show that it requires some skill,
  Such difficulties in it?
We would things, yet we know not what,
  And let our will be granted,

Yet instantly we find in that
  Something unthought of wanted.
Our joys and hopes such shadows are
  As with our motions vary,
Which when we oft have fetched from far,
  With us they never tarry.
Some worldly cross doth still attend
  What long we have been spinning,
And ere we fully get the end,
  We lose of our beginning.
Our policies so peevish are
  That with themselves they wrangle,
And many times become the snare
  That soonest us entangle;
For that the love we bear our friends,
  Though ne'er so strongly grounded,
Hath in it certain oblique ends,
  If to the bottom sounded;
Our own well wishing making it
  A pardonable treason,
For that it is derived from wit,
  And underpropped with reason.
For our dear selves' beloved sake,
  Even in the depth of passion,
Our centre though ourselves we make
  Yet is not that our station;
For whilst our brows ambitious be,
  And youth at hand awaits us,
It is a pretty thing to see
  How finely beauty cheats us;
And whilst with time we trifling stand
  To practise antique graces,
Age with a pale and withered hand
  Draws furrows in our faces.

*Drayton.*

189

# A Woman's Heart

O faithless world, and thy most faithless part,
　　　A woman's heart!
The true shop of variety, where sits
　　　Nothing but fits
And fevers of desire, and pangs of love,
　　　Which toys remove.
Why was she born to please? or I to trust
　　　Words writ in dust,
Suffering her eyes to govern my despair,
　　　My pain for air;
And fruit of time rewarded with untruth,
　　　The food of youth?
Untrue she was; yet I believed her eyes,
　　　Instructed spies,
Till I was taught that love was but a school
　　　To breed a fool.
Or sought she more, by triumphs of denial,
　　　To make a trial
How far her smiles commanded my weakness?
　　　Yield and confess!
Excuse no more thy folly; but, for cure,
　　　Blush and endure
As well thy shame as passions that were vain;
　　　And think, 'tis gain,
To know that love lodged in a woman's breast
　　　Is but a guest.

*Wotton.*

190

## 190

# Of Women

If women could be fair, and yet not fond,
Or that their love were firm, not fickle, still,
I would not marvel that they make men bond
By service long to purchase their good will;
But when I see how frail those creatures are,
I muse that men forget themselves so far.

To mark the choice they make, and how they change,
How oft from Phoebus they do flee to Pan,
Unsettled still, like haggards wild, they range,
These gentle birds that fly from man to man;
Who would not scorn and shake them from the fist,
And let them fly, fair fools, which way they list?

Yet, for disport, we fawn and flatter both,
To pass the time when nothing else can please;
And train them to our lure with subtle oath,
Till, weary of their wiles, ourselves we ease:
And then we say, when we their fancy try,
To play with fools, O what a fool was I!

*Edward de Vere, Earl of Oxford.*

## 191

Follow a shadow, it still flies you;
Seem to fly it, it will pursue:
So court a mistress, she denies you;
Let her alone, she will court you;
Say are not women truly, then,
Styled but the shadows of us men?

At morn and even shades are longest;
At noon they are or short, or none:
So men at weakest, they are strongest,
But grant us perfect, they 're not known.
Say are not women truly, then,
Styled but the shadows of us men?

*Ben Jonson.*

## 192

Shall I, wasting in despair,
Die because a woman 's fair?
Or make pale my cheeks with care
Cause another 's rosy are?
Be she fairer than the day,
Or the flowery meads in May,
If she think not well of me,
What care I how fair she be?

Shall my silly heart be pined
Cause I see a woman kind?
Or a well-disposed nature
Joined with a lovely feature?
Be she meeker, kinder, than
Turtle-dove or pelican,
If she be not so to me,
What care I how kind she be?

Shall a woman's virtues move
Me to perish for her love?
Or her well-deservings known
Make me quite forget my own?

Be she with that goodness blest
Which may merit name of best,
If she be not such to me,
What care I how good she be?

'Cause her fortune seems too high,
Shall I play the fool and die?
She that bears a noble mind,
If not outward helps she find,
Thinks what with them he would do
Who without them dares her woo;
And unless that mind I see,
What care I how great she be?

Great, or good, or kind, or fair,
I will ne'er the more despair;
If she love me, this believe,
I will die ere she shall grieve;
If she slight me when I woo,
I can scorn and let her go;
For if she be not for me,
What care I for whom she be?

*Wither.*

## 193

Shall I tell you whom I love?
Hearken then awhile to me;
And if such a woman move,
As I now shall versify,
Be assured 'tis she or none
That I love, and love alone.

Nature did her so much right,
As she scorns the help of Art;
In as many virtues dight
As e'er yet embraced a heart.

So much good so truly tried,
Some for less were deified.

Wit she hath without desire
To make known how much she hath;
And her anger flames no higher
Than may fitly sweeten wrath.
Full of pity as may be,
Though perhaps not so to me.

Reason masters every sense,
And her virtues grace her birth:
Lovely as all excellence,
Modest in her most of mirth:
Likelihood enough to prove,
Only worth could kindle love.

Such she is: and if you know
Such a one as I have sung;
Be she brown, or fair, or so,
That she be but somewhat young;
Be assured, 'tis she, or none,
That I love, and love alone.

*Browne.*

## 194

# What Kind of Mistress He Would Have

Be the mistress of my choice
Clean in manners, clear in voice;
Be she witty, more than wise,
Pure enough, though not precise;

Be she showing in her dress
Like a civil wilderness;
That the curious may detect
Order in a sweet neglect;
Be she rolling in her eye,
Tempting all the passers-by;
And each ringlet of her hair
An enchantment, or a snare
For to catch the lookers-on;
But herself held fast by none.
Let her Lucrece all day be,
Thais in the night to me.
Be she such as neither will
Famish me nor overfill.

*Herrick.*

## 195

Love who will, for I'll love none,
There's fools enough beside me:
Yet if each woman have not one,
Come to me where I hide me,
And if she can the place attain,
For once I'll be her fool again.

It is an easy place to find,
And women sure should know it;
Yet thither serves not every wind,
Nor many men can show it:
It is the storehouse, where doth lie
All women's truth and constancy

If the journey be so long,
No woman will adventer;

But dreading her weak vessel's wrong,
The voyage will not enter:
Then may she sigh and lie alone,
In love with all, yet loved of none.

*Browne.*

196

## On Love

Love bade me ask a gift,
And I no more did move
But this, that I might shift
Still with my clothes my love:
That favour granted was:
Since which, though I love many,
Yet it so comes to pass
That long I love not any.

*Herrick.*

197

## The Indifferent

I can love both fair and brown;
Her whom abundance melts, and her whom want betrays;
Her who loves loneness best, and her who masks and plays;
Her whom the country formed, and whom the town;
Her who believes, and her who tries;
Her who still weeps with spongy eyes,
And her who is dry cork, and never cries.

I can love her, and her, and you, and you;
I can love any, so she be not true.

Will no other vice content you?
Will it not serve your turn to do as did your mothers?
Or have you all old vices spent and now would find out others?
Or doth a fear that men are true torment you?
O we are not, be not you so;
Let me—and do you—twenty know;
Rob me, but bind me not, and let me go.
Must I, who came to travel thorough you,
Grow your fixed subject, because you are true?

Venus heard me sigh this song;
And by love's sweetest part, variety, she swore,
She heard not this till now; it should be so no more.
She went, examined, and returned ere long,
And said, "Alas! some two or three
Poor heretics in love there be,
Which think to stablish dangerous constancy.
But I have told them, 'Since you will be true,
You shall be true to them who're false to you.'"

*Donne.*

198

## Community

Good we must love, and must hate ill,
For ill is ill, and good good still;
But there are things indifferent,

Which we may neither hate, nor love,
But one, and then another prove,
    As we shall find our fancy bent.

If then at first wise Nature had
Made women either good or bad,
    Then some we might hate, and some choose;
But since she did them so create,
That we may neither love, nor hate,
    Only this rests, all all may use.

If they were good, it would be seen;
Good is as visible as green,
    And to all eyes itself betrays.
If they were bad, they could not last;
Bad doth itself and others waste;
    So they deserve nor blame, nor praise.

But they are ours as fruits are ours;
He that but tastes, he that devours,
    And he that leaves all, doth as well;
Changed loves are but changed sorts of meat;
And when he hath the kernel eat,
    Who doth not fling away the shell?

*Donne.*

199

# To Virgins

Hear, ye virgins, and I'll teach
What the times of old did preach
Rosamond was in a bower
Kept, as Danae in a tower:

But yet love, who subtle is,
Crept to that, and came to this.
Be ye locked up like to these,
Or the rich Hesperides,
Or those babies in your eyes,
In their crystal nunneries;
Notwithstanding love will win,
Or else force a passage in:
And as coy be as you can,
Gifts will get ye, or the man.

*Herrick.*

200

## Upon Love, by Way of Question and Answer

I bring ye love: *Quest.* What will love do?
*Ans.* Like and dislike ye.
I bring ye love: *Quest.* What will love do?
*Ans.* Stroke ye to strike ye.
I bring ye love: *Quest.* What will love do?
*Ans.* Love will befool ye.
I bring ye love: *Quest.* What will love do?
*Ans.* Heat ye to cool ye.
I bring ye love: *Quest.* What will love do?
*Ans.* Love gifts will send ye.
I bring ye love: *Quest.* What will love do?
*Ans.* Stock ye to spend ye.
I bring ye love: *Quest.* What will love do?
*Ans.* Love will fulfil ye.
I bring ye love: *Quest.* What will love do?
*Ans.* Kiss ye to kill ye.

*Herrick.*

201

# The Shepherd's Description of Love

*Meliboeus.* Shepherd, what's love, I pray thee tell?
*Faustus.* It is that fountain and that well
Where pleasure and repentance dwell;
It is perhaps that sauncing bell
That tolls all into heaven or hell;
And this is love, as I heard tell.

*Meliboeus.* Yet what is love, I prithee say?
*Faustus.* It is a work on holiday;
It is December matched with May,
When lusty bloods, in fresh array,
Hear ten months after of the play;
And this is love, as I hear say.

*Meliboeus.* Yet what is love, good shepherd, sain?
*Faustus.* It is a sunshine mixed with rain;
It is a tooth-ache, or like pain;
It is a game where none doth gain;
The lass saith no, and would full fain;
And this is love, as I hear sain.

*Meliboeus.* Yet, shepherd, what is love, I pray?
*Faustus.* It is a yea, it is a nay,
A pretty kind of sporting fray;
It is a thing will soon away;
Then, nymphs, take vantage while ye may;
And this is love, as I hear say.

*Meliboeus.* Yet what is love, good shepherd, show?
*Faustus.* A thing that creeps; it cannot go;
A prize that passeth to and fro;
A thing for one, a thing for moe;
And he that proves shall find it so;
And, shepherd, this is love, I trow.

*Raleigh.*

## 202

Kind are her answers,
But her performance keeps no day;
Breaks time, as dancers
From their own music when they stray.
All her free favours
And smooth words wing my hopes in vain.
O did ever voice so sweet but only feign?
Can true love yield such delay,
Converting joy to pain?

Lost is our freedom,
When we submit to women so:
Why do we need them
When, in their best they work our woe?
There is no wisdom
Can alter ends, by Fate prefixt.
O why is the good of man with evil mixt?
Never were days yet called two,
But one night went betwixt.

*Campion.*

203

While that the sun with his beams hot
Scorched the fruits in vale and mountain,
Philon, the shepherd, late forgot,
Sitting beside a crystal fountain
In shadow of a green oak-tree,
Upon his pipe this song played he:
Adieu, Love! adieu, Love! untrue Love!
Untrue Love, untrue Love! adieu, Love!
Your mind is light, soon lost for new love.

So long as I was in your sight,
I was your heart, your soul, your treasure;
And evermore you sobbed and sighed,
Burning in flames beyond all measure.
Three days endured your love for me,
And it was lost in other three.
Adieu, Love! adieu, Love! untrue Love!
Untrue Love, untrue Love! adieu, Love!
Your mind is light, soon lost for new love.

Another shepherd you did see,
To whom your heart was soon enchained;
Full soon your love was leapt from me,
Full soon my place he had obtained:
Soon came a third your love to win;
And we were out, and he was in.
Adieu, Love! adieu, Love! untrue Love!
Untrue Love, untrue Love! adieu, Love!
Your mind is light, soon lost for new love.

Sure, you have made me passing glad
That you your mind so soon removed,

Before that I the leisure had
To choose you for my best beloved:
For all my love was passed and done
Two days, before it was begun.
Adieu, Love! adieu, Love! untrue Love!
Untrue Love, untrue Love! adieu, Love!
Your mind is light, soon lost for new love.

*Anonymous.*

## 204

Once did I love and yet I live,
Though love and truth be now forgotten;
Then did I joy, now do I grieve
That holy vows must now be broken.

Hers be the blame that caused it so,
Mine be the grief though it be mickle;
She shall have shame, I cause to know
What 'tis to love a dame so fickle.

Love her that list, I am content
For that chameleon-like she changeth,
Yielding such mists as may prevent
My sight to view her when she rangeth.

Let him not vaunt that gains my loss,
For when that he and time hath proved her,
She may him bring to Weeping-Cross:
I say no more, because I loved her.

*Anonymous.*

# 205

Once did my thoughts both ebb and flow,
As passion did them move;
Once did I hope, straight fear again,—
And then I was in love.

Once did I waking spend the night,
And tell how many minutes move;
Once did I wishing waste the day,—
And then I was in love.

Once, by my carving true love's knot,
The weeping trees did prove
That wounds and tears were both our lot,—
And then I was in love.

Once did I breathe another's breath
And in my mistress move,
Once was I not mine own at all,—
And then I was in love.

Once wore I bracelets made of hair,
And collars did approve,
Once wore my clothes made out of wax,—
And then I was in love.

Once did I sonnet to my saint,
My soul in numbers move,
Once did I tell a thousand lies,—
And then I was in love.

Once in my ear did dangling hang
A little turtle-dove,
Once, in a word, I was a fool,—
And then I was in love. *Anonymous.*

## 206

Now have I learned with much ado at last
By true disdain to kill desire;
This was the mark at which I shot so fast,
Unto this height I did aspire:
Proud Love, now do thy worst and spare not,
For thee and all thy shafts I care not.

What hast thou left wherewith to move my mind?
What life to quicken dead desire?
I count thy words and oaths as light as wind,
I feel no heat in all thy fire:
Go, change thy bow and get a stronger,
Go, break thy shafts and buy thee longer.

In vain thou bait'st thy hook with beauty's blaze,
In vain thy wanton eyes allure;
These are but toys for them that love to gaze,
I know what harm thy looks procure:
Some strange conceit must be devised,
Or thou and all thy skill despised.

*Anonymous.*

## 207

Now let her change and spare not!
Since she proves strange I care not:
Feigned love charmed so my delight
That still I doted on her sight.
But she is gone, new joys embracing
And my desires disgracing.

When did I err in blindness,
Or vex her with unkindness?

If my cares served her alone,
Why is she thus untimely gone?
True love abides to the hour of dying:
False love is ever flying.

False! then, farewell for ever!
Once false proves faithful never:
He that boasts now of thy love,
Shall soon my present fortunes prove.
Were he as fair as bright Adonis,
Faith is not had, where none is.

*Campion.*

## 208

Dear, if I with guile would gild a true intent,
Heaping flatteries that in heart were never meant:
Easily could I then obtain
What now in vain I force;
Falsehood much doth gain,
Truth yet holds the better course.

Love forbid that through dissembling I should thrive,
Or in praising you myself of truth deprive!
Let not your high thoughts debase
A simple truth in me:
Great is Beauty's grace,
Truth is yet as fair as she!

Praise is but the wind of pride, if it exceeds;
Wealth, prized in itself, no outward value needs.
Fair you are, and passing fair;
You know it, and 'tis true:
Yet let none despair
But to find as fair as you.

*Campion.*

209

Go and catch a falling star,
  Get with child a mandrake root,
Tell me where all past years are,
  Or who cleft the devil's foot,
Teach me to hear mermaids singing,
Or to keep off envy's stinging,
      And find
      What wind
Serves to advance an honest mind.

If thou be'st born to strange sights,
  Things invisible to see,
Ride ten thousand days and nights,
  Till age snow white hairs on thee,
Thou, when thou return'st, wilt tell me
      And swear,
      No where
Lives a woman true and fair.

If thou find'st one, let me know;
  Such a pilgrimage were sweet.
Yet do not, I would not go,
  Though at next door we might meet.
Though she were true when you met her,
And last till you write your letter,
      Yet she
      Will be
False, ere I come, to two or three.

*Donne.*

210

How easily wert thou chained,
Fond heart, by favours feigned!
Why lived thy hopes in grace,
Straight to die disdained?
But since thou art now beguiled
By love that falsely smiled,
In some less happy place
Mourn alone exiled!
My love still here increaseth,
And with my love my grief,
While her sweet bounty ceaseth,
That gave my woes relief.
Yet 'tis no woman leaves me,
For such may prove unjust;
A goddess thus deceives me,
Whose faith who could mistrust?

A goddess so much graced,
That Paradise is placed
In her most heavenly breast,
Once by love embraced:
But love, that so kind proved,
Is now from her removed,
Nor will he longer rest
Where no faith is loved.
If powers celestial wound us
And will not yield relief,
Woe then must needs confound us,
For none can cure our grief.
No wonder if I languish
Through burden of my smart:
It is no common anguish
From Paradise to part.

*Campion.*

## 211

So quick, so hot, so mad is thy fond suit,
  So rude, so tedious grown, in urging me,
That fain I would, with loss, make thy tongue mute,
  And yield some little grace to quiet thee:
An hour with thee I care not to converse,
For I would not be counted too perverse.

But roofs too hot would prove for me all fire;
  And hills too high for my unused pace;
The grove is charged with thorns and the bold briar;
  Gray snakes the meadows shroud in every place:
A yellow frog, alas, will fright me so,
As I should start and tremble as I go.

Since then I can on earth no fit room find,
  In heaven I am resolved with you to meet:
Till then, for hope's sweet sake, rest your tired mind
  And not so much as see me in the street:
A heavenly meeting one day we shall have,
But never, as you dream, in bed, or grave.

*Campion.*

## 212

# Myra

I, with whose colours Myra dressed her head,
  I, that wear posies of her own hand-making,
I, that mine own name in the chimneys read
  By Myra finely wrought ere I was waking:
Must I look on, in hope time coming may
With change bring back my turn again to play?

I, that on Sunday at the church-stile found
  A garland sweet, with true love-knots in flowers,
Which I to wear about mine arms was bound,
  That each of us might know that all was ours:
Must I now lead an idle life in wishes,
And follow Cupid for his loaves and fishes?

I, that did wear the ring her mother left,
  I, for whose love she gloried to be blamed,
I, with whose eyes her eyes committed theft,
  I, who did make her blush when I was named:
Must I lose ring, flowers, blush, theft, and go naked,
Watching with sighs, till dead love be awaked?

I, that when drowsy Argus fell asleep,
  Like jealousy o'erwatched with desire,
Was ever warned modesty to keep,
  While her breath speaking kindled Nature's fire:
Must I look on a-cold, while others warm them?
Do Vulcan's brothers in such fine nets arm them?

Was it for this that I might Myra see
  Washing the water with her beauties white?
Yet would she never write her love to me;
  Thinks wit of change while thoughts are in delight?
Mad girls must safely love, as they may leave;
No man can print a kiss; lines may deceive.

*Fulke Greville, Lord Brooke.*

213

# The Blossom

Little think'st thou, poor flower,
Whom I've watched six or seven days,
And seen thy birth, and seen what every hour
Gave to thy growth, thee to this height to raise,
And now dost laugh and triumph on this bough,
Little think'st thou,
That it will freeze anon, and that I shall
To-morrow find thee fallen, or not at all.

Little think'st thou, poor heart,
That labourest yet to nestle thee,
And think'st by hovering here to get a part
In a forbidden or forbidding tree,
And hop'st her stiffness by long siege to bow,
Little think'st thou,
That thou to-morrow, ere that sun doth wake,
Must with this sun and me a journey take.

But thou which lovest to be
Subtle to plague thyself, wilt say,
Alas! if you must go, what's that to me?
Here lies my business, and here I will stay;
You go to friends, whose love and means present
Various content
To your eyes, ears, and taste, and every part;
If then your body go, what need your heart?

Well then, stay here; but know,
When thou hast stayed, and done thy most,
A naked thinking heart, that makes no show,
Is to a woman but a kind of ghost.

How shall she know my heart; or having none,
Know thee for one?
Practice may make her know some other part;
But take my word, she doth not know a heart.

Meet me at London, then,
Twenty days hence, and thou shalt see
Me fresher, and more fat, by being with men,
Than if I had stayed still with her and thee.
For God's sake, if you can, be you so too;
I will give you
There to another friend, whom we shall find
As glad to have my body as my mind.

*Donne.*

## 214

Farewell, dear love! since thou wilt needs be gone:
Mine eyes do show my life is almost done.
—Nay I will never die,
So long as I can spy;
There be many mo
Though that she do go.
There be many mo, I fear not;
Why, then, let her go, I care not.

Farewell, farewell! since this I find is true,
I will not spend more time in wooing you.
—But I will seek elsewhere
If I may find her there
Shall I bid her go?
What and if I do?
Shall I bid her go and spare not?
O no, no, no, no, I dare not.

Ten thousand times farewell! yet stay awhile.
Sweet, kiss me once, sweet kisses time beguile.
        —I have no power to move:
        How now, am I in love!—
        Wilt thou needs be gone?
        Go then, all is one.
Wilt thou needs be gone? O hie thee!
Nay; stay, and do no more deny me.

Once more farewell! I see "Loth to depart"
Bids oft adieu to her that holds my heart:
        But seeing I must lose
        Thy love which I did choose,
        Go thy ways for me,
        Since it may not be:
Go thy ways for me, but whither
Go?—oh, but where I may come thither.

What shall I do? my love is now departed,
She is as fair as she is cruel-hearted:
        She would not be entreated
        With prayers oft repeated.
        If she come no more,
        Shall I die therefore?
If she come no more, what care I?
—Faith, let her go, or come, or tarry.

*Anonymous.*

## 215

Though your strangeness frets my heart,
    Yet may not I complain:
You persuade me, 't is but art,
    That secret love must feign.

If another you affect,
'T is but a show, to avoid suspect.
Is this fair excusing? O, no! all is abusing!

Your wished sight if I desire,
Suspicions you pretend:
Causeless you yourself retire,
While I in vain attend.
This a lover whets, you say,
Still made more eager by delay.
Is this fair excusing? O, no! all is abusing!

When another holds your hand,
You swear I hold your heart:
When my rivals close do stand,
And I sit far apart,
I am nearer yet than they,
Hid in your bosom, as you say.
Is this fair excusing? O, no! all is abusing!

Would my rival then I were,
Or else your secret friend:
So much lesser should I fear,
And not so much attend.
They enjoy you, every one,
Yet I must seem your friend alone.
Is this fair excusing? O, no! all is abusing!

*Campion.*

216

Think'st thou to seduce me then with words that
have no meaning?
Parrots so can learn to prate, our speech by pieces
gleaning:
Nurses teach their children so about the time of
weaning.

Learn to speak first, then to woo: to wooing, much
pertaineth:
He that courts us wanting art, soon falters when he
feigneth,
Looks asquint on his discourse, and smiles, when he
complaineth.

Skilful anglers hide their hooks, fit baits for every
season;
But with crooked pins fish thou, as babes do, that
want reason:
Gudgeons only can be caught with such poor tricks of
treason.

Ruth forgive me, if I erred from human heart's compassion,
When I laughed sometimes too much to see thy
foolish fashion:
But, alas, who less could do that found so good
occasion!

*Campion.*

217

# To his Rival

Her loved I most,
By thee that 's lost,
Though she were won with leisure;
She was my gain,
But to my pain
Thou spoil'st me of my treasure.

The ship full fraught
With gold, far sought,
Though ne'er so wisely helmed,
May suffer wrack
In sailing back
By tempest overwhelmed.

But she, good sir,
Did not prefer
You, for that I was ranging;
But for that she
Found faith in me,
And she loved to be changing.

Therefore boast not
Your happy lot,
Be silent now you have her;
The time I knew
She slighted you,
When I was in her favour.

None stands so fast
But may be cast
By fortune, and disgraced:

Once did I wear
Her garter there
Where you her glove have placed.

I had the vow
That thou hast now
And glances to discover
Her love to me,
And she to thee
Reads but old lessons over.

She hath no smile
That can beguile,
But as my thought I know it;
Yea, to a hair,
Both when and where
And how she will bestow it.

What now is thine
Was only mine,
And first to me was given;
Thou laugh'st at me,
I laugh at thee,
And thus we two are even.

But I'll not mourn,
But stay my turn,
The wind may come about, sir,
And once again
May bring me in
And help to bear you out, sir.

*Drayton.*

218

## Chop-Cherry

Thou gav'st me leave to kiss,
  Thou gav'st me leave to woo;
Thou mad'st me think, by this
  And that, thou lov'dst me too.

But I shall ne'er forget
  How, for to make thee merry,
Thou mad'st me chop, but yet
  Another snapped the cherry.

*Herrick.*

219

## A Canzonet to his Coy Love

I pray thee, leave, love me no more,
  Call home the heart you gave me,
I but in vain that saint adore,
  That can, but will not save me:
These poor half kisses kill me quite;
  Was ever man thus served?
Amidst an ocean of delight,
  For pleasure to be starved.

Show me no more those snowy breasts
  With azure riverets branched,
Where whilst mine eye with plenty feasts,
  Yet is my thirst not stanched.

O Tantalus, thy pains ne'er tell,
By me thou art prevented;
'T is nothing to be plagued in hell,
But thus in heaven tormented.

Clip me no more in those dear arms,
Nor thy life's comfort call me;
O, these are but too powerful charms,
And do but more enthrall me.
But see how patient I am grown,
In all this coil about thee;
Come, nice thing, let thy heart alone;
I cannot live without thee.

*Drayton.*

## 220

Take, O, take those lips away,
That so sweetly were forsworn;
And those eyes, the break of day,
Lights that do mislead the morn;
But my kisses bring again, bring again;
Seals of love, but sealed in vain, sealed in vain.

*Shakespeare.*

## 221

Sigh no more, ladies, sigh no more,
Men were deceivers ever,
One foot in sea and one on shore,
To one thing constant never:
Then sigh not so, but let them go,
And be you blithe and bonny,
Converting all your sounds of woe
Into Hey nonny, nonny.

Sing no more ditties, sing no moe,
Of dumps so dull and heavy;
The fraud of men was ever so,
Since summer first was leavy:
Then sigh not so, but let them go,
And be you blithe and bonny,
Converting all your sounds of woe
Into Hey nonny, nonny.

*Shakespeare.*

222

## The Message

Send home my long strayed eyes to me,
Which, O! too long have dwelt on thee;
Yet since there they have learned such ill,
Such forced fashions,
And false passions,
That they be
Made by thee
Fit for no good sight, keep them still.

Send home my worthless heart again,
Which no unworthy thought could stain;
But if it be taught by thine
To make jestings
Of protestings,
And break both
Word and oath,
Keep it, for then 'tis none of mine.

Yet send me back my heart and eyes,
That I may know, and see thy lies,

And may laugh and joy, when thou
Art in anguish
And dost languish
For some one
That will none,
Or prove as false as thou art now.

*Donne.*

223

When thou must home to shades of underground,
And there arrived, a new admired guest,
The beauteous spirits do engirt thee round,
White Iope, blithe Helen, and the rest,
To hear the stories of thy finished love
From that smooth tongue whose music hell can move;
Then wilt thou speak of banqueting delights,
Of masques and revels which sweet youth did make,
Of tourneys and great challenges of knights,
And all those triumphs for thy beauty's sake:
When thou hast told these honours done to thee,
Then tell, O tell, how thou didst murder me.

*Campion.*

224

# The Prohibition

Take heed of loving me;
At least remember, I forbade it thee;
Not that I shall repair my unthrifty waste
Of breath and blood, upon thy sighs and tears,
By being to thee then what to me thou wast;
But so great joy our life at once outwears.

Then, lest thy love by my death frustrate be,
If thou love me, take heed of loving me.

Take heed of hating me,
Or too much triumph in the victory;
Not that I shall be mine own officer,
And hate with hate again retaliate;
But thou wilt lose the style of conqueror,
If I, thy conquest, perish by thy hate.
Then, lest my being nothing lessen thee,
If thou hate me, take heed of hating me.

Yet love and hate me too;
So these extremes shall ne'er their office do;
Love me, that I may die the gentler way;
Hate me, because thy love's too great for me:
Or let these two, themselves, not me, decay;
So shall I live thy stage, not triumph be.
Lest thou thy love and hate, and me undo,
O let me live, yet love and hate me too.

*Donne.*

## 225

There's nothing grieves me, but that age should haste,
That in my days I may not see thee old,
That where those two clear sparkling eyes are placed,
Only two loopholes then I might behold:
That lovely, arched, ivory, polished brow
Defaced with wrinkles, that I might but see;
Thy dainty hair, so curled and crisped now,
Like grizzled moss upon some aged tree;
Thy cheek, now flush with roses, sunk and lean,
Thy lips with age as any wafer thin,

Thy pearly teeth out of thy head so clean,
That, when thou feed'st, thy nose shall touch thy chin.
These lines that now thou scornst, which should delight thee,
Then would I make thee read, but to despite thee.

*Drayton.*

## 226

Why should your fair eyes, with such sovereign grace,
Disperse their rays on every vulgar spirit,
Whilst I in darkness, in the self-same place,
Get not one glance to recompense my merit?
So doth the plowman gaze the wandering star,
And only rest contented with the light,
That never learned what constellations are,
Beyond the bent of his unknowing sight.
O why should beauty, custom to obey,
To their gross sense apply herself so ill?
Would God I were as ignorant as they,
When I am made unhappy by my skill!
Only compelled on this poor good to boast,
Heavens are not kind to them that know them most.

*Drayton.*

## 227

You're not alone when you are still alone:
O God, from you that I could private be!
Since you one were, I never since was one;
Since you in me, my self since out of me,
Transported from my self into your being,
Though either distant, present yet to either;

Senseless with too much joy, each other seeing,
And only absent when we are together.
Give me myself, and take yourself again;
Devise some means but how I may forsake you;
So much is mine that doth with you remain,
That taking what is mine, with me I take you
You do bewitch me: O that I could fly
From my self you, or from your own self I!

*Drayton.*

## 228

Ring out your bells, let mourning shows be spread;
For Love is dead.
All love is dead, infected
With plague of deep disdain;
Worth, as not worth, rejected,
And Faith, fair scorn doth gain.
From so ungrateful fancy,
From such a female frenzy,
From them that use men thus,
Good Lord, deliver us!

Weep, neighbours, weep, do you not hear it said
That Love is dead?
His deathbed, peacock's folly;
His winding-sheet is shame;
His will, false-seeming holy;
His sole executor, blame.
From so ungrateful fancy,
From such a female frenzy,
From them that use men thus,
Good Lord, deliver us!

Let dirge be sung, and trentals rightly read,
For Love is dead.
Sir Wrong his tomb ordaineth,
My mistress' marble heart;
Which epitaph containeth,
"Her eyes were once his dart".
From so ungrateful fancy,
From such a female frenzy,
From them that use men thus,
Good Lord, deliver us!

Alas! I lie; rage hath this error bred,
Love is not dead.
Love is not dead, but sleepeth
In her unmatched mind,
Where she his counsel keepeth,
Till due desert she find.
Therefore from so vile fancy,
To call such wit a frenzy,
Who love can temper thus,
Good Lord, deliver us!

*Sidney.*

229

Harden now thy tired heart, with more than flinty rage!
Ne'er let her false tears henceforth thy constant grief assuage!
Once true happy days thou saw'st when she stood firm and kind,
Both as one then lived and held one ear, one tongue, one mind:
But now those bright hours be fled, and never may return;
What then remains but her untruths to mourn?

Silly traitoress, who shall now thy careless tresses
place?
Who thy pretty talk supply, whose ear thy music
grace?
Who shall thy bright eyes admire? what lips triumph
with thine?
Day by day who'll visit thee and say: "Thou art
only mine"?
Such a time there was, God wot, but such shall never
be:
Too oft, I fear, thou wilt remember me.

*Campion.*

230

# The Apparition

When by thy scorn, O murderess, I am dead,
And that thou think'st thee free
From all solicitation from me,
Then shall my ghost come to thy bed,
And thee, feigned vestal, in worse arms shall see:
Then thy sick taper will begin to wink,
And he, whose thou art then, being tired before,
Will, if thou stir, or pinch to wake him, think
Thou call'st for more,
And, in false sleep, will from thee shrink:
And then, poor aspen wretch, neglected thou
Bathed in a cold quicksilver sweat wilt lie
A verier ghost than I.
What I will say, I will not tell thee now,
Lest that preserve thee; and since my love is spent,
I'd rather thou shouldst painfully repent,
Than by my threatenings rest still innocent.

*Donne.*

## 231

An evil spirit, your beauty, haunts me still,
Wherewith, alas, I have been long possesst;
Which ceaseth not to tempt me to each ill,
Nor give me once but one poor minute's rest.
In me it speaks, whether I sleep or wake,
And when by means to drive it out I try,
With greater torments then it me doth take,
And tortures me in most extremity.
Before my face it lays down my despairs,
And hastes me on unto a sudden death;
Now tempting me to drown myself in tears,
And then in sighing to give up my breath.
Thus am I still provoked to every evil,
By this good wicked spirit, sweet angel devil.

*Drayton.*

## 232

The expense of spirit in a waste of shame
Is lust in action; and till action, lust
Is perjured, murderous, bloody, full of blame,
Savage, extreme, rude, cruel, not to trust,
Enjoyed no sooner but despised straight,
Past reason hunted, and no sooner had
Past reason hated, as a swallowed bait
On purpose laid to make the taker mad;
Mad in pursuit and in possession so;
Had, having, and in quest to have, extreme;
A bliss in proof, and proved, a very woe;
Before, a joy proposed; behind, a dream.
All this the world well knows; yet none knows well
To shun the heaven that leads men to this hell.

*Shakespeare.*

## 233

Thou blind man's mark, thou fool's self-chosen snare,
Fond fancy's scum, and dregs of scattered thought;
Band of all evils, cradle of causeless care,
Thou web of will, whose end is never wrought;
Desire, Desire, I have too dearly bought,
With prize of mangled mind, thy worthless ware;
Too long, too long asleep thou hast me brought,
Who should my mind to higher things prepare.
But yet in vain thou hast my ruin sought;
In vain thou mad'st me to vain things aspire;
In vain thou kindlest all thy smoky fire;
For virtue hath this better lesson taught:
  Within myself to seek my only hire,
  Desiring nought, but how to kill Desire.

*Sidney.*

## 234

Leave me, O Love, which reachest but to dust;
And thou, my mind, aspire to higher things;
Grow rich in that which never taketh rust;
Whatever fades, but fading pleasure brings.
Draw in thy beams, and humble all thy might
To that sweet yoke where lasting freedoms be;
Which breaks the clouds, and opens forth the light,
That doth both shine and give us sight to see.
O take fast hold; let that light be thy guide
In this small course which birth brings out to death;
And think how evil becometh him to slide,
Who seeketh heaven, and comes of heavenly breath.
  Then farewell, world; thy uttermost I see:
  Eternal Love, maintain thy life in me.

*Sidney.*

Doubt you to whom my Muse these notes intendeth,
Which now my breast o'ercharged to music lendeth?
To you, to you, all song of praise is due:
Only in you my song begins and endeth.

Who hath the eyes which marry state with pleasure?
Who keeps the key of Nature's chiefest treasure?
To you, to you, all song of praise is due:
Only for you the heaven forgat all measure.

Who hath the lips, where wit in fairness reigneth?
Who womankind at once both decks and staineth?
To you, to you, all song of praise is due:
Only by you Cupid his crown maintaineth.

Who hath the feet, whose step of sweetness planteth?
Who else, for whom Fame worthy trumpets wanteth?
To you, to you, all song of praise is due:
Only to you her sceptre Venus granteth.

Who hath the breast, whose milk doth passions nourish?
Whose grace is such, that when it chides doth cherish?
To you, to you, all song of praise is due:
Only through you the tree of life doth flourish.

Who hath the hand, which without stroke subdueth?
Who long dead beauty with increase reneweth?
To you, to you, all song of praise is due:
Only at you all envy hopeless rueth.

Who hath the hair, which, loosest, fastest tieth?
Who makes a man live then glad when he dieth?
To you, to you, all song of praise is due:
Only of you the flatterer never lieth.

Who hath the voice, which soul from senses sunders?
Whose force but yours the bolts of beauty thunders?
To you, to you, all song of praise is due:
Only with you not miracles are wonders.

Doubt you to whom my Muse these notes intendeth,
Which now my breast o'ercharged to music lendeth?
To you, to you, all song of praise is due:
Only in you my song begins and endeth.

*Sidney.*

## 236

Only Joy, now here you are,
Fit to hear and ease my care,
Let my whispering voice obtain
Sweet reward for sharpest pain;
Take me to thee, and thee to me.
"No, no, no, no, my dear, let be."

Night hath closed all in her cloak,
Twinkling stars love-thoughts provoke,
Danger hence, good care doth keep,
Jealousy itself doth sleep;
Take me to thee, and thee to me.
"No, no, no, no, my dear, let be."

Better place no wit can find,
Cupid's yoke to loose or bind;

These sweet flowers on fine bed too,
Us in their best language woo;
Take me to thee, and thee to me.
"No, no, no, no, my dear, let be."

This small light the moon bestows
Serves thy beams but to disclose,
So to raise my hap more high;
Fear not else, none can us spy;
Take me to thee, and thee to me.
"No, no, no, no, my dear, let be."

That you heard was but a mouse,
Dumb Sleep holdeth all the house;
Yet asleep methinks they say,
"Young fools, take time while you may";
Take me to thee, and thee to me.
"No, no, no, no, my dear, let be."

Niggard time threats, if we miss
This large offer of our bliss,
Long stay ere he grant the same:
Sweet, then, while each thing doth frame,
Take me to thee, and thee to me.
"No, no, no, no, my dear, let be."

Your fair mother is abed,
Candles out, and curtains spread;
She thinks you do letters write;
Write, but let me first endite:
Take me to thee, and thee to me.
"No, no, no, no, my dear, let be."

Sweet, alas, why strive you thus?
Concord better fitteth us;

Leave to Mars the force of hands,
Your power in your beauty stands;
Take me to thee, and thee to me.
"No, no, no, no, my dear, let be."

Woe to me, and do you swear
Me to hate? but I forbear;
Cursed be my destinies all,
That brought me so high to fall;
Soon with my death I will please thee.
"No, no, no, no, my dear, let be."

*Sidney.*

## 237

In a grove most rich of shade,
Where birds wanton music made,
May, then young, his pied weeds showing,
New perfumed with flowers fresh growing;

Astrophel with Stella sweet
Did for mutual comfort meet,
Both within themselves oppressed,
But each in the other blessed.

Him great harms had taught much care,
Her fair neck a foul yoke bare;
But her sight his cares did banish
In his sight her yoke did vanish.

Wept they had, alas, the while,
But now tears themselves did smile,
While their eyes, by love directed,
Interchangeably reflected.

Sigh they did, but now betwixt
Sighs of woe were glad sighs mixt;
With arms crossed, yet testifying
Restless rest, and living dying.

Their ears hungry of each word
Which the dear tongue would afford;
But their tongues restrained from walking,
Till their hearts had ended talking.

But when their tongues could not speak,
Love itself did silence break:
Love did set his lips asunder,
Thus to speak in love and wonder.

" Stella, sovereign of my joy,
Fair triumpher of annoy;
Stella, star of heavenly fire,
Stella, loadstar of desire;

" Stella, in whose shining eyes
Are the lights of Cupid's skies,
Whose beams, where they once are darted,
Love therewith is straight imparted;

" Stella, whose voice, when it speaks,
Senses all asunder breaks;
Stella, whose voice, when it singeth,
Angels to acquaintance bringeth;

" Stella, in whose body is
Writ each character of bliss;
Whose face all, all beauty passeth,
Save thy mind, which yet surpasseth;

"Grant, O grant; but speech, alas,
Fails me, fearing on to pass:
Grant—O me, what am I saying?
But no fault there is in praying.

"Grant, O dear! on knees I pray"
(Knees on ground he then did stay),
"That, not I, but since I love you,
Time and place for me may move you.

"Never season was more fit,
Never room more apt for it;
Smiling air allows my reason;
These birds sing: now use the season.

"This small wind, which so sweet is,
See how it the leaves doth kiss;
Each tree in his best attiring,
Sense of love to love inspiring.

"Love makes earth the water drink,
Love to earth makes water sink;
And, if dumb things be so witty,
Shall a heavenly grace want pity?"

There his hands, in their speech, fain
Would have made tongue's language plain;
But her hands, his hands repelling,
Gave repulse, all grace excelling.

Then she spake; her speech was such,
As not ears, but heart did touch;
While such wise she love denied,
As yet love she signified.

"Astrophel," said she, "my love,
Cease, in these effects, to prove;
Now be still, yet still believe me,
Thy grief more than death would grieve me.

"If that any thought in me
Can taste comfort but of thee,
Let me, fed with hellish anguish,
Joyless, hopeless, endless languish.

"If those eyes you praised, be
Half so dear as you to me,
Let me home return, stark blinded
Of those eyes, and blinder minded.

"If to secret of my heart,
I do any wish impart,
Where thou art not foremost placed,
Be both wish and I defaced.

"If more may be said, I say
All my bliss in thee I lay;
If thou love, my love content thee,
For all love, all faith is meant thee.

"Trust me, while I thee deny,
In myself the smart I try;
Tyrant Honour doth thus use thee,
Stella's self might not refuse thee.

"Therefore, dear, this no more move,
Lest, though I leave not thy love,
Which too deep in me is framed,
I should blush when thou art named."

Therewithal away she went,
Leaving him to passion, rent
With what she had done and spoken,
That therewith my song is broken.

*Sidney.*

## 238

O dear life, when shall it be
That mine eyes thine eyes may see,
And in them thy mind discover,
Whether absence have had force
Thy remembrance to divorce
From the image of the lover?

Or if I myself find not,
After parting, ought forgot,
Nor debarred from Beauty's treasure,
Let no tongue aspire to tell
In what high joys I shall dwell:
Only Thought aims at the pleasure.

Thought, therefore, I will send thee
To take up the place for me;
Long I will not after tarry;
There, unseen, thou mayest be bold,
Those fair wonders to behold,
Which in them my hopes do carry.

Thought see thou no place forbear,
Enter bravely everywhere,
Seize on all to her belonging;
But if thou wouldst guarded be,
Fearing her beams, take with thee
Strength of liking, rage of longing.

Think of that most grateful time
When my leaping heart will climb
In thy lips to have his biding,
There those roses for to kiss,
Which do breathe a sugared bliss,
Opening rubies, pearls dividing.

Think of my most princely power,
When I blessed shall devour
With my greedy lickorous senses
Beauty, music, sweetness, love,
While she doth against me prove
Her strong darts but weak defences.

Think, think of those dallyings,
When with dovelike murmurings,
With glad moaning, passed anguish,
We change eyes, and heart for heart
Each to other do depart,
Joying till joy makes us languish.

O my Thought, my thoughts surcease,
Thy delights my woes increase,
My life melts with too much thinking;
Think no more, but die in me,
Till thou shalt revived be,
At her lips my nectar drinking.

*Sidney.*

## 239

Who is it that this dark night,
Underneath my window plaineth?
It is one who from thy sight,
Being, ah! exiled, disdaineth
Every other vulgar light.

Why, alas! and are you he?
Be not yet those fancies changed?
Dear, when you find change in me,
Though from me you be estranged,
Let my change to ruin be.

Well, in absence this will die;
Leave to see, and leave to wonder.
Absence sure will help, if I
Can learn how myself to sunder
From what in my heart doth lie.

But time will these thoughts remove:
Time doth work what no man knoweth.
Time doth as the subject prove,
With time still the affection groweth
In the faithful turtle dove.

What if you new beauties see!
Will not they stir new affection?
I will think they pictures be
(Image-like, of saints' perfection)
Poorly counterfeiting thee.

But your reason's purest light
Bids you leave such minds to nourish!
Dear, do reason no such spite;
Never doth thy beauty flourish
More than in my reason's sight.

But the wrongs love bears will make
Love at length leave undertaking.
No, the more fools it do shake,
In a ground of so firm making
Deeper still they drive the stake.

Peace, I think that some give ear;
Come no more, lest I get anger.
Bliss, I will my bliss forbear;
Fearing, sweet, you to endanger;
But my soul shall harbour there.

Well, be gone; be gone, I say,
Lest that Argus' eyes perceive you.
O unjust Fortune's sway,
Which can make me thus to leave you,
And from louts to run away.

*Sidney.*

## 240

Let me not to the marriage of true minds
Admit impediments. Love is not love
Which alters when it alteration finds,
Or bends with the remover to remove:
O, no! it is an ever-fixed mark
That looks on tempests and is never shaken;
It is the star to every wandering bark,
Whose worth's unknown, although his height be
taken.
Love's not Time's fool, though rosy lips and cheeks
Within his bending sickle's compass come;
Love alters not with his brief hours and weeks,
But bears it out even to the edge of doom.
If this be error and upon me proved,
I never writ, nor no man ever loved.

*Shakespeare.*

241

## The Bargain

My true love hath my heart, and I have his,
By just exchange one for another given:
I hold his dear, and mine he cannot miss,
There never was a better bargain driven:
My true love hath my heart, and I have his.

His heart in me keeps him and me in one,
My heart in him his thoughts and senses guides:
He loves my heart, for once it was his own,
I cherish his because in me it bides:
My true love hath my heart, and I have his.

*Sidney.*

242

As you came from the holy land
  Of Walsinghame,
Met you not with my true love
  By the way as you came?

How shall I know your true love,
  That have met many one,
As I went to the holy land,
  That have come, that have gone?

She is neither white nor brown,
  But as the heavens fair;
There is none hath a form so divine
  In the earth or the air.

Such a one did I meet, good sir,
  Such an angelic face,
Who like a queen, like a nymph, did appear,
  By her gait, by her grace.

She hath left me here all alone,
  All alone, as unknown,
Who sometimes did me lead with herself,
  And me loved as her own.

What's the cause that she leaves you alone,
  And a new way doth take,
Who loved you once as her own,
  And her joy did you make?

I have loved her all my youth,
  But now old, as you see:
Love likes not the falling fruit
  From the withered tree.

Know that Love is a careless child,
  And forgets promise past;
He is blind, he is deaf when he list,
  And in faith never fast.

His desire is a dureless content
  And a trustless joy;
He is won with a world of despair,
  And is lost with a toy.

Of womenkind such indeed is the love,
  Or the word love abused,
Under which many childish desires
  And conceits are excused.

But true love is a durable fire,
In the mind ever burning,
Never sick, never old, never dead,
From itself never turning.

*Raleigh.*

243

## The Undertaking

I have done one braver thing
Than all the Worthies did;
And yet a braver thence doth spring,
Which is, to keep that hid.

It were but madness now to impart
The skill of specular stone,
When he, which can have learned the art
To cut it, can find none.

So, if I now should utter this,
Others—because no more
Such stuff to work upon, there is—
Would love but as before.

But he who loveliness within
Hath found, all outward loathes,
For he who colour loves, and skin,
Loves but their oldest clothes.

If, as I have, you also do
Virtue in woman see,

And dare love that, and say so too,
  And forget the He and She;

And if this love, though placed so,
  From profane men you hide,
Which will no faith on this bestow,
  Or, if they do, deride;

Then you have done a braver thing
  Than all the Worthies did;
And a braver thence will spring,
  Which is, to keep that hid.

*Donne.*

244

## To Anthea, who may Command him Anything

Bid me to live, and I will live
  Thy Protestant to be,
Or bid me love, and I will give
  A loving heart to thee.

A heart as soft, a heart as kind,
  A heart as sound and free
As in the whole world thou canst find,
  That heart I'll give to thee.

Bid that heart stay, and it will stay
  To honour thy decree:
Or bid it languish quite away,
  And 't shall do so for thee.

Bid me to weep, and I will weep
   While I have eyes to see:
And, having none, yet I will keep
   A heart to weep for thee.

Bid me despair, and I'll despair
   Under that cypress-tree:
Or bid me die, and I will dare
   E'en death to die for thee.

Thou art my life, my love, my heart,
   The very eyes of me:
And hast command of every part
   To live and die for thee.

*Herrick.*

## 245

Being your slave, what should I do but tend
Upon the hours and times of your desire?
I have no precious time at all to spend,
Nor services to do, till you require.
Nor dare I chide the world-without-end hour
Whilst I, my sovereign, watch the clock for you,
Nor think the bitterness of absence sour
When you have bid your servant once adieu;
Nor dare I question with my jealous thought
Where you may be, or your affairs suppose,
But, like a sad slave, stay and think of nought
Save, where you are how happy you make those.
   So true a fool is love that in your will,
   Though you do anything, he thinks no ill.

*Shakespeare.*

246

Absence, hear thou my protestation
    Against thy strength,
    Distance, and length;
Do what thou canst for alteration,
    For hearts of truest mettle
    Absence doth join and time doth settle.

Who loves a mistress of such quality,
    His mind hath found
    Affection's ground
Beyond time, place, and all mortality;
    To hearts that cannot vary
    Absence is present, Time doth tarry.

My senses want their outward motion,
    Which now within
    Reason doth win,
Redoubled by her secret notion;
    Like rich men that take pleasure
    In hiding more than handling treasure.

By absence this good means I gain,
    That I can catch her,
    Where none can watch her,
In some close corner of my brain;
    There I embrace and kiss her,
    And so I both enjoy and miss her.

*Donne.*

## 247

Love me or not, love her I must or die;
Leave me or not, follow her, needs must I.
O that her grace would my wished comforts give!
How rich in her, how happy should I live!

All my desire, all my delight should be,
Her to enjoy, her to unite to me:
Envy should cease, her would I love alone:
Who loves by looks is seldom true to one.

Could I enchant, and that it lawful were,
Her would I charm softly that none should hear.
But love enforced rarely yields firm content;
So would I love that neither should repent.

*Campion.*

## 248

Since there's no help, come, let us kiss and part.
Nay, I have done, you get no more of me,
And I am glad, yea, glad with all my heart,
That thus so cleanly I myself can free.
Shake hands for ever, cancel all our vows,
And when we meet at any time again,
Be it not seen in either of our brows
That we one jot of former love retain.
Now at the last gasp of Love's latest breath,
When, his pulse failing, Passion speechless lies,
When Faith is kneeling by his bed of death,
And Innocence is closing up his eyes,
Now, if thou wouldst, when all have given him over,
From death to life thou might'st him yet recover.

*Drayton.*

## 249

Fain would I change that note
To which fond love hath charmed me
Long, long to sing by rote,
Fancying that that harmed me:
Yet when this thought doth come,
" Love is the perfect sum
Of all delight",
I have no other choice
Either for pen or voice
To sing or write.

O Love, they wrong thee much
That say thy sweet is bitter,
When thy ripe fruit is such
As nothing can be sweeter
Fair house of joy and bliss,
Where truest pleasure is,
I do adore thee;
I know thee what thou art,
I serve thee with my heart,
And fall before thee.

*Anonymous.*

## 250

Shall I look to ease my grief?
No, my sight is lost with eying:
Shall I speak and beg relief?
No, my voice is hoarse with crying:
What remains but only dying?

Love and I of late did part,
  But the boy, my peace envying,
Like a Parthian threw his dart
  Backward, and did wound me flying:
  What remains but only dying?

She whom then I looked on,
  My remembrance beautifying,
Stays with me though I am gone,
  Gone, and at her mercy lying:
  What remains but only dying?

Shall I try her thoughts and write?
  No, I have no means of trying:
If I should, yet at first sight
  She would answer with denying:
  What remains but only dying?

Thus my vital breath doth waste,
  And, my blood with sorrow drying,
Sighs and tears make life to last
  For a while, their place supplying:
  What remains but only dying?

*Anonymous.*

## 251

There is none, O none but you,
  That from me estrange your sight,
Whom mine eyes affect to view
  Or chained ears hear with delight.

Other beauties others move,
  In you I all graces find;
Such is the effect of love,
  To make them happy that are kind.

Women in frail beauty trust,
  Only seem you fair to me:
Yet prove truly kind and just,
  For that may not dissembled be.

Sweet, afford me then your sight,
  That, surveying all your looks,
Endless volumes I may write
  And fill the world with envied books:

Which when after-ages view,
  All shall wonder and despair,
Woman to find man so true,
  Or man a woman half so fair.

*Campion.*

252

## The Canonization

For God's sake hold your tongue, and let me love;
    Or chide my palsy, or my gout;
    My five grey hairs, or ruined fortune flout;
With wealth your state, your mind with arts improve;
    Take you a course, get you a place,
    Observe his Honour, or his Grace;
Or the king's real, or his stamped face
    Contemplate; what you will, approve,
    So you will let me love.

Alas! alas! who's injured by my love?
What merchant's ships have my sighs drowned?
Who says my tears have overflowed his ground?
When did my colds a forward spring remove?
When did the heats which my veins fill
Add one more to the plaguy bill?
Soldiers find wars, and lawyers find out still
Litigious men, which quarrels move,
Though she and I do love.

Call's what you will, we are made such by love;
Call her one, me another fly,
We're tapers too, and at our own cost die,
And we in us find the eagle and the dove.
The phoenix riddle hath more wit
By us; we two being one, are it;
So, to one neutral thing both sexes fit.
We die and rise the same, and prove
Mysterious by this love.

We can die by it, if not live by love,
And if unfit for tomb and hearse
Our legend be, it will be fit for verse;
And if no piece of chronicle we prove,
We'll build in sonnets pretty rooms;
As well a well-wrought urn becomes
The greatest ashes, as half-acre tombs,
And by these hymns all shall approve
Us canonized for love;

And thus invoke us, "You, whom reverend love
Made one another's hermitage;
You, to whom love was peace, that now is rage;

Who did the whole world's soul contract, and drove
Into the glasses of your eyes;
So made such mirrors, and such spies,
That they did all to you epitomize—
Countries, towns, courts beg from above
A pattern of your love."

*Donne.*

253

## The Good-Morrow

I wonder, by my troth, what thou and I
Did, till we loved? were we not weaned till then?
But sucked on country pleasures, childishly?
Or snorted we in the Seven Sleepers' den?
'T was so; but this, all pleasures fancies be;
If ever any beauty I did see,
Which I desired, and got, 't was but a dream of thee.

And now good-morrow to our waking souls,
Which watch not one another out of fear;
For love all love of other sights controls,
And makes one little room an everywhere.
Let sea-discoverers to new worlds have gone;
Let maps to other worlds on worlds have shown;
Let us possess one world; each hath one, and is one.

My face in thine eye, thine in mine appears,
And true plain hearts do in the faces rest;
Where can we find two better hemispheres
Without sharp north, without declining west?

Whatever dies, was not mixed equally;
If our two loves be one, or thou and I
Love so alike that none can slacken, none can die.

*Donne.*

## 254

Follow thy fair sun, unhappy shadow!
Though thou be black as night,
And she made all of light,
Yet follow thy fair sun, unhappy shadow!

Follow her whose light thy light depriveth;
Though here thou livest disgraced,
And she in heaven is placed,
Yet follow her whose light the world reviveth!

Follow those pure beams whose beauty burneth,
That so have scorched thee,
As thou still black must be,
Till her kind beams thy black to brightness turneth.

Follow her! while yet her glory shineth:
There comes a luckless night,
That will dim all her light;
And this the black unhappy shade divineth.

Follow still! since so thy fates ordained;
The sun must have his shade,
Till both at once do fade;
The sun still proved, the shadow still disdained.

*Campion.*

## 255

At her fair hands how have I grace entreated,
With prayers oft repeated!
Yet still my love is thwarted:
Heart, let her go, for she 'll not be converted.
Say, shall she go?
Oh, no, no, no, no, no!
She is most fair, though she be marble-hearted.

How often have my sighs declared mine anguish,
Wherein I daily languish!
Yet still she doth procure it:
Heart, let her go, for I cannot endure it.
Say, shall she go?
O, no, no, no, no, no!
She gave the wound, and she alone must cure it.

The trickling tears that down my cheeks have flowed
My love have often showed;
Yet still unkind I prove her:
Heart, let her go, for nought I do can move her.
Say, shall she go?
O, no, no, no, no, no!
Though me she hate I cannot choose but love her.

But shall I still a true affection owe her,
Which prayers, sighs, tears do show her,
And shall she still disdain me?
Heart, let her go, if they no grace can gain me.
Say, shall she go?
O, no, no, no, no, no!
She made me hers, and hers she will retain me.

But if the love that hath and still doth burn me
No love at length return me,
Out of my thoughts I 'll set her:
Heart, let her go, O heart, I pray thee, let her.
Say, shall she go?
O, no, no, no, no, no!
Fixed in the heart, how can the heart forget her?

But if I weep and sigh and often wail me
Till tears, sighs, prayers fail me,
Shall yet my love persèver?
Heart, let her go, if she will right thee never.
Say, shall she go?
O, no, no, no, no, no!
Tears, sighs, prayers fail, but true love lasteth ever.

*Anonymous.*

## 256

Come, O come, my life's delight,
Let me not in languor pine!
Love loves no delay; thy sight,
The more enjoyed, the more divine:
O come, and take from me
The pain of being deprived of thee!

Thou all sweetness dost enclose,
Like a little world of bliss.
Beauty guards thy looks: the rose
In them pure and eternal is.
Come, then, and make thy flight
As swift to me as heavenly light.

*Campion.*

## 257

Sweetest love, I do not go,
  For weariness of thee,
Nor in hope the world can show
  A fitter love for me;
    But since that I
At the last must part, 't is best,
Thus to use myself in jest
  By feigned deaths to die.

Yesternight the sun went hence,
  And yet is here to-day;
He hath no desire nor sense,
  Nor half so short a way;
    Then fear not me,
But believe that I shall make
Speedier journeys, since I take
  More wings and spurs than he.

O how feeble is man's power,
  That if good fortune fall,
Cannot add another hour,
  Nor a lost hour recall;
    But come bad chance,
And we join to it our strength,
And we teach it art and length,
  Itself o'er us to advance.

When thou sigh'st, thou sigh'st not wind,
  But sigh'st my soul away;
When thou weep'st, unkindly kind,
  My life's blood doth decay.
    It cannot be
That thou lovest me as thou say'st,

If in thine my life thou waste,
  That art the best of me.

Let not thy divining heart
  Forethink me any ill;
Destiny may take thy part,
  And may thy fears fulfil.
    But think that we
Are but turned aside to sleep,
They who one another keep
  Alive, ne'er parted be.

*Donne.*

## 258

My sweetest Lesbia, let us live and love;
And though the sager sort our deeds reprove,
Let us not weigh them: heaven's great lamps do dive
Into their west, and straight again revive:
But soon as once set is our little light,
Then must we sleep one ever-during night.

If all would lead their lives in love like me,
Then bloody swords and armour should not be;
No drum nor trumpet peaceful sleeps should move,
Unless alarm came from the camp of love:
But fools do live, and waste their little light,
And seek with pain their ever-during night.

When timely death my life and fortune ends,
Let not my hearse be vext with mourning friends;
But let all lovers, rich in triumph, come
And with sweet pastimes grace my happy tomb:
And, Lesbia, close up thou my little light,
And crown with love my ever-during night.

*Campion.*

## 259

# To Celia

Drink to me only with thine eyes,
  And I will pledge with mine;
Or leave a kiss but in the cup,
  And I 'll not look for wine.
The thirst that from the soul doth rise,
  Doth ask a drink divine:
But might I of Jove's nectar sup,
  I would not change for thine.

I sent thee late a rosy wreath,
  Not so much honouring thee,
As giving it a hope that there
  It could not withered be.
But thou thereon didst only breathe,
  And sent'st it back to me:
Since when it grows, and smells, I swear,
  Not of itself, but thee.

*Ben Jonson.*

## 260

# The Invitation

Live with me still, and all the measures
  Played to by the spheres I'll teach thee;
Let's but thus dally, all the pleasures
  The moon beholds, her man shall reach thee.

Dwell in mine arms, aloft we'll hover,
And see fields of armies fighting:
O, part not from me! I'll discover
There all the books of fancy's writing.

Be but my darling, age to free thee
From her curse, shall fall a-dying;
Call me thy empress, Time to see thee
Shall forget his art of flying.

*Dekker.*

261

## To Oenone

What, conscience, say is it in thee,
When I a heart had one,
To take away that heart from me,
And to retain thy own?

For shame or pity now incline
To play a loving part;
Either to send me kindly thine,
Or give me back my heart.

Covet not both; but if thou dost
Resolve to part with neither,
Why! yet to show that thou art just
Take me and mine together.

*Herrick.*

# The Legacy

When last I died, (and, dear, I die
As often as from thee I go,
Though it be but an hour ago,
And lovers' hours be full eternity)
I can remember yet, that I
Something did say, and something did bestow;
Though I be dead, which sent me, I might be
Mine own executor and legacy.

I heard me say, " Tell her anon,
That myself," that is you, not I,
" Did kill me," and when I felt me die,
I bid me send my heart, when I was gone;
But I alas! could there find none;
When I had ripped, and searched where hearts should
lie,
It killed me again, that I who still was true
In life, in my last will should cozen you.

Yet I found something like a heart,
But colours it, and corners had;
It was not good, it was not bad,
It was entire to none, and few had part;
As good as could be made by art
It seemed, and therefore for our loss be sad.
I meant to send that heart instead of mine,
But O! no man could hold it, for 'twas thine.

*Donne.*

## 263

Shall I come, sweet love, to thee,
  When the evening beams are set?
Shall I not excluded be?
  Will you find no feigned let?
Let me not, for pity, more,
Tell the long hours at your door!

Who can tell what thief or foe,
  In the covert of the night,
For his prey will work my woe,
  Or through wicked foul despite?
So may I die unredrest,
Ere my long love be possest.

But to let such dangers pass,
  Which a lover's thoughts disdain,
'Tis enough in such a place
  To attend love's joys in vain.
Do not mock me in thy bed,
While these cold nights freeze me dead.

*Campion.*

## 264

# The Dream

Dear love, for nothing less than thee
Would I have broke this happy dream;
    It was a theme
For reason, much too strong for fantasy.
Therefore thou waked'st me wisely; yet
My dream thou brokest not, but continued'st it.

Thou art so true that thoughts of thee suffice
To make dreams truths, and fables histories;
Enter these arms, for since thou thought'st it best,
Not to dream all my dream, let's act the rest.

As lightning, or a taper's light,
Thine eyes, and not thy noise waked me;
Yet I thought thee
(For thou lovest truth) an angel, at first sight;
But when I saw thou saw'st my heart,
And knew'st my thoughts beyond an angel's art,
When thou knew'st what I dreamt, when thou knew'st
when
Excess of joy would wake me, and camest then,
I must confess, it could not choose but be
Profane, to think thee anything but thee.

Coming and staying showed thee, thee,
But rising makes me doubt, that now
Thou art not thou.
That love is weak where fear's as strong as he;
'T is not all spirit, pure and brave,
If mixture it of fear, shame, honour have;
Perchance as torches, which must ready be,
Men light and put out, so thou deal'st with me;
Thou camest to kindle, go'st to come; then I
Will dream that hope again, but else would die.

*Donne.*

265

# Phyllida's Love-call

*Phyllida.* Corydon, arise, my Corydon,
Titan shineth clear.
*Corydon.* Who is it that calleth Corydon,
Who is it that I hear?
*Phyllida.* Phyllida, thy true love, calleth thee,
Arise then, arise then;
Arise and keep thy flock with me.
*Corydon.* Phyllida, my true love, is it she?
I come then, I come then,
I come and keep my flock with thee.

*Phyllida.* Here are cherries ripe for my Corydon,
Eat them for my sake.
*Corydon.* Here 's my oaten pipe, my lovely one,
Sport for thee to make.
*Phyllida.* Here are threads, my true love, fine as silk,
To knit thee, to knit thee,
A pair of stockings white as milk.
*Corydon.* Here are reeds, my true love, fine and neat,
To make thee, to make thee,
A bonnet to withstand the heat.

*Phyllida.* I will gather flowers, my Corydon,
To set in thy cap.
*Corydon.* I will gather pears, my lovely one,
To put in thy lap.
*Phyllida.* I will buy my true love garters gay,
For Sundays, for Sundays,
To wear about his legs so tall.

*Corydon.* I will buy my true love yellow say,
For Sundays, for Sundays,
To wear about her middle small.

*Phyllida.* When my Corydon sits on a hill
Making melody—
*Corydon.* When my lovely one goes to her wheel,
Singing cheerily—
*Phyllida.* Sure methinks my true love doth excel
For sweetness, for sweetness,
Our Pan, that old Arcadian knight.
*Corydon.* And methinks my true love bears the bell
For clearness, for clearness,
Beyond the nymphs that be so bright.

*Phyllida.* Had my Corydon, my Corydon,
Been, alack, her swain—
*Corydon.* Had my lovely one, my lovely one,
Been in Ida plain—
*Phyllida.* Cynthia Endymion had refused,
Preferring, preferring,
My Corydon to play withal.
*Corydon.* The queen of love had been excused,
Bequeathing, bequeathing,
My Phyllida the golden ball.

*Phyllida.* Yonder comes my mother, Corydon,
Whither shall I fly?
*Corydon.* Under yonder beech, my lovely one,
While she passeth by.
*Phyllida.* Say to her thy true love was not here:
Remember, remember,
To-morrow is another day.

*Corydon.* Doubt me not, my true love, do not fear:
Farewell then, farewell then,
Heaven keep our loves alway.

*Anonymous.*

266

See, see, mine own sweet jewel,
What I have for my darling:
A robin red-breast and a starling.
These I give both in hope to move thee;
Yet thou say'st I do not love thee.

*Anonymous.*

267

Fain I would, but oh I dare not,
Speak my thoughts at full to praise her:
"Speak the best," cries Love, "and spare not;
Thy speech can no higher raise her:
Thy speech than thy thoughts are lower,
Yet thy thoughts doth not half know her."

*Anonymous.*

268

How many new years have grown old
Since first your servant old was new!
How many long hours have I told
Since first my love was vowed to you!
And yet, alas! she doth not know
Whether her servant love or no.

How many walls as white as snow,
  And windows clear as any glass,
Have I conjured to tell you so,
  Which faithfully performed was!
And yet you 'll swear you do not know
Whether your servant love or no.

How often hath my pale lean face,
  With true characters of my love,
Petitioned to you for grace,
  Whom neither sighs nor tears can move!
O cruel, yet do you not know
Whether your servant love or no?

And wanting oft a better token,
  I have been fain to send my heart,
Which now your cold disdain hath broken,
  Nor can you heal't by any art:
O look upon 't, and you shall know
Whether your servant love or no.

*Anonymous.*

## 269

O Night, O jealous Night, repugnant to my measures!
  O Night so long desired, yet cross to my content!
There's none but only thou that can perform my pleasures,
  Yet none but only thou that hindereth my intent.

Thy beams, thy spiteful beams, thy lamps that burn too brightly,
  Discover all my trains, and naked lay my drifts,

That night by night I hope, yet fail my purpose
nightly;
Thy envious glaring gleam defeateth so my shifts.

Sweet Night, withhold thy beams, withhold them till
to-morrow!
Whose joy's in lack so long a hell of torment
breeds.
Sweet Night, sweet gentle Night, do not prolong my
sorrow:
Desire is guide to me, and Love no lodestar needs.

Let sailors gaze on Stars and Moon so freshly shining;
Let them that miss the way be guided by the light;
I know my Lady's bower, there needs no more divining;
Affection sees in dark, and Love hath eyes by
night.

Dame Cynthia, couch awhile! hold in thy horns for
shining,
And glad not lowering Night with thy too glorious
rays;
But be she dim and dark, tempestuous and repining,
That in her spite my sport may work thy endless
praise.

And when my will is wrought, then, Cynthia, shine,
good lady,
All other nights and days in honour of that night,
That happy, heavenly night, that night so dark and
shady,
Wherein my Love had eyes that lighted my delight.

*Anonymous.*

270

Let me not Chloris think, because
She hath envassalled me,
That her beauty can give laws
To others that are free.
I was made to be the prey
And booty of her eyes:
In my bosom, she may say,
Her greatest kingdom lies.

Though others may her brow adore,
Yet more must I that therein see far more
Than any other's eyes have power to see;
She is to me
More than to any others she can be.

I can discern more secret notes
That in the margin of her cheeks Love quotes
Than any else besides have art to read;
No looks proceed
From those fair eyes but to me wonder breed.

O then why
Should she fly
From him to whom her sight
Doth add so much above her might?
Why should not she
Still joy to reign in me?

*Anonymous.*

271

Sweet love, mine only treasure,
For service long unfeigned
Wherein I nought have gained,
Vouchsafe this little pleasure,
To tell me in what part
My Lady keeps my heart.

If in her hair so slender,
Like golden nets entwined
Which fire and art have 'fined,
Her thrall my heart I render
For ever to abide
With locks so dainty tied.

If in her eyes she bind it,
Wherein that fire was framed
By which it is enflamed,
I dare not look to find it:
I only wish it sight
To see that pleasant light.

But if her breast have deigned
With kindness to receive it,
I am content to leave it
Though death thereby were gained.
Then, Lady, take your own
That lives by you alone.

*Anonymous.*

272

Why canst thou not, as others do,
  Look on me with unwounding eyes?
And yet look sweet, but yet not so;
  Smile, but not in killing wise;
Arm not thy graces to confound;
Only look, but do not wound.

Why should mine eyes see more in you
  Than they can see in all the rest?
For I can others' beauties view
  And not find my heart opprest.
O be as others are to me,
Or let me be more to thee.

*Anonymous.*

273

# A Conjuration to Electra

By those soft tods of wool
With which the air is full;
By all those tinctures there,
That paint the hemisphere;
By dews and drizzling rain
That swell the golden grain;
By all those sweets that be
I' the flowery nunnery;
By silent nights, and the
Three forms of Hecate;
By all aspects that bless
The sober sorceress,

While juice she strains, and pith
To make her philters with;
By time that hastens on
Things to perfection;
And by yourself, the best
Conjurement of the rest:
O my Electra! be
In love with none, but me.

*Herrick.*

274

## The Ecstasy

Where, like a pillow on a bed,
  A pregnant bank swelled up, to rest
That violet's reclining head,
  Sat we two, one another's best.

Our hands were firmly cemented
  By a fast balm, which thence did spring;
Our eye-beams twisted, and did thread
  Our eyes upon one double string.

So to engraft our hands, as yet
  Was all the means to make us one;
And pictures in our eyes to get
  Was all our propagation.

As, 'twixt two equal armies, Fate
  Suspends uncertain victory,
Our souls, which to advance their state
  Were gone out, hung 'twixt her and me.

And whilst our souls negotiate there,
  We like sepulchral statues lay;
All day, the same our postures were,
  And we said nothing, all the day.

If any, so by love refined,
  That he soul's language understood,
And by good love were grown all mind,
  Within convenient distance stood,

He, though he knew not which soul spake,
  Because both meant, both spake the same,
Might thence a new concoction take,
  And part far purer than he came.

This ecstasy doth unperplex
  (We said) and tell us what we love;
We see by this, it was not sex;
  We see, we saw not, what did move:

But as all several souls contain
  Mixture of things they know not what,
Love these mixed souls doth mix again,
  And makes both one, each this, and that.

A single violet transplant,
  The strength, the colour, and the size,
All which before was poor and scant,
  Redoubles still, and multiplies.

When love with one another so
  Interanimates two souls,
That abler soul, which thence doth flow,
  Defects of loneliness controls.

We then, who are this new soul, know,
Of what we are composed, and made,
For the atomies of which we grow
Are souls, whom no change can invade.

But, O alas! so long, so far,
Our bodies why do we forbear?
They are ours, though not we; we are
The intelligences, they the spheres.

We owe them thanks, because they thus
Did us, to us, at first convey,
Yielded their senses' force to us,
Nor are dross to us, but allay.

On man heaven's influence works not so,
But that it first imprints the air;
For soul into the soul may flow,
Though it to body first repair.

As our blood labours to beget
Spirits, as like souls as it can;
Because such fingers need to knit
That subtle knot, which makes us man;

So must pure lovers' souls descend
To affections, and to faculties,
Which sense may reach and apprehend,
Else a great prince in prison lies.

To our bodies turn we then, that so
Weak men on love revealed may look;
Love's mysteries in souls do grow,
But yet the body is his book.

And if some lover, such as we,
  Have heard this dialogue of one,
Let him still mark us, he shall see
  Small change when we're to bodies grown.

*Donne.*

275

## The Phoenix and the Turtle

Let the bird of loudest lay,
On the sole Arabian tree,
Herald sad and trumpet be,
To whose sound chaste wings obey.

But thou shrieking harbinger,
Foul precurrer of the fiend,
Augur of the fever's end,
To this troop come thou not near!

From this session interdict
Every fowl of tyrant wing,
Save the eagle, feathered king:
Keep the obsequy so strict.

Let the priest in surplice white,
That defunctive music can,
Be the death-divining swan,
Lest the requiem lack his right.

And thou treble-dated crow,
That thy sable gender makest
With the breath thou givest and takest,
'Mongst our mourners shalt thou go.

Here the anthem doth commence;
Love and constancy is dead;
Phoenix and the turtle fled
In a mutual flame from hence.

So they loved, as love in twain
Had the essence but in one;
Two distincts, division one:
Number there in love was slain.

Hearts remote, yet not asunder;
Distance, and no space was seen
'Twixt the turtle and his queen:
But in them it were a wonder.

So between them love did shine,
That the turtle saw his right
Flaming in the phoenix' sight;
Either was the other's mine.

Property was thus appalled,
That the self was not the same;
Single nature's double name
Neither two nor one was called.

Reason, in itself confounded,
Saw division grow together,
To themselves yet either neither,
Simple were so well compounded,

That it cried, How true a twain
Seemeth this concordant one!
Love hath reason, reason none,
If what parts can so remain.

Whereupon it made this threne
To the phoenix and the dove,
Co-supremes and stars of love,
As chorus to their tragic scene.

## Threnos

Beauty, truth, and rarity,
Grace in all simplicity,
Here enclosed in cinders lie.

Death is now the phoenix' nest:
And the turtle's loyal breast
To eternity doth rest,

Leaving no posterity:
'T was not their infirmity,
It was married chastity.

Truth may seem, but cannot be:
Beauty brag, but 't is not she;
Truth and beauty buried be.

To this urn let those repair
That are either true or fair;
For these dead birds sigh a prayer.

*Shakespeare.*

# The Relic

When my grave is broke up again
Some second guest to entertain,
(For graves have learned that woman-head,
To be to more than one a bed)
And he that digs it, spies
A bracelet of bright hair about the bone,
Will not he let us alone,
And think that there a loving couple lies,
Who thought that this device might be some way
To make their souls at the last busy day
Meet at this grave, and make a little stay?

If this fall in a time, or land,
Where mass-devotion doth command,
Then he that digs us up will bring
Us to the bishop or the king,
To make us relics; then
Thou shalt be a Mary Magdalen, and I
A something else thereby;
All women shall adore us, and some men.
And, since at such times miracles are sought,
I would have that age by this paper taught
What miracles we harmless lovers wrought.

First we loved well and faithfully,
Yet knew not what we loved, nor why;
Difference of sex we never knew,
No more than guardian angels do;
Coming and going we
Perchance might kiss, but not between those meals;
Our hands ne'er touched the seals,

Which nature, injured by late law, sets free.
These miracles we did; but now alas!
All measure, and all language, I should pass,
Should I tell what a miracle she was.

*Donne.*

277

# The Anniversary

All kings, and all their favourites,
All glory of honours, beauties, wits,
The sun itself, which makes time, as they pass,
Is elder by a year now than it was
When thou and I first one another saw.
All other things to their destruction draw,
Only our love hath no decay;
This no to-morrow hath, nor yesterday;
Running it never runs from us away,
But truly keeps his first, last, everlasting day.

Two graves must hide thine and my corse;
If one might, death were no divorce.
Alas! as well as other princes, we
(Who prince enough in one another be)
Must leave at last in death these eyes and ears,
Oft fed with true oaths, and with sweet salt tears;
But souls where nothing dwells but love
(All other thoughts being inmates) then shall prove
This or a love increased there above,
When bodies to their graves, souls from their graves remove.

And then we shall be throughly blest;
But now no more than all the rest.
Here upon earth we 're kings, and none but we
Can be such kings, nor of such subjects be.
Who is so safe as we? where none can do
Treason to us, except one of us two.
True and false fears let us refrain,
Let us love nobly, and live, and add again
Years and years unto years, till we attain
To write threescore; this is the second of our reign.

*Donne.*

## 278

The glorious image of the Maker's beauty,
My sovereign saint, the idol of my thought,
Dare not henceforth, above the bounds of duty,
To accuse of pride, or rashly blame for aught.
For being, as she is, divinely wrought,
And of the brood of Angels heavenly born;
And with the crew of blessed Saints upbrought,
Each of which did her with their gifts adorn;
The bud of joy, the blossom of the morn,
The beam of light, whom mortal eyes admire;
What reason is it then but she should scorn
Base things, that to her love too bold aspire?
Such heavenly forms ought rather worshipped be,
Than dare be loved by men of mean degree.

*Spenser.*

## 279

Since first I saw your face I resolved to honour and
renown ye;
If now I be disdained I wish my heart had never
known ye.
What? I that loved and you that liked shall we
begin to wrangle?
No, no, no, my heart is fast, and cannot disentangle.

If I admire or praise you too much, that fault you
may forgive me,
Or if my hands had strayed but a touch, then justly
might you leave me.
I asked you leave, you bade me love; is 't now a
time to chide me?
No, no, no, I'll love you still what fortune e'er betide me.

The sun whose beams most glorious are rejecteth no
beholder,
And your sweet beauty past compare made my poor
eyes the bolder:
Where beauty moves, and wit delights, and signs of
kindness bind me,
There, O there! where'er I go I'll leave my heart
behind me.

*Anonymous.*

## 280

When like an eaglet I first found my love,
For that the virtue I thereof would know,
Upon the nest I set it forth, to prove
If it were of that kingly kind or no:

But it no sooner saw my sun appear,
But on her rays with open eyes it stood,
To show that I had hatched it for the air,
And rightly came from that brave-mounting brood.
And, when the plumes were summed with sweet desire
To prove the pinions, it ascends the skies;
Do what I could, it need'sly would aspire
To my soul's sun, those two celestial eyes.
Thus from my breast, where it was bred alone,
It after thee is like an eaglet flown.

*Drayton.*

## 281

Loving in truth, and fain in verse my love to show,
That She, dear She, might take some pleasure of my pain;
Pleasure might cause her read, reading might make her know,
Knowledge might pity win, and pity grace obtain;
I sought fit words to paint the blackest face of woe,
Studying inventions fine, her wits to entertain;
Oft turning others' leaves, to see if thence would flow
Some fresh and fruitful showers upon my sunburned brain.
But words came halting forth, wanting Invention's stay;
Invention, Nature's child, fled step-dame Study's blows;

And others' feet still seemed but strangers in my
way.
Thus, great with child to speak, and helpless in my
throes,
Biting my truant pen, beating myself for spite,
"Fool," said my Muse to me, "look in thy
heart, and write!"

*Sidney.*

## 282

In truth, O Love, with what a boyish kind
Thou dost proceed in thy most serious ways,
That when the heaven to thee his best displays
Yet of that best thou leav'st the best behind.
For, like a child that some fair book doth find,
With gilded leaves or coloured vellum plays,
Or, at the most, on some fair picture stays,
But never heeds the fruit of writer's mind;
So when thou saw'st in Nature's cabinet
Stella, thou straight look'st babies in her eyes,
In her cheek's pit thou didst thy pitfold set,
And in her breast bo-peep or couching lies,
Playing and shining in each outward part;
But, fool, seek'st not to get into her heart.

*Sidney.*

## 283

Alas, have I not pain enough, my friend,
Upon whose breast a fiercer gripe doth tire
Than did on him who first stole down the fire,
While Love on me doth all his quiver spend;

But with your rhubarb words ye must contend
To grieve me worse in saying, that Desire
Doth plunge my well-formed soul even in the mire
Of sinful thoughts, which do in ruin end?
If that be sin which doth the manners frame,
Well stayed with truth in word and faith of deed,
Ready of wit, and fearing nought but shame;
If that be sin which in fixt hearts doth breed
  A loathing of all loose unchastity,
  Then love is sin, and let me sinful be!

*Sidney.*

## 284

The curious wits, seeing dull pensiveness
Bewray itself in my long settled eyes,
Whence those same fumes of melancholy rise,
With idle pains and missing aim, do guess.
Some that know how my spring I did address,
Deem that my Muse some fruit of knowledge plies;
Others, because the Prince my service tries,
Think that I think state errors to redress.
But harder judges judge ambition's rage,
Scourge of itself, still climbing slippery place,
Holds my young brain captived in golden cage.
O fools, or overwise: alas, the race
  Of all my thoughts hath neither stop nor start,
  But only Stella's eyes and Stella's heart.

*Sidney.*

## 285

Though dusty wits do scorn astrology,
And fools can think those lamps of purest light,
Whose number, ways, greatness, eternity,
Promising wonders, wonder do invite,
To have for no cause birthright in the sky
But for to spangle the black weeds of night;
Or for some brawl which in that chamber high
They should still dance to please a gazer's sight:
For me, I do Nature unidle know,
And know great causes great effects procure;
And know those bodies high reign on the low.
And if these rules did fail, proof makes me sure,
  Who oft fore-judge my after-following race,
  By only those two stars in Stella's face.

*Sidney.*

## 286

With how sad steps, O Moon, thou climb'st the skies!
How silently, and with how wan a face!
What, may it be that even in heavenly place
That busy archer his sharp arrows tries?
Sure, if that long with love-acquainted eyes
Can judge of love, thou feel'st a lover's case;
I read it in thy looks; thy languisht grace,
To me that feel the like, thy state descries.
Then, even of fellowship, O Moon, tell me,
Is constant love deemed there but want of wit?
Are beauties there as proud as here they be?
Do they above love to be loved, and yet
  Those lovers scorn whom that love doth possess?
  Do they call virtue there, ungratefulness?

*Sidney.*

## 287

Come Sleep! O Sleep, the certain knot of peace,
The baiting place of wit, the balm of woe,
The poor man's wealth, the prisoner's release,
The indifferent judge between the high and low;
With shield of proof, shield me from out the prease
Of those fierce darts Despair at me doth throw;
O make in me those civil wars to cease;
I will good tribute pay, if thou do so.
Take thou of me smooth pillows, sweetest bed,
A chamber deaf to noise and blind to light,
A rosy garland and a weary head:
And if these things, as being thine by right,
  Move not thy heavy grace, thou shalt in me,
  Livelier than elsewhere, Stella's image see.

*Sidney.*

## 288

Having this day my horse, my hand, my lance
Guided so well, that I obtained the prize,
Both by the judgment of the English eyes,
And of some sent by that sweet enemy, France;
Horsemen my skill in horsemanship advance,
Townfolks my strength; a daintier judge applies
His praise to sleight, which from good use doth rise;
Some lucky wits impute it but to chance;
Others, because of both sides I do take
My blood from them who did excel in this,
Think Nature me a man of arms did make.
How far they shot awry! the true cause is,
  Stella looked on, and from her heavenly face
  Sent forth the beams which made so fair my race.

*Sidney.*

## 289

Highway, since you my chief Parnassus be,
And that my Muse, to some ears not unsweet,
Tempers her words to trampling horses' feet
More oft than to a chamber melody;
Now, blessed you, bear onward blessed me
To her, where I my heart safe left shall meet;
My Muse and I must you of duty greet
With thanks and wishes, wishing thankfully.
Be you still fair, honoured by public heed,
By no encroachment wronged, nor time forgot,
Nor blamed for blood, nor shamed for sinful deed;
And that you know I envy you no lot
  Of highest wish, I wish you so much bliss:
  Hundreds of years you Stella's feet may kiss.

*Sidney.*

## 290

No more, my dear, no more these counsels try;
O give my passions leave to run their race;
Let Fortune lay on me her worst disgrace;
Let folk o'ercharged with brain against me cry;
Let clouds bedim my face, break in mine eye;
Let me no steps but of lost labour trace;
Let all the earth with scorn recount my case;
But do not will me from my love to fly!
I do not envy Aristotle's wit,
Nor do aspire to Caesar's bleeding fame;
Nor aught do care though some above me sit;
Nor hope nor wish another course to frame,
  But that which once may win thy cruel heart:
  Thou art my Wit, and thou my Virtue art.

*Sidney.*

## 291

Good brother Philip, I have borne thee long;
I was content you should in favour creep,
While craftily you seemed your cut to keep,
As though that soft fair hand did you great wrong:
I bare, with envy, yet I bare, your song,
When in her neck you did love ditties peep;
Nay, more fool I! oft suffered you to sleep
In lilies' nest, where Love's self lies along.
What, doth high place ambitious thoughts augment?
Is sauciness reward of courtesy?
Cannot such grace your silly self content,
But you must needs with those lips billing be,
And through those lips drink nectar from that tongue?
Leave that, Sir Phip, lest off your neck be wrung!

*Sidney.*

## 292

Be your words made, good Sir, of Indian ware,
That you allow me them by so small rate?
Or do you cutted Spartans imitate?
Or do you mean my tender ears to spare
That to my questions you so total are?
When I demand of Phoenix Stella's state,
You say, forsooth, you left her well of late:
O God, think you that satisfies my care?
I would know whether she did sit or walk;
How clothed; how waited on; sighed she or smiled;
Whereof, with whom, how often did she talk;
With what pastime time's journey she beguiled;
If her lips deigned to sweeten my poor name:
Say all; and, all well said, still say the same.

*Sidney.*

# 293

# Epithalamion

Ye learned sisters, which have oftentimes
Been to me aiding, others to adorn,
Whom ye thought worthy of your graceful rhymes,
That even the greatest did not greatly scorn
To hear their names sung in your simple lays,
But joyed in their praise;
And when ye list your own mishaps to mourn,
Which death, or love, or fortune's wreck did raise,
Your string could soon to sadder tenor turn,
And teach the woods and waters to lament
Your doleful dreriment:
Now lay those sorrowful complaints aside,
And having all your heads with garland crowned,
Help me mine own love's praises to resound;
Ne let the same of any be envied:
So Orpheus did for his own bride,
So I unto myself alone will sing;
The woods shall to me answer, and my echo ring.

Early, before the world's light-giving lamp
His golden beam upon the hills doth spread,
Having disperst the night's uncheerful damp,
Do ye awake; and with fresh lustihead
Go to the bower of my beloved love
My truest turtle dove:
Bid her awake; for Hymen is awake,
And long since ready forth his mask to move,
With his bright tead that flames with many a flake,
And many a bachelor to wait on him,
In their fresh garments trim.
Bid her awake therefore, and soon her dight,

For lo! the wished day is come at last,
That shall for all the pains and sorrows past
Pay to her usury of long delight:
And, whilst she doth her dight,
Do ye to her of joy and solace sing,
That all the woods may answer, and your echo ring.

Bring with you all the Nymphs that you can hear,
Both of the rivers and the forests green,
And of the sea that neighbours to her near;
All with gay garlands goodly well beseen.
And let them also with them bring in hand
Another gay garland,
For my fair love, of lilies and of roses,
Bound truelove-wise, with a blue silk riband.
And let them make great store of bridal posies
And let them eke bring store of other flowers,
To deck the bridal bowers.
And let the ground whereas her foot shall tread,
For fear the stones her tender foot should wrong,
Be strewed with fragrant flowers all along,
And diapered like the discoloured mead.
Which done, do at her chamber door await,
For she will waken strait,
The whiles do ye this song unto her sing;
The woods shall to you answer, and your echo ring.

Ye Nymphs of Mulla, which with careful heed
The silver scaly trouts do tend full well,
And greedy pikes which use therein to feed
(Those trouts and pikes all others do excel);
And ye likewise, which keep the rushy lake
Where none do fishes take,
Bind up the locks the which hang scattered light,
And in his waters, which your mirror make,

Behold your faces as the crystal bright,
That when you come whereas my love doth lie,
No blemish she may spy.
And eke, ye lightfoot maids, which keep the door,
That on the hoary mountain used to tower,
And the wild wolves which seek them to devour
With your steel darts do chase from coming near;
Be also present here,
To help to deck her, and to help to sing,
That all the woods may answer, and your echo ring.

Wake now, my love, awake! for it is time;
The rosy Morn long since left Tithon's bed,
All ready to her silver coach to climb;
And Phoebus 'gins to show his glorious head.
Hark! how the cheerful birds do chant their lays,
And carol of love's praise.
The merry Lark his matins sings aloft;
The Thrush replies; the Mavis descant plays;
The Ouzel shrills; the Ruddock warbles soft;
So goodly all agree with sweet consent
To this day's merriment.
Ah! my dear love, why do ye sleep thus long,
When meeter were that ye should now awake,
To await the coming of your joyous make,
And hearken to the birds' lovelearned song,
The dewy leaves among?
For they of joy and pleasance to you sing,
That all the woods them answer, and their echo ring.

My love is now awake out of her dreams,
And her fair eyes, like stars that dimmed were
With darksome cloud, now show their goodly beams
More bright than Hesperus his head doth rear.

Come now, ye damsels, daughters of delight,
Help quickly her to dight:
But first come ye, fair hours, which were begot,
In Jove's sweet paradise, of Day and Night;
Which do the seasons of the year allot,
And all that ever in this world is fair
Do make and still repair:
And ye three handmaids of the Cyprian Queen,
The which do still adorn her beauty's pride,
Help to adorn my beautifullest bride:
And, as ye her array, still throw between
Some graces to be seen;
And, as ye use to Venus, to her sing,
The whiles the woods shall answer, and your echo
ring.

Now is my love all ready forth to come:
Let all the virgins therefore well await;
And ye, fresh boys, that tend upon her groom,
Prepare yourselves, for he is coming straight.
Set all your things in seemly good array,
Fit for so joyful day:
The joyful'st day that ever Sun did see.
Fair Sun! show forth thy favourable ray,
And let thy lifefull heat not fervent be,
For fear of burning her sunshiny face,
Her beauty to disgrace.
O fairest Phoebus! father of the Muse!
If ever I did honour thee aright,
Or sing the thing that mote thy mind delight,
Do not thy servant's simple boon refuse;
But let this day, let this one day, be mine;
Let all the rest be thine:
Then I thy sovereign praises loud will sing,
That all the woods shall answer, and their echo ring.

Hark! how the Minstrels 'gin to shrill aloud
Their merry music that resounds from far,
The pipe, the tabor, and the trembling crowd,
That well agree withouten breach or jar.
But most of all the Damsels do delight,
When they their timbrels smite,
And thereunto do dance and carol sweet,
That all the senses they do ravish quite;
The whiles the boys run up and down the street,
Crying aloud with strong confused noise,
As if it were one voice,
Hymen! ïo Hymen! Hymen! they do shout;
That even to the heavens their shoutings shrill
Doth reach, and all the firmament doth fill:
To which the people standing all about,
As in approvance, do thereto applaud,
And loud advance her laud;
And evermore they Hymen, Hymen, sing,
That all the woods them answer, and their echo ring.

Lo! where she comes along with portly pace,
Like Phoebe, from her chamber of the East,
Arising forth to run her mighty race,
Clad all in white, that 'seems a virgin best.
So well it her beseems, that ye would ween
Some Angel she had been.
Her long loose yellow locks like golden wire,
Sprinkled with pearl, and pearling flowers a-tween,
Do like a golden mantle her attire;
And being crowned with a garland green,
Seem like some maiden Queen.
Her modest eyes, abashed to behold
So many gazers as on her do stare,
Upon the lowly ground affixed are,
Ne dare lift up her countenance too bold,

But blush to hear her praises sung so loud,
So far from being proud.
Nathless, do ye still loud her praises sing,
That all the woods may answer, and your echo ring.

Tell me, ye merchants' daughters, did ye see
So fair a creature in your town before,
So sweet, so lovely, and so mild as she,
Adorned with beauty's grace and virtue's store?
Her goodly eyes like sapphires shining bright,
Her forehead ivory white,
Her cheeks like apples which the sun hath rudded,
Her lips like cherries charming men to bite,
Her breast like to a bowl of cream uncrudded,
Her paps like lilies budded,
Her snowy neck like to a marble tower;
And all her body like a palace fair,
Ascending up, with many a stately stair,
To honour's seat and chastity's sweet bower.
Why stand ye still, ye Virgins, in amaze
Upon her so to gaze,
Whiles ye forget your former lay to sing,
To which the woods did answer, and your echo ring?

But if ye saw that which no eyes can see,
The inward beauty of her lively spright,
Garnished with heavenly gifts of high degree,
Much more then would ye wonder at that sight,
And stand astonished like to those which read
Medusa's mazeful head.
There dwells sweet love, and constant chastity,
Unspotted faith, and comely womanhood,
Regard of honour, and mild modesty;
There virtue reigns as Queen in royal throne,
And giveth laws alone,

The which the base affections do obey,
And yield their services unto her will;
Ne thought of thing uncomely ever may
Thereto approach to tempt her mind to ill.
Had ye once seen these her celestial treasures,
And unrevealed pleasures,
Then would ye wonder, and her praises sing,
That all the woods should answer, and your echo
ring.

Open the temple gates unto my love!
Open them wide that she may enter in,
And all the posts adorn as doth behove,
And all the pillars deck with garlands trim,
For to receive this Saint with honour due
That cometh in to you.
With trembling steps, and humble reverence,
She cometh in before the Almighty's view:
Of her, ye virgins, learn obedience,
When so ye come into those holy places,
To humble your proud faces.
Bring her up to the high altar, that she may
The sacred ceremonies there partake,
The which do endless matrimony make;
And let the roaring Organs loudly play
The praises of the Lord in lively notes;
The whiles, with hollow throats,
The Choristers the joyous Anthem sing,
That all the woods may answer, and their echo ring.

Behold, whiles she before the altar stands,
Hearing the holy priest that to her speaks,
And blesseth her with his two happy hands
How the red roses flush up in her cheeks,

And the pure snow, with goodly vermeil stain,
Like crimson dyed in grain;
That even the Angels, which continually
About the sacred altar do remain,
Forget their service and about her fly,
Oft peeping in her face, that seems more fair,
The more they on it stare.
But her sad eyes, still fastened on the ground,
Are governed with goodly modesty,
That suffers not one look to glance awry,
Which may let in a little thought unsound.
Why blush ye, love, to give to me your hand,
The pledge of all our band?
Sing, ye sweet Angels, Alleluia sing,
That all the woods may answer, and your echo ring.

Now all is done: bring home the Bride again;
Bring home the triumph of our victory;
Bring home with you the glory of her gain,
With joyance bring her and with jollity.
Never had man more joyful day than this,
Whom heaven would heap with bliss.
Make feast therefore now all this live-long day;
This day for ever to me holy is.
Pour out the wine without restraint or stay,
Pour not by cups but by the belly-full,
Pour out to all that wull,
And sprinkle all the posts and walls with wine,
That they may sweat, and drunken be withal.
Crown ye God Bacchus with a coronal,
And Hymen also crown with wreaths of vine:
And let the Graces dance unto the rest,
For they can do it best:
The whiles the maidens do their carol sing,
To which the woods shall answer, and their echo ring.

Ring ye the bells, ye young men of the town,
And leave your wonted labours for this day:
This day is holy; do ye write it down,
That ye for ever it remember may.
This day the sun is in his chiefest height,
With Barnaby the bright,
From whence declining daily by degrees,
He somewhat loseth of his heat and light,
When once the Crab behind his back he sees.
But for this time it ill ordained was,
To choose the longest day in all the year,
And shortest night, when longest fitter were:
Yet never day so long but late would pass.
Ring ye the bells, to make it wear away,
And bonfires make all day;
And dance about them, and about them sing,
That all the woods may answer, and your echo
ring.

Ah! when will this long weary day have end,
And lend me leave to come unto my love?
How slowly do the hours their numbers spend;
How slowly does sad Time his feathers move!
Haste thee, O fairest Planet! to thy home
Within the Western foam:
Thy tired steeds long since have need of rest.
Long though it be, at last I see it gloom,
And the bright evening star with golden crest
Appear out of the East.
Fair child of beauty! glorious lamp of love!
That all the host of heaven in ranks dost lead,
And guidest lovers through the night's sad dread,
How cheerfully thou lookest from above,
And seemst to laugh atween thy twinkling light,
As joyous in the sight

Of these glad many, which for joy do sing,
That all the woods them answer, and their echo ring.

Now cease, ye damsels, your delights forepast;
Enough is it that all the day was yours:
Now day is done, and night is nighing fast,
Now bring the Bride into the bridal bowers.
Now night is come, now soon her disarray,
And in her bed her lay;
Lay her in lilies and in violets,
And silken curtains over her display,
And odoured sheets, and Arras coverlets.
Behold how goodly my fair love does lie,
In proud humility!
Like unto Maia, when as Jove her took
In Tempe, lying on the flowery grass,
Twixt sleep and wake, after she weary was,
With bathing in the Acidalian brook.
Now it is night, ye damsels may be gone,
And leave my love alone;
And leave likewise your former lay to sing:
The woods no more shall answer, nor your echo
ring.

Now welcome, night! thou night so long expected,
That long day's labour dost at last defray,
And all my cares, which cruel love collected,
Has summed in one, and cancelled for aye:
Spread thy broad wing over my love and me,
That no man may us see;
And in thy sable mantle us enwrap,
From fear of peril and foul horror free.
Let no false treason seek us to entrap,
Nor any dread disquiet once annoy
The safety of our joy;

But let the night be calm and quietsome,
Without tempestuous storms or sad affray:
Like as when Jove with fair Alcmena lay,
When he begot the great Tirynthian groom:
Or like as when he with thyself did lie,
And begot Majesty.
And let the maids and young men cease to sing;
Ne let the woods them answer, nor their echo ring.

Let no lamenting cries, nor doleful tears,
Be heard all night within, nor yet without:
Ne let false whispers, breeding hidden fears,
Break gentle sleep with misconceived doubt.
Let no deluding dreams, nor dreadful sights,
Make sudden sad affrights;
Ne let housefires, nor lightning's helpless harms,
Ne let the Pouke, nor other evil sprights,
Ne let mischievous witches with their charms,
Ne let hob-goblins, names whose sense we see not,
Fray us with things that be not;
Let not the Screech-Owl, nor the Stork, be heard;
Nor the night Raven, that still deadly yells;
Nor damned ghosts, called up with mighty spells;
Nor grisly vultures make us once affeared:
Ne let the unpleasant quire of Frogs still croaking
Make us to wish their choking.
Let none of these their dreary accents sing;
Ne let the woods them answer, nor their echo ring.

But let still Silence true night watches keep,
That sacred peace may in assurance reign,
And timely sleep, when it is time to sleep,
May pour his limbs forth on your pleasant plain;
The whiles an hundred little winged loves,
Like divers-feathered doves,

Shall fly and flutter round about your bed,
And in the secret dark, that none reproves,
Their pretty stealths shall work, and snares shall spread
To filch away sweet snatches of delight,
Concealed through covert night.
Ye sons of Venus, play your sports at will;
For greedy pleasure, careless of your toys,
Thinks more upon her paradise of joys,
Than what we do, albeit good or ill.
All night therefore attend your merry play,
For it will soon be day:
Now none doth hinder you, that say or sing;
Ne will the woods now answer, nor your echo ring.

Who is the same, which at my window peeps,
Or whose is that fair face that shines so bright?
Is it not Cynthia, she that never sleeps,
But walks about high heaven all the night?
O, fairest goddess! do thou not envy
My Love with me to spy;
For thou likewise didst love, though now unthought,
And for a fleece of wool, which privily
The Latmian shepherd once unto thee brought,
His pleasures with thee wrought.
Therefore to us be favourable now;
And sith of women's labours thou hast charge,
And generation goodly dost enlarge,
Encline thy will to effect our wishful vow,
And the chaste womb inform with timely seed,
That may our comfort breed:
Till which we cease our hopeful hap to sing;
Ne let the woods us answer, nor our echo ring.

And thou, great Juno, which with awful might
The laws of wedlock still doth patronize,

And the religion of the faith first plight
With sacred rites hast taught to solemnize;
And eke for comfort often called art
Of women in their smart;
Eternally bind thou this lovely band,
And all thy blessings unto us impart.
And thou, glad Genius, in whose gentle hand
The bridal bower and genial bed remain,
Without blemish or stain;
And the sweet pleasures of their loves' delight
With secret aid dost succour and supply,
Till they bring forth the fruitful progeny;
Send us the timely fruit of this same night:
And thou, fair Hebe, and thou, Hymen free,
Grant that it may so be!
Till which we cease your further praise to sing;
Ne any woods shall answer, nor your echo ring.

And ye high heavens, the temple of the gods,
In which a thousand torches flaming bright
Do burn, that to us wretched earthly clods
In dreadful darkness lend desired light;
And all ye powers which in the same remain,
More than we men can fain,
Pour out your blessing on us plenteously,
And happy influence upon us rain,
That we may raise a large posterity,
Which from the earth, which they may long possess
With lasting happiness,
Up to your haughty palaces may mount:
And, for the guerdon of their glorious merit,
May heavenly tabernacles there inherit,
Of blessed Saints for to increase the count.
So let us rest, sweet love, in hope of this,

And cease till then our timely joys to sing;
The woods no more us answer, nor our echo ring.

Song! made in lieu of many ornaments,
With which my love should duly have been decked,
Which cutting off through hasty accidents,
Ye would not stay your due time to expect,
But promised both to recompense;
Be unto her a goodly ornament,
And for short time an endless monument!

*Spenser.*

## 294

Roses, their sharp spines being gone,
Not royal in their smells alone,
But in their hue;
Maiden pinks, of odour faint,
Daisies smell-less, yet most quaint,
And sweet thyme true;

Primrose, firstborn child of Ver;
Merry springtime's harbinger,
With her bells dim;
Oxlips in their cradles growing,
Marigolds on deathbeds blowing,
Larks'-heels trim.

All dear Nature's children sweet,
Lie 'fore bride and bridegroom's feet,
Blessing their sense!
Not an angel of the air,
Bird melodious, or bird fair,
Be absent hence!

The crow, the slanderous cuckoo, nor
The boding raven, nor chough hoar,
Nor chattering pie,
May on our bride-house perch or sing,
Or with them any discord bring,
But from it fly!

*Fletcher.*

## 295

Hold back thy hours, dark Night, till we have done;
The Day will come too soon;
Young maids will curse thee, if thou steal'st away
And leav'st their losses open to the day:
Stay, stay, and hide
The blushes of the bride.

Stay, gentle Night, and with thy darkness cover
The kisses of her lover;
Stay, and confound her tears and her shrill cryings,
Her weak denials, vows, and often-dyings;
Stay, and hide all:
But help not, though she call.

*Beaumont and Fletcher.*

## 296

Hark, hark! the lark at heaven's gate sings,
And Phoebus 'gins arise,
His steeds to water at those springs
On chaliced flowers that lies;

And winking Mary-buds begin
To ope their golden eyes:
With every thing that pretty is,
My lady sweet, arise:
Arise, arise.

*Shakespeare.*

## 297

Stay, O sweet, and do not rise;
The light that shines comes from thine eyes;
The day breaks not, it is my heart,
Because that you and I must part.
Stay, or else my joys will die
And perish in their infancy.

*Donne.*

## 298

Rise, lady mistress, rise!
The night hath tedious been;
No sleep hath fallen into my eyes,
Nor slumbers made me sin.
Is not she a saint, then, say,
Thought of whom keeps sin away?

Rise, madam, rise and give me light,
Whom darkness still will cover,
And ignorance darker than night,
Till thou shine on thy lover.
All want day till thy beauty rise,
For the grey morn breaks from thine eyes.

*Field.*

## 299

Pack, clouds, away, and welcome, day!
  With night we banish sorrow.
Sweet air, blow soft; mount, lark, aloft
  To give my love good morrow.
Wings from the wind to please her mind,
  Notes from the lark I'll borrow:
Bird, prune thy wing, nightingale, sing,
  To give my love good morrow.
    To give my love good morrow,
    Notes from them all I'll borrow.

Wake from thy nest, robin redbreast!
  Sing, birds, in every furrow,
And from each bill let music shrill
  Give my fair love good morrow.
Blackbird and thrush in every bush,
  Stare, linnet, and cock-sparrow,
You pretty elves, amongst yourselves
  Sing my fair love good morrow.
    To give my love good morrow,
    Sing, birds, in every furrow.

*Heywood.*

## 300

You spotted snakes with double tongue,
  Thorny hedgehogs, be not seen;
Newts and blind-worms, do no wrong,
  Come not near our fairy queen.
    Philomel, with melody
    Sing in our sweet lullaby;

Lulla, lulla, lullaby, lulla, lulla, lullaby.
Never harm,
Nor spell nor charm,
Come our lovely lady nigh;
So, good-night, with lullaby.

Weaving spiders, come not here;
Hence, you long-legged spinners, hence!
Beetles black, approach not near;
Worm nor snail, do no offence.
Philomel, with melody
Sing in our sweet lullaby;
Lulla, lulla, lullaby, lulla, lulla, lullaby.
Never harm,
Nor spell nor charm,
Come our lovely lady nigh;
So, good-night, with lullaby.

*Shakespeare.*

## 301

Golden slumbers kiss your eyes,
Smiles awake you when you rise.
Sleep, pretty wantons, do not cry,
And I will sing a lullaby:
Rock them, rock them, lullaby.

Care is heavy, therefore sleep you;
You are care, and care must keep you.
Sleep, pretty wantons, do not cry,
And I will sing a lullaby;
Rock them, rock them, lullaby.

*Dekker.*

302

## To the Tune of Basciami vita mia

Sleep, Baby mine, Desire's nurse, Beauty, singeth;
Thy cries, O baby, set mine head on aching.
The babe cries, "'Way, thy love doth keep me waking."

Lully, lully, my babe, Hope cradle bringeth
Unto my children alway good rest taking.
The babe cries, "'Way, thy love doth keep me waking."

Since, baby mine, from me thy watching springeth,
Sleep then a little; pap, Content is making.
The babe cries, "Nay, for that abide I waking."

*Sidney.*

303

Come, little babe, come, silly soul,
  Thy father's shame, thy mother's grief,
Born as I doubt to all our dole,
  And to thyself unhappy chief:
    Sing lullaby, and lap it warm,
    Poor soul that thinks no creature harm.

Thou little think'st and less dost know
  The cause of this thy mother's moan;
Thou want'st the wit to wail her woe,
  And I myself am all alone:
    Why dost thou weep? why dost thou wail?
    And knowest not yet what thou dost ail.

Come, little wretch, ah, silly heart!
Mine only joy, what can I more?
If there be any wrong thy smart,
That may the destinies implore:
'T was I, I say, against my will,
I wail the time, but be thou still.

And dost thou smile? O, thy sweet face!
Would God himself he might thee see!
No doubt thou wouldst soon purchase grace,
I know right well, for thee and me:
But come to mother, babe, and play,
For father false is fled away.

Sweet boy, if it by fortune chance
Thy father home again to send,
If death do strike me with his lance,
Yet mayst thou me to him commend:
If any ask thy mother's name,
Tell how by love she purchased blame.

*Nicholas Breton.*

304

## Sephestia's Cradle Song

Weep not, my wanton, smile upon my knee;
When thou art old there's grief enough for thee.
Mother's wag, pretty boy,
Father's sorrow, father's joy;
When thy father first did see
Such a boy by him and me,
He was glad, I was woe;
Fortune changed made him so,
When he left his pretty boy,
Last his sorrow, first his joy.

Weep not, my wanton, smile upon my knee;
When thou art old there's grief enough for thee.
Streaming tears that never stint,
Like pearl-drops from a flint,
Fell by course from his eyes,
That one another's place supplies;
Thus he grieved in every part,
Tears of blood fell from his heart,
When he left his pretty boy,
Father's sorrow, father's joy.

Weep not, my wanton, smile upon my knee;
When thou art old there's grief enough for thee.
The wanton smiled, father wept,
Mother cried, baby leapt;
More he crowed, more we cried,
Nature could not sorrow hide:
He must go, he must kiss
Child and mother, baby bliss,
For he left his pretty boy,
Father's sorrow, father's joy.
Weep not, my wanton, smile upon my knee;
When thou art old there's grief enough for thee.

*Greene.*

305

# Our Blessed Lady's Lullaby

Upon my lap my Sovereign sits,
And sucks upon my breast;
Meanwhile his love sustains my life,
And gives my body rest.
Sing, lullaby, my little boy,
Sing, lullaby, my livës joy.

When thou hast taken thy repast,
  Repose, my babe, on me.
So may thy mother and thy nurse,
  Thy cradle also be.
    Sing, lullaby, my little boy,
    Sing, lullaby, my livës joy.

I grieve that duty doth not work
  All that my wishing would,
Because I would not be to thee
  But in the best I should.
    Sing, lullaby, my little boy,
    Sing, lullaby, my livës joy.

Yet as I am and as I may,
  I must and will be thine,
Though all too little for thyself
  Vouchsafing to be mine.
    Sing, lullaby, my little boy,
    Sing, lullaby, my livës joy.

My wits, my words, my deeds, my thoughts,
  And else what is in me,
I rather will not wish to use,
  If not in serving thee.
    Sing, lullaby, my little boy,
    Sing, lullaby, my livës joy.

My babe, my bliss, my child, my choice,
  My fruit, my flower, and bud,
My Jesus, and my only joy,
  The sum of all my good.
    Sing, lullaby, my little boy,
    Sing, lullaby, my livës joy.

My sweetness, and the sweetest most
  That heaven could earth deliver,
Soul of my love, spirit of my life,
  Abide with me for ever.
    Sing, lullaby, my little boy,
    Sing, lullaby, my livës joy.

Live still with me, and be my love,
  And death will me refrain,
Unless thou let me die with thee,
  To live with thee again.
    Sing, lullaby, my little boy,
    Sing, lullaby, my livës joy.

Leave now to wail, thou luckless wight
  That wrought'st thy race's woe,
Redress is found, and foiled is
  Thy fruit-alluring foe.
    Sing, lullaby, my little boy,
    Sing, lullaby, my livës joy.

The fruit of death from Paradise
  Made thee exiled mourn;
My fruit of life to Paradise
  Makes joyful thy return.
    Sing, lullaby, my little boy,
    Sing, lullaby, my livës joy.

Grow up, good fruit, be nourished by
  These fountains two of me,
That only flow with maiden's milk,
  The only meat for thee.
    Sing, lullaby, my little boy,
    Sing, lullaby, my livës joy.

The earth is now a heaven become,
And this base bower of mine,
A princely palace unto me,
My son doth make to shine.
Sing, lullaby, my little boy,
Sing, lullaby, my livës joy.

His sight gives clearness to my sight,
When waking I him see,
And sleeping, his mild countenance
Gives favour unto me.
Sing, lullaby, my little boy,
Sing, lullaby, my livës joy.

When I him in mine arms embrace,
I feel my heart embraced,
Even by the inward grace of his,
Which he in me hath placed.
Sing, lullaby, my little boy,
Sing, lullaby, my livës joy.

And when I kiss his loving lips,
Then his sweet-smelling breath
Doth yield a savour to my soul,
That feeds love, hope, and faith.
Sing, lullaby, my little boy,
Sing, lullaby, my livës joy.

The shepherds left their keeping sheep,
For joy to see my lamb;
How may I more rejoice to see
Myself to be the dam.
Sing, lullaby, my little boy,
Sing, lullaby, my livës joy.

Three kings their treasures hither brought
Of incense, myrrh, and gold;
The heaven's treasure and the king
That here they might behold.
Sing, lullaby, my little boy,
Sing, lullaby, my livës joy.

One sort an angel did direct,
A star did guide the other,
And all the fairest son to see
That ever had a mother.
Sing, lullaby, my little boy,
Sing, lullaby, my livës joy.

This sight I see, this child I have,
This infant I embrace,
O endless comfort of the earth,
And heaven's eternal grace.
Sing, lullaby, my little boy,
Sing, lullaby, my livës joy.

Thee sanctity herself doth serve,
Thee goodness doth attend,
Thee blessedness doth wait upon,
And virtues all commend.
Sing, lullaby, my little boy,
Sing, lullaby, my livës joy.

Great kings and prophets wished have
To see that I possess,
Yet wish I never thee to see,
If not in thankfulness.
Sing, lullaby, my little boy,
Sing, lullaby, my livës joy.

Let heaven and earth, and saints and men,
  Assistance give to me,
That all their most occurring aid
  Augment my thanks to thee.
    Sing, lullaby, my little boy,
    Sing, lullaby, my livës joy.

And let the ensuing blessed race,
  Thou wilt succeeding raise,
Join all their praises unto mine,
  To multiply thy praise.
    Sing, lullaby, my little boy,
    Sing, lullaby, my livës joy.

And take my service well in worth,
  And Joseph's here with me,
Who of my husband bears the name,
  Thy servant for to be.
    Sing, lullaby, my little boy,
    Sing, lullaby, my livës joy.

*Richard Verstegen.*

306

# The Virgin Mary

To work a wonder, God would have her shown
At once a bud and yet a rose full-blown.

*Herrick.*

# The Burning Babe

As I in hoary winter's night stood shivering in the snow,
Surprised was I with sudden heat which made my heart to glow:
And lifting up a fearful eye to view what fire was near,
A pretty babe all burning bright did in the air appear;
Who, scorched with excessive heat, such floods of tears did shed
As though His floods should quench His flames with which His tears were fed:
"Alas!" quoth He, "but newly born in fiery heats I fry,
Yet none approach to warm their hearts or feel my fire but I!

"My faultless breast the furnace is; the fuel, wounding thorns;
Love is the fire, and sighs the smoke; the ashes, shames and scorns;
The fuel Justice layeth on, and Mercy blows the coals,
The metal in this furnace wrought are men's defiled souls:
For which, as now on fire I am to work them to their good,
So will I melt into a bath, to wash them in my blood."

With this He vanished out of sight and swiftly
shrunk away,
And straight I called unto mind that it was Christmas Day.

*Southwell.*

## 308

# A Child my Choice

Let folly praise that fancy loves, I praise and love
that Child
Whose heart no thought, whose tongue no word,
whose hand no deed defiled.
I praise Him most, I love Him best, all praise and
love is His;
While Him I love, in Him I live, and cannot live
amiss.
Love's sweetest mark, laud's highest theme, man's
most desired light,
To love Him life, to leave Him death, to live in
Him delight.
He mine by gift, I His by debt, thus each to other
due,
First friend He was, best friend He is, all times will
try Him true.
Though young, yet wise, though small, yet strong;
though man, yet God He is;
As wise He knows, as strong He can, as God He
loves to bless.
His knowledge rules, His strength defends, His love
doth cherish all;
His birth our joy, His life our light, His death our
end of thrall.

Alas! He weeps, He sighs, He pants, yet do His
angels sing;
Out of His tears, His sighs and throbs, doth bud a
joyful spring.
Almighty Babe, whose tender arms can force all foes
to fly,
Correct my faults, protect my life, direct me when I
die!

*Southwell.*

309

## To his Saviour, a Child: a Present by a Child

Go, pretty child, and bear this flower
Unto thy little Saviour;
And tell Him, by that bud now blown,
He is the Rose of Sharon known.
When thou hast said so, stick it there
Upon His bib or stomacher;
And tell Him, for good handsel too,
That thou hast brought a whistle new,
Made of a clean straight oaten reed,
To charm His cries at time of need.
Tell Him, for coral, thou hast none,
But if thou hadst, He should have one;
But poor thou art, and known to be
Even as moneyless as He.
Lastly, if thou canst win a kiss
From those mellifluous lips of His;
Then never take a second on,
To spoil the first impression.

*Herrick.*

310

## Another Grace for a Child

Here a little child I stand
Heaving up my either hand;
Cold as paddocks though they be,
Here I lift them up to Thee,
For a benison to fall
On our meat and on us all. Amen.

*Herrick.*

311

Yet if his majesty our sovereign lord
Should of his own accord
Friendly himself invite,
And say "I'll be your guest to-morrow night",
How should we stir ourselves, call and command
All hands to work! "Let no man idle stand.
Set me fine Spanish tables in the hall,
See they be fitted all;
Let there be room to eat,
And order taken that there want no meat.
See every sconce and candlestick made bright,
That without tapers they may give a light.
Look to the presence: are the carpets spread,
The dais o'er the head,
The cushions in the chairs,
And all the candles lighted on the stairs?
Perfume the chambers, and in any case
Let each man give attendance in his place."
Thus if the king were coming would we do,
And 't were good reason too;

For 't is a duteous thing
To show all honour to an earthly king,
And after all our travail and our cost,
So he be pleased to think no labour lost.
But at the coming of the King of Heaven
All's set at six and seven:
We wallow in our sin,
Christ cannot find a chamber in the inn.
We entertain him always like a stranger,
And as at first still lodge him in the manger.

*Anonymous.*

## 312

Most glorious Lord of life, that, on this day,
Did'st make thy triumph over death and sin,
And, having harrowed hell, did'st bring away
Captivity thence captive, us to win:
This joyous day, dear Lord, with joy begin,
And grant that we, for whom thou diddest die,
Being with thy dear blood clean washed from sin,
May live for ever in felicity;
And that thy love we, weighing worthily,
May likewise love thee for the same again;
And for thy sake, that all like dear did'st buy,
With love may one another entertain.
So let us love, dear love, like as we ought:
Love is the lesson which the Lord us taught.

*Spenser.*

313

## For the Baptist

The last and greatest herald of heaven's King,
Girt with rough skins, hies to the desert wild,
Among that savage brood the woods forth bring,
Which he than man more harmless found and mild:
His food was locusts, and what young doth spring,
With honey that from virgin hives distilled;
Parched body, hollow eyes, some uncouth thing
Made him appear, long since from earth exiled.
Then burst he forth: "All ye, whose hopes rely
On God, with me amidst these deserts mourn;
Repent, repent, and from old errors turn."
Who listened to his voice, obeyed his cry?
  Only the echoes, which he made relent,
  Rung from their marble caves, "Repent, repent!"

*Drummond.*

314

At the round earth's imagined corners blow
Your trumpets, angels, and arise, arise
From death, you numberless infinities
Of souls, and to your scattered bodies go;
All whom the flood did, and fire shall, o'erthrow,
All whom war, death, age, agues, tyrannies,
Despair, law, chance hath slain, and you, whose eyes
Shall behold God, and never taste death's woe.
But let them sleep, Lord, and me mourn a space;
For, if above all these my sins abound,

'T is late to ask abundance of Thy grace,
When we are there. Here on this lowly ground,
Teach me how to repent, for that's as good
As if Thou hadst sealed my pardon with Thy
blood.

*Donne.*

315

## A Hymn to God the Father

I

Wilt Thou forgive that sin where I begun,
Which was my sin, though it were done before?
Wilt Thou forgive that sin, through which I run,
And do run still, though still I do deplore?
When Thou hast done, Thou hast not done,
For I have more.

II

Wilt Thou forgive that sin which I have won
Others to sin, and made my sin their door?
Wilt Thou forgive that sin which I did shun
A year or two, but wallowed in a score?
When Thou hast done, Thou hast not done,
For I have more.

III

I have a sin of fear, that when I have spun
My last thread, I shall perish on the shore;
But swear by Thyself, that at my death Thy Son
Shall shine as He shines now, and heretofore;
And, having done that, Thou hast done;
I fear no more.

*Donne.*

## 316

Let not the sluggish sleep
  Close up thy waking eye,
Until with judgment deep
  Thy daily deeds thou try:
He that one sin in conscience keeps
  When he to quiet goes,
More venturous is than he that sleeps
  With twenty mortal foes.

*Anonymous.*

## 317

Awake, awake, thou heavy sprite,
  That sleep'st the deadly sleep of sin!
Rise now and walk the ways of light!
  'T is not too late yet to begin.
Seek heaven early, seek it late:
True Faith still finds an open gate.

Get up, get up, thou leaden man!
  Thy track to endless joy or pain
Yields but the model of a span;
  Yet burns out thy life's lamp in vain!
One minute bounds thy bane or bliss!
Then watch and labour, while time is.

*Campion.*

318

# A Thanksgiving to God for his House

Lord, Thou hast give me a cell
  Wherein to dwell;
And little house, whose humble roof
  Is weather-proof;
Under the spars of which I lie
  Both soft and dry;
Where Thou my chamber for to ward
  Hast set a guard
Of harmless thoughts, to watch and keep
  Me, while I sleep.
Low is my porch, as is my fate,
  Both void of state;
And yet the threshold of my door
  Is worn by the poor,
Who thither come, and freely get
  Good words or meat;
Like as my parlour, so my hall
  And kitchen 's small;
A little buttery, and therein
  A little bin
Which keeps my little loaf of bread
  Unchipt, unflead.
Some brittle sticks of thorn or briar
  Make me a fire,
Close by whose living coal I sit,
  And glow like it.
Lord, I confess, too, when I dine,
  The pulse is Thine,

And all those other bits, that be
There placed by Thee;
The worts, the purslain, and the mess
Of water-cress,
Which of Thy kindness Thou hast sent;
And my content
Makes those, and my beloved beet,
To be more sweet.
'T is Thou that crown'st my glittering hearth
With guiltless mirth;
And giv'st me wassail bowls to drink,
Spiced to the brink.
Lord, 't is Thy plenty-dropping hand,
That soils my land;
And giv'st me for my bushel sown,
Twice ten for one.
Thou mak'st my teeming hen to lay
Her egg each day;
Besides my healthful ewes to bear
Me twins each year,
The while the conduits of my kine
Run cream for wine.
All these, and better Thou dost send
Me, to this end,
That I should render, for my part,
A thankful heart;
Which, fired with incense, I resign,
As wholly Thine;
But the acceptance, that must be,
My Christ, by Thee.

*Herrick.*

## 319

The man of life upright,
Whose guiltless heart is free
From all dishonest deeds,
Or thought of vanity;

The man whose silent days
In harmless joys are spent,
Whom hopes cannot delude
Nor sorrow discontent;

That man needs neither towers
Nor armour for defence,
Nor secret vaults to fly
From thunder's violence:

He only can behold
With unaffrighted eyes
The horrors of the deep
And terrors of the skies.

Thus, scorning all the cares
That fate or fortune brings,
He makes the heaven his book,
His wisdom heavenly things;

Good thoughts his only friends,
His wealth a well-spent age,
The earth his sober inn
And quiet pilgrimage.

*Campion.*

# A Hymn to Christ, at the Author's last going into Germany

In what torn ship so ever I embark,
That ship shall be my emblem of Thy ark;
What sea soever swallow me, that flood
Shall be to me an emblem of Thy blood;
Though Thou with clouds of anger do disguise
Thy face, yet through that mask I know those eyes,
Which, though they turn away sometimes,
They never will despise

I sacrifice this island unto Thee,
And all whom I love there, and who love me;
When I have put our seas 'twixt them and me,
Put Thou Thy seas betwixt my sins and Thee.
As the tree's sap doth seek the root below
In winter, in my winter now I go,
Where none but Thee, the eternal root
Of true love, I may know.

Nor Thou nor Thy religion dost control
The amorousness of an harmonious soul;
But Thou wouldst have that love Thyself; as Thou
Art jealous, Lord, so I am jealous now;
Thou lovest not, till from loving more Thou free
My soul; Whoever gives, takes liberty;
Oh, if Thou carest not whom I love,
Alas! Thou lovest not me.

Seal then this bill of my divorce to all,
On whom those fainter beams of love did fall;

Marry those loves, which in youth scattered be
On fame, wit, hopes, false mistresses, to Thee.
Churches are best for prayer, that have least light;
To see God only, I go out of sight;
　　And to escape stormy days, I choose
　　　　An everlasting night.

*Donne.*

321

## Of Misery

Corpse, clad with carefulness;
Heart, heaped with heaviness;
Purse, poor and penniless;
Back, bare in bitterness;
O get my grave in readiness;
Fain would I die to end this stress.

*Thomas Howell.*

322

## The Wood, the Weed, the Wag

Three things there be that prosper all apace,
　And flourish while they are asunder far;
But on a day, they meet all in a place,
　And when they meet, they one another mar.

And they be these: the Wood, the Weed, the Wag:
　The Wood is that that makes the gallows tree;
The Weed is that that strings the hangman's bag;
　The Wag, my pretty knave, betokens thee.

Now mark, dear boy, while these assemble not,
Green springs the tree, hemp grows, the wag is wild;
But when they meet, it makes the timber rot,
It frets the halter, and it chokes the child.
God Bless the Child!

*Raleigh.*

323

When that I was and a little tiny boy,
With hey, ho, the wind and the rain,
A foolish thing was but a toy,
For the rain it raineth every day.

But when I came to man's estate,
With hey, ho, the wind and the rain,
'Gainst knaves and thieves men shut their gate,
For the rain it raineth every day.

But when I came, alas! to wive,
With hey, ho, the wind and the rain,
By swaggering could I never thrive,
For the rain it raineth every day.

But when I came unto my beds,
With hey, ho, the wind and the rain,
With toss-pots still had drunken heads,
For the rain it raineth every day.

A great while ago the world begun,
With hey, ho, the wind and the rain,
But that's all one, our play is done,
And we'll strive to please you every day.

*Shakespeare.*

## 324

Whether men do laugh or weep,
Whether they do wake or sleep,
Whether they die young or old,
Whether they feel heat or cold;
There is, underneath the sun,
Nothing in true earnest done.

All our pride is but a jest:
None are worst, and none are best;
Grief and joy, and hope and fear,
Play their pageants everywhere:
Vain opinion all doth sway,
And the world is but a play.

Powers above in clouds do sit,
Mocking our poor apish wit;
That so lamely, with such state,
Their high glory imitate:
No ill can be felt but pain,
And that happy men disdain.

*Campion.*

## 325

# The Lie

Go, Soul, the body's guest,
  Upon a thankless arrant;
Fear not to touch the best,
  The truth shall be thy warrant:
Go, since I needs must die,
And give the world the lie.

Say to the court, it glows
  And shines like rotten wood;
Say to the church, it shows
  What 's good, and doth no good:
If church and court reply,
Then give them both the lie.

Tell potentates, they live
  Acting by others' action;
Not loved unless they give,
  Not strong but by a faction:
If potentates reply,
Give potentates the lie.

Tell men of high condition,
  That manage the estate,
Their purpose is ambition,
  Their practice only hate:
And if they once reply,
Then give them all the lie.

Tell them that brave it most,
  They beg for more by spending,
Who, in their greatest cost,
  Seek nothing but commending:
And if they make reply,
Then give them all the lie.

Tell zeal it wants devotion;
  Tell love it is but lust;
Tell time it is but motion;
  Tell flesh it is but dust:
And wish them not reply,
For thou must give the lie.

Tell age it daily wasteth;
  Tell honour how it alters;
Tell beauty how she blasteth;
  Tell favour how it falters:
And as they shall reply,
Give every one the lie.

Tell wit how much it wrangles
  In tickle points of niceness;
Tell wisdom she entangles
  Herself in over-wiseness:
And when they do reply,
Straight give them both the lie.

Tell physic of her boldness;
  Tell skill it is pretension;
Tell charity of coldness;
  Tell law it is contention:
And as they do reply,
So give them still the lie.

Tell fortune of her blindness;
  Tell nature of decay;
Tell friendship of unkindness;
  Tell justice of delay:
And if they will reply,
Then give them all the lie.

Tell arts they have no soundness,
  But vary by esteeming;
Tell schools they want profoundness,
  And stand too much on seeming:
If arts and schools reply,
Give arts and schools the lie.

Tell faith it's fled the city;
  Tell how the country erreth;
Tell manhood shakes off pity;
  Tell virtue least preferreth:
And if they do reply,
Spare not to give the lie.

So when thou hast, as I
  Commanded thee, done blabbing,
Although to give the lie
  Deserves no less than stabbing,
Stab at thee he that will,
No stab the soul can kill.

*Raleigh.*

326

## The World

The world's a bubble and the life of man
  Less than a span;
In his conception wretched, from the womb,
  So to the tomb;
Curst from his cradle, and brought up to years
  With cares and fears.
Who then to frail mortality shall trust
But limns on water, or but writes in dust.

Yet, whilst with sorrow here we live oppressed,
  What life is best?
Courts are but only superficial schools,
  To dandle fools;

The rural part is turned into a den
Of savage men;
And where 's a city from foul vice so free
But may be termed the worst of all the three?

Domestic cares afflict the husband's bed,
Or pains his head:
Those that live single take it for a curse,
Or do things worse:
These would have children; those that have them moan,
Or wish them gone:
What is it, then, to have or have no wife,
But single thraldom or a double strife?

Our own affections still at home to please
Is a disease;
To cross the seas to any foreign soil,
Peril and toil;
Wars with their noise affright us; when they cease,
We're worse in peace:
What then remains, but that we still should cry
For being born, and, being born, to die?

*Bacon.*

327

# The Happy Life

How happy is he born and taught
That serveth not another's will;
Whose armour is his honest thought,
And simple truth his utmost skill;

Whose passions not his masters are;
Whose soul is still prepared for death,
Untied unto the world by care
Of public fame or private breath;

Who envies none that chance doth raise,
Nor vice; who never understood
How deepest wounds are given by praise;
Nor rules of state, but rules of good;

Who hath his life from rumours freed;
Whose conscience is his strong retreat;
Whose state can neither flatterers feed,
Nor ruin make oppressors great;

Who God doth late and early pray
More of his grace than gifts to lend;
And entertains the harmless day
With a religious book or friend.

This man is freed from servile bands,
Of hope to rise or fear to fall:
Lord of himself, though not of lands,
And, having nothing, yet hath all.

*Wotton.*

## 328

# Epistle to the Lady Margaret, Countess of Cumberland

He that of such a height hath built his mind,
And reared the dwelling of his thoughts so strong,
As neither fear nor hope can shake the frame
Of his resolved powers; nor all the wind

Of vanity or malice pierce to wrong
His settled peace, or to disturb the same:
What a fair seat hath he, from whence he may
The boundless wastes and wilds of man survey!

And with how free an eye doth he look down
Upon these lower regions of turmoil!
Where all the storms of passions mainly beat
On flesh and blood: where honour, power, renown
Are only gay afflictions, golden toil;
Where greatness stands upon as feeble feet
As frailty doth; and only great doth seem
To little minds, who do it so esteem.

He looks upon the mightiest monarchs' wars
But only as on stately robberies;
Where evermore the fortune that prevails
Must be the right: the ill-succeeding mars
The fairest and the best-faced enterprise.
Great pirate Pompey lesser pirates quails:
Justice, he sees (as if seduced), still
Conspires with power, whose cause must not be ill.

He sees the face of Right as manifold
As are the passions of uncertain man;
Who puts it in all colours, all attires,
To serve his ends, and make his courses hold.
He sees, that let deceit work what it can,
Plot and contrive base ways to high desires,
That the all-guiding providence doth yet
All disappoint, and mocks this smoke of wit.

Nor is he moved with all the thunder-cracks
Of tyrants' threats, or with the surly brow
Of power, that proudly sits on others' crimes;
Charged with more crying sins than those he checks.

The storms of sad confusion, that may grow
Up in the present for the coming times,
Appal not him; that hath no side at all,
But of himself, and knows the worst can fall.

Although his heart, so near allied to earth,
Cannot but pity the perplexed state
Of troublous and distressed mortality,
That thus make way unto the ugly birth
Of their own sorrows, and do still beget
Affliction upon imbecility:
Yet seeing thus the course of things must run,
He looks thereon not strange, but as fore-done.

And whilst distraught ambition compasses,
And is encompassed; whilst as craft deceives,
And is deceived; whilst man doth ransack man,
And builds on blood, and rises by distress;
And the inheritance of desolation leaves
To great-expecting hopes: he looks thereon,
As from the shore of peace, with unwet eye,
And bears no venture in impiety.

Thus, madam, fares the man that hath prepared
A rest for his desires; and sees all things
Beneath him; and hath learnt this book of man,
Full of the notes of frailty; and compared
The best of glory with her sufferings:
By whom, I see, you labour, all you can,
To plant your heart; and set your thoughts as near
His glorious mansion, as your powers can bear.

Which, madam, are so soundly fashioned
By that clear judgment, that hath carried you
Beyond the feeble limits of your kind,
As they can stand against the strongest head

Passion can make; inured to any hue
The world can cast; that cannot cast that mind
Out of her form of goodness, that doth see
Both what the best and worst of earth can be.

Which makes, that whatsoever here befals,
You in the region of yourself remain:
Where no vain breath of the impudent molests,
That hath secured within the brazen walls
Of a clear conscience, that without all stain
Rises in peace, in innocency rests;
Whilst all what malice from without procures,
Shows her own ugly heart, but hurts not yours.

And whereas none rejoice more in revenge
Than women use to do; yet you well know,
That wrong is better checked by being contemned
Than being pursued; leaving to him to avenge,
To whom it appertains. Wherein you show,
How worthily your clearness had condemned
Base malediction, living in the dark,
That at the rays of goodness still doth bark.

Knowing the heart of man is set to be
The centre of his world, about the which
These revolutions of disturbances
Still roll; where all the aspects of misery
Predominate; whose strong effects are such,
As he must bear, being powerless to redress:
And that unless above himself he can
Erect himself, how poor a thing is man!

And how turmoiled they are that level lie
With earth, and cannot lift themselves from thence,
That never are at peace with their desires,
But work beyond their years; and even deny

Dotage her rest, and hardly will dispense
With death. That when ability expires,
Desire lives still: so much delight they have,
To carry toil and travail to the grave.

Whose ends you see; and what can be the best
They reach unto, when they have cast the sum
And reckonings of their glory. And you know,
This floating life hath but this port of rest,
A heart prepared, that fears no ill to come.
And that man's greatness rests but in his show,
The best of all whose days consumed are,
Either in war, or peace conceiving war.

This concord, madam, of a well-tuned mind
Hath been so set by that all-working hand
Of heaven, that though the world hath done his worst
To put it out by discords most unkind;
Yet doth it still in perfect union stand
With God and man; nor ever will be forced
From that most sweet accord; but still agree,
Equal in fortune's inequality.

And this note, madam, of your worthiness
Remains recorded in so many hearts,
As time nor malice cannot wrong your right,
In the inheritance of fame you must possess:
You that have built you by your great deserts,
Out of small means, a far more exquisite
And glorious dwelling for your honoured name,
Than all the gold of leaden mines can frame.

*Daniel.*

329

What is a day, what is a year
  Of vain delight and pleasure?
Like to a dream it endless dies,
  And from us like a vapour flies:
And this is all the fruit that we find,
  Which glory in worldly treasure.

He that will hope for true delight,
  With virtue must be graced;
Sweet folly yields a bitter taste,
  Which ever will appear at last:
But if we still in virtue delight,
  Our souls are in heaven placed.

*Campion.*

330

# Ballad of Agincourt

Fair stood the wind for France,
When we our sails advance,
Nor now to prove our chance
    Longer will tarry;
But putting to the main
At Kaux, the mouth of Seine,
With all his martial train
    Landed King Harry.

And taking many a fort
Furnished in warlike sort,
Marcheth towards Agincourt
    In happy hour;

Skirmishing day by day
With those that stopped his way
Where the French general lay
With all his power.

Which in his height of pride
King Henry to deride,
His ransom to provide
To the king sending;
Which he neglects the while
As from a nation vile,
Yet with an angry smile
Their fall portending.

And turning to his men
Quoth our brave Henry then:
"Though they to one be ten,
Be not amazed:
Yet have we well begun,
Battles so bravely won
Have ever to the sun
By fame been raised.

"And for myself (quoth he)
This my full rest shall be,
England ne'er mourn for me
Nor more esteem me:
Victor I will remain
Or on this earth lie slain,
Never shall she sustain
Loss to redeem me.

"Poitiers and Cressy tell,
When most their pride did swell,
Under our swords they fell:
No less our skill is

Than when our grandsire great,
Claiming the regal seat,
By many a warlike feat
Lopped the French Lilies."

The Duke of York so dread
The eager vaward led;
With the main Henry sped
Amongst his henchmen;
Exeter had the rear,
A braver man not there;
O Lord, how hot they were
On the false Frenchmen!

They now to fight are gone;
Armour on armour shone,
Drum now to drum did groan:
To hear was wonder.
That with the cries they make
The very earth did shake;
Trumpet to trumpet spake,
Thunder to thunder.

Well it thine age became,
O noble Erpingham,
Which did'st the signal aim
To our hid forces;
When from a meadow by,
Like a storm suddenly,
The English archery
Struck the French horses,

With Spanish yew so strong,
Arrows a cloth-yard long,
That like to serpents stung
Piercing the weather;

None from his fellows starts,
But playing manly parts,
And like true English hearts,
    Stuck close together.

When down their bows they threw
And forth their bilboes drew
And on the French they flew,
    Not one was tardy;
Arms were from shoulders sent,
Scalps to the teeth were rent,
Down the French peasants went,
    Our men were hardy.

This while our noble king,
His broad-sword brandishing,
Down the French host did ding,
    As to o'erwhelm it;
And many a deep wound lent,
His arms with blood besprent,
And many a cruel dent
    Bruised his helmet.

Gloster, that duke so good,
Next of the royal blood,
For famous England stood
    With his brave brother;
Clarence, in steel so bright,
Though but a maiden knight,
Yet in that furious fight
    Scarce such another.

Warwick in blood did wade,
Oxford the foe invade,
And cruel slaughter made
    Still as they ran up:

Suffolk his axe did ply,
Beaumont and Willoughby
Bare them right doughtily,
    Ferrers and Fanhope.

Upon Saint Crispin's day
Fought was this noble fray
Which fame did not delay
    To England to carry:
O when shall English men
With such acts fill a pen,
Or England breed again
    Such a King Harry!

*Drayton.*

## 331

What pleasure have great princes
  More dainty to their choice
Than herdsmen wild, who careless,
  In quiet life rejoice,
And fortune's fate not fearing
Sing sweet in summer morning?

Their dealings plain and rightful,
  Are void of all deceit;
They never know how spiteful
  It is to kneel and wait
On favourite presumptuous
Whose pride is vain and sumptuous.

All day their flocks each tendeth;
  At night they take their rest;

More quiet than who sendeth
His ship into the East,
Where gold and pearl are plenty;
But getting, very dainty.

For lawyers and their pleading,
They 'steem it not a straw;
They think that honest meaning
Is of itself a law:
Whence conscience judgeth plainly,
They spend no money vainly.

O happy who thus liveth!
Not caring much for gold;
With clothing which sufficeth
To keep him from the cold.
Though poor and plain his diet,
Yet merry it is, and quiet.

*Anonymous.*

332

# To the Virginian Voyage

You brave heroic minds,
Worthy your country's name,
That honour still pursue;
Go and subdue,
Whilst loitering hinds
Lurk here at home with shame.

Britons, you stay too long;
Quickly aboard bestow you,
  And with a merry gale
  Swell your stretched sail,
With vows as strong
As the winds that blow you.

Your course securely steer,
West and by south forth keep;
  Rocks, lee-shores, nor shoals,
  When Eolus scowls,
You need not fear;
So absolute the deep.

And cheerfully at sea
Success you still entice
  To get the pearl and gold,
  And ours to hold
Virginia,
Earth's only Paradise.

When nature hath in store
Fowl, venison, and fish,
  And the fruitful'st soil,
  Without your toil,
Three harvests more,
All greater than you wish.

And the ambitious vine
Crowns with his purple mass
  The cedar reaching high
  To kiss the sky,
The cypress, pine,
And useful sassafras.

To whom the golden age
Still nature's laws doth give,
    No other cares attend
    But them to defend
From winter's rage,
That long there doth not live.

When as the luscious smell
Of that delicious land,
    Above the seas that flows,
    The clear wind throws
Your hearts to swell
Approaching the dear strand;

In kenning of the shore
(Thanks to God first given),
    O you, the happiest men,
    Be frolic then;
Let cannons roar,
Frighting the wide heaven.

And in regions far,
Such heroes bring ye forth,
    As those from whom we came;
    And plant our name
Under that star
Not known unto our North

And as there plenty grows
Of laurel everywhere,
    Apollo's sacred tree,
    You it may see,
A poet's brows
To crown, that may sing there.

Thy voyages attend
Industrious Hackluit,
    Whose reading shall inflame
    Men to seek fame,
And much commend
To after-times thy wit.

*Drayton.*

333

Desire, that is of things ungot,
  See what travail it procureth,
  And how much the mind endureth,
To gain what yet it gaineth not:
    For never was it paid,
    The charge defrayed,
According to the price of thought.

*Daniel.*

334

## Change should Breed Change

New doth the sun appear,
The mountains' snows decay,
Crowned with frail flowers forth comes the baby year.
My soul, yet in that frost
Which flower and fruit hath lost,
As if all here immortal were, dost stay:
For shame! thy powers awake,
Look to that heaven which never night makes black,
And there, at that immortal sun's bright rays,
Deck thee with flowers which fear not rage of days.

*Drummond.*

## 335

Oft, when my spirit doth spread her bolder wings,
In mind to mount up to the purest sky,
It down is weighed with thought of earthly things,
And clogged with burden of mortality;
Where, when that sovereign beauty it doth spy,
Resembling heaven's glory in her light,
Drawn with sweet pleasure's bait, it back doth fly,
And unto heaven forgets her former flight.
There my frail fancy, fed with full delight,
Doth bathe in bliss, and mantleth most at ease;
Ne thinks of other heaven, but how it might
Her heart's desire with most contentment please.
  Heart need not wish none other happiness,
  But here on earth to have such heaven's bliss.

*Spenser.*

## 336

They that have power to hurt and will do none,
That do not do the thing they most do show,
Who, moving others, are themselves as stone,
Unmoved, cold, and to temptation slow,
They rightly do inherit heaven's graces
And husband nature's riches from expense;
They are the lords and owners of their faces,
Others but stewards of their excellence.
The summer's flower is to the summer sweet,
Though to itself it only live and die,
But if that flower with base infection meet,
The basest weed outbraves his dignity:
  For sweetest things turn sourest by their deeds;
  Lilies that fester smell far worse than weeds.

*Shakespeare.*

## 337

As Love and I late harboured in one inn,
With proverbs thus each other entertain:
In love there is no lack, thus I begin;
Fair words make fools, replieth he again:
Who spares to speak doth spare to speed, quoth I;
As well, saith he, too forward as too slow:
Fortune assists the boldest, I reply;
A hasty man, quoth he, ne'er wanted woe:
Labour is light where love, quoth I, doth pay;
Saith he, Light burden's heavy, if far borne:
Quoth I, The main lost, cast the bye away:
You have spun a fair thread, he replies in scorn.
  And having thus awhile each other thwarted,
  Fools as we met, so fools again we parted.

*Drayton.*

## 338

# Madrigal

This life, which seems so fair,
Is like a bubble blown up in the air
By sporting children's breath,
Who chase it everywhere,
And strive who can most motion it bequeath:
And though it sometime seem of its own might,
Like to an eye of gold, to be fixed there,
And firm to hover in that empty height,
That only is because it is so light.
But in that pomp it doth not long appear;
  For even when most admired, it in a thought,
  As swelled from nothing, doth dissolve in nought.

*Drummond.*

339

## To be Merry

Let's now take our time
While we're in our prime,
And old, old age is afar off:
For the evil, evil days
Will come on apace,
Before we can be aware of.

*Herrick.*

340

That time of year thou mayst in me behold
When yellow leaves, or none, or few, do hang
Upon those boughs which shake against the cold,
Bare ruined choirs, where late the sweet birds sang.
In me thou see'st the twilight of such day
As after sunset fadeth in the west,
Which by and by black night doth take away,
Death's second self, that seals up all in rest.
In me thou see'st the glowing of such fire
That on the ashes of his youth doth lie,
As the death-bed whereon it must expire
Consumed with that which it was nourished by.
This thou perceivest, which makes thy love more strong,
To love that well which thou must leave ere long.

*Shakespeare.*

## 341

# A Farewell to Arms

(To Queen Elizabeth)

His golden locks time hath to silver turned;
  O time too swift, O swiftness never ceasing!
His youth 'gainst time and age hath ever spurned,
  But spurned in vain; youth waneth by increasing;
Beauty, strength, youth are flowers but fading seen;
Duty, faith, love are roots, and ever green.

His helmet now shall make a hive for bees;
  And, lovers' sonnets turned to holy psalms,
A man-at-arms must now serve on his knees,
  And feed on prayers, which are age his alms:
But though from court to cottage he depart,
His saint is sure of his unspotted heart.

And when he saddest sits in homely cell,
  He'll teach his swains this carol for a song:
"Blest be the hearts that wish my sovereign well,
  Curst be the souls that think her any wrong."
Goddess, allow this aged man his right,
To be your beadsman now that was your knight.

*Peele.*

342

# His Age, Dedicated to his Peculiar Friend, Mr. John Wickes, under the Name of Posthumus

Ah Posthumus! our years hence fly,
And leave no sound; nor piety
Or prayers, or vow
Can keep the wrinkle from the brow;
But we must on,
As fate does lead or draw us; none,
None, Posthumus, could e'er decline
The doom of cruel Proserpine.

The pleasing wife, the house, the ground,
Must all be left, no one plant found
To follow thee,
Save only the cursed cypress tree;
A merry mind
Looks forward, scorns what's left behind;
Let's live, my Wickes, then, while we may,
And here enjoy our holiday.

We've seen the past best times, and these
Will ne'er return; we see the seas
And moons to wane,
But they fill up their ebbs again;
But vanished man,
Like to a lily lost, ne'er can,
Ne'er can repullulate, or bring
His days to see a second spring.

But on we must, and thither tend,
Where Anchus and rich Tullus blend
Their sacred seed:
Thus has infernal Jove decreed;
We must be made,
Ere long a song, ere long a shade.
Why then, since life to us is short,
Let's make it full up by our sport.

Crown we our heads with roses then,
And 'noint with Tyrian balm; for when
We two are dead,
The world with us is buried.
Then live we free
As is the air, and let us be
Our own fair wind, and mark each one
Day with the white and lucky stone.

We are not poor, although we have
No roofs of cedar, nor our brave
Baiae, nor keep
Account of such a flock of sheep;
Nor bullocks fed
To lard the shambles: barbels bred
To kiss our hands; nor do we wish
For Pollio's lampreys in our dish.

If we can meet and so confer
Both by a shining salt-cellar,
And have our roof,
Although not arched, yet weather-proof,
And ceiling free
From that cheap candle bawdery;
We'll eat our bean with that full mirth
As we were lords of all the earth.

Well then, on what seas we are tossed,
Our comfort is, we can't be lost.
        Let the wind drive
Our barque, yet she will keep alive
        Amidst the deeps;
'Tis constancy, my Wickes, which keeps
The pinnace up; which though she errs
I' the seas she saves her passengers.

Say we must part (sweet mercy bless
Us both i' the sea, camp, wilderness),
        Can we so far
Stray to become less circular
        Than we are now?
No, no, that self-same heart, that vow
Which made us one, shall ne'er undo,
Or ravel so to make us two.

Live in thy peace; as for myself
When I am bruised on the shelf
        Of time and show
My locks behung with frost and snow;
        When with the rheum,
The cough, the ptisick, I consume
Unto an almost nothing; then
The ages fled I'll call again,

And with a tear compare these last
Lame and bad times with those are past;
        While Baucis by,
My old lean wife, shall kiss it dry.
        And so we'll sit
By the fire, foretelling snow and sleet,
And weather by our aches, grown
Now old enough to be our own

True calendars, as puss's ear
Washed o'er's, to tell what change is near:
Then to assuage
The gripings of the chine by age
I'll call my young
Iulus to sing such a song
I made upon my Julia's breast;
And of her blush at such a feast.

Then shall be read that flower of mine,
Enclosed within a crystal shrine;
A primrose next;
A piece, then, of a higher text,
For to beget
In me a more transcendent heat
Than that insinuating fire,
Which crept into each aged sire,

When the fair Helen, from her eyes,
Shot forth her loving sorceries;
At which I'll rear
Mine aged limbs above my chair,
And, hearing it,
Flutter and crow as in a fit
Of fresh concupiscence, and cry:
No lust there's like to poetry.

Thus, frantic, crazy man, God wot,
I'll call to mind things half-forgot,
And oft between
Repeat the things that I have seen!
Thus ripe with tears,
And twisting my Iulus' hairs;
Doting, I'll weep and say, in truth,
Baucis, these were my sins of youth.

Then next I'll cause my hopeful lad,
If a wild apple can be had,
To crown the hearth,
Lar thus conspiring with our mirth;
Then to infuse
Our browner ale into the cruse,
Which sweetly spiced, we'll first carouse
Unto the genius of the house.

Then the next health of friends of mine,
Loving the brave Burgundian wine,
High sons of pith,
Whose fortunes I have frolicked with;
Such as could well
Bear up the magic bough and spell;
And dancing 'bout the mystic thyrse,
Give up the just applause to verse:

To those, and then again to thee,
We'll drink, my Wickes, until we be
Plump as the cherry,
Though not so fresh, yet full as merry
As the cricket,
The untamed heifer, or the pricket,
Until our tongues shall tell our ears
We're younger by a score of years.

Thus, till we see the fire less shine
From the embers than the kitling's eyne,
We'll still sit up,
Sphering about the wassail-cup
To all those times
Which gave me honour for my rhymes.
The coal once spent, we'll then to bed,
Far more than night-bewearied. *Herrick.*

343

## To a Gentlewoman objecting to Him his Gray Hairs

Am I despised because you say,
And I dare swear, that I am gray?
Know, lady, you have but your day:
And time will come when you shall wear
Such frost and snow upon your hair;
And when (though long, it comes to pass)
You question with your looking-glass;
And in that sincere crystal seek,
But find no rose-bud in your cheek;
Nor any bed to give the show
Where such a rare carnation grew.
Ah! then too late, close in your chamber keeping,
It will be told
That you are old,
By those true tears you're weeping.

*Herrick.*

344

## To Perilla

Ah, my Perilla, dost thou grieve to see
Me, day by day, to steal away from thee?
Age calls me hence, and my gray hairs bid come,
And haste away to mine eternal home;
'T will not be long, Perilla, after this,
That I must give thee the supremest kiss:

Dead when I am, first cast in salt, and bring
Part of the cream from that religious spring;
With which, Perilla, wash my hands and feet;
That done, then wind me in that very sheet
Which wrapt thy smooth limbs when thou didst
implore
The gods' protection but the night before.
Follow me weeping to my turf, and there
Let fall a primrose, and with it a tear:
Then, lastly, let some weekly-strewings be
Devoted to the memory of me:
Then shall my ghost not walk about, but keep
Still in the cool and silent shades of sleep.

*Herrick.*

345

# A Lament in Time of Plague

Adieu! farewell earth's bliss,
This world uncertain is:
Fond are life's lustful joys,
Death proves them all but toys.
None from his darts can fly:
I am sick, I must die.
Lord have mercy on us!

Rich men, trust not in wealth
Gold cannot buy you health;
Physic himself must fade;
All things to end are made;
The plague full swift goes by;
I am sick, I must die.
Lord have mercy on us!

Beauty is but a flower,
Which wrinkles will devour:
Brightness falls from the air;
Queens have died young and fair;
Dust hath closed Helen's eye:
I am sick, I must die.
    Lord have mercy on us!

Strength stoops unto the grave,
Worms feed on Hector brave:
Swords may not fight with fate:
Earth still holds ope her gate.
Come, come, the bells do cry:
I am sick, I must die.
    Lord have mercy on us!

Wit with his wantonness
Tasteth death's bitterness:
Hell's executioner
Hath no ears for to hear
What vain art can reply;
I am sick, I must die.
    Lord have mercy on us!

Haste therefore each degree
To welcome destiny:
Heaven is our heritage,
Earth but a player's stage.
Mount we unto the sky;
I am sick, I must die.
    Lord have mercy on us!

*Nashe.*

## 346

When, in disgrace with fortune and men's eyes,
I all alone beweep my outcast state
And trouble deaf heaven with my bootless cries
And look upon myself and curse my fate,
Wishing me like to one more rich in hope,
Featured like him, like him with friends possessed,
Desiring this man's art and that man's scope,
With what I most enjoy contented least;
Yet in these thoughts myself almost despising,
Haply I think on thee, and then my state,
Like to the lark at break of day arising
From sullen earth, sings hymns at heaven's gate;
For thy sweet love remembered such wealth brings
That then I scorn to change my state with kings.

*Shakespeare.*

## 347

When to the sessions of sweet silent thought
I summon up remembrance of things past,
I sigh the lack of many a thing I sought,
And with old woes new wail my dear time's waste:
Then can I drown an eye, unused to flow,
For precious friends hid in death's dateless night,
And weep afresh love's long since cancelled woe,
And moan the expense of many a vanished sight:
Then can I grieve at grievances foregone,
And heavily from woe to woe tell o'er
The sad account of fore-bemoaned moan,
Which I new pay as if not paid before.
But if the while I think on thee, dear friend,
All losses are restored and sorrows end.

*Shakespeare.*

## 348

Alas, 't is true I have gone here and there
And made myself a motley to the view.
Gored mine own thoughts, sold cheap what is most
    dear,
Made old offences of affections new:
Most true it is that I have looked on truth
Askance and strangely: but, by all above,
These blenches gave my heart another youth,
And worse essays proved thee my best of love.
Now all is done, have what shall have no end:
Mine appetite I never more will grind
On newer proof, to try an older friend,
A god in love, to whom I am confined.
  Then give me welcome, next my heaven the best,
  Even to thy pure and most most loving breast.

*Shakespeare.*

## 349

O, for my sake do you with Fortune chide,
The guilty goddess of my harmful deeds,
That did not better for my life provide
Than public means which public manners breeds.
Thence comes it that my name receives a brand,
And almost thence my nature is subdued
To what it works in, like the dyer's hand:
Pity me then and wish I were renewed;
Whilst, like a willing patient, I will drink
Potions of eisel 'gainst my strong infection;
No bitterness that I will bitter think,
Nor double penance, to correct correction.
  Pity me then, dear friend, and I assure ye
  Even that your pity is enough to cure me.

*Shakespeare.*

## 350

Urns and odours bring away!
Vapours, sighs, darken the day!
Our dole more deadly looks than dying:
Balms, and gums, and heavy cheers,
Sacred vials filled with tears,
And clamours through the wild air flying

Come, all sad and solemn shows,
That are quick-eyed Pleasure's foes!
We convent nought else but woes.

*Fletcher.*

## 351

Hence, all you vain delights,
As short as are the nights
Wherein you spend your folly!
There's nought in this life sweet,
If man were wise to see't,
But only melancholy,
Oh, sweetest melancholy!
Welcome, folded arms, and fixed eyes,
A sight that piercing mortifies,
A look that's fastened to the ground,
A tongue chained up without a sound!

Fountain-heads, and pathless groves,
Places which pale passion loves!
Moonlight walks, when all the fowls
Are warmly housed, save bats and owls!
A midnight bell, a parting groan!
These are the sounds we feed upon;
Then stretch our bones in a still gloomy valley
Nothing's so dainty sweet as lovely melancholy.

*Fletcher.*

352

Slow, slow, fresh fount, keep time with my salt tears;
Yet slower, yet; O faintly, gentle springs;
List to the heavy part the music bears,
Woe weeps out her division when she sings.
Droop herbs and flowers;
Fall grief in showers,
Our beauties are not ours;
O, I could still,
Like melting snow upon some craggy hill,
Drop, drop, drop, drop,
Since nature's pride is now a withered daffodil.

*Jonson.*

353

The hour of sweety night decays apace,
And now warm beds are better than this place.
All time is long that is unwilling spent,
But hours are minutes when they yield content.
The gathered flowers we love that breathe sweet scent,
But loathe them, their sweet odours being spent.
It is a life is never ill
To lie and sleep in roses still.

The rarer pleasure is it is more sweet,
And friends are kindest when they seldom meet.
Who would not hear the nightingale still sing,
Or who grew ever weary of the spring?
The day must have her night, the spring her fall,
All is divided, none is lord of all.
It were a most delightful thing
To live in a perpetual spring.

*Marston.*

354

# On the Tombs in Westminster Abbey

Mortality, behold and fear!
What a change of flesh is here!
Think how many royal bones
Sleep within these heaps of stones;
Here they lie had realms and lands,
Who now want strength to stir their hands;
Where from their pulpits sealed with dust
They preach, In greatness is no trust.
Here's an acre sown indeed
With the richest royallest seed
That the Earth did e'er suck in
Since the first man died for sin:
Here the bones of birth have cried,
Though gods they were, as men they died!
Here are sands, ignoble things,
Dropt from the ruined sides of kings:
Here's a world of pomp and state
Buried in dust, once dead by fate.

*Beaumont.*

355

All the flowers of the spring
Meet to perfume our burying;
These have but their growing prime,
And man does flourish but his time:
Survey our progress from our birth;
We are set, we grow, we turn to earth.

Courts adieu, and all delights,
All bewitching appetites!
Sweetest breath and clearest eye,
Like perfumes, go out and die;
And consequently this is done
As shadows wait upon the sun.
Vain the ambition of kings
Who seek by trophies and dead things
To leave a living name behind,
And weave but nets to catch the wind.

*Webster.*

## 356

Full fathom five thy father lies;
  Of his bones are coral made;
Those are pearls that were his eyes:
  Nothing of him that doth fade
But doth suffer a sea-change
Into something rich and strange.
Sea-nymphs hourly ring his knell:
                    Ding-dong.
Hark! now I hear them: Ding-dong, bell.

*Shakespeare.*

## 357

Come away, come away, Death,
And in sad cypress let me be laid;
Fly away, fly away, breath;
I am slain by a cruel, fair maid.
My shroud of white stuck all with yew,
        O prepare it!
My part of death, no one so true
        Did share it.

Not a flower, not a flower sweet,
On my black coffin let there be strown;
Not a friend, not a friend greet
My poor corpse where my bones shall be thrown:
A thousand thousand sighs to save,
    Lay me O where
Sad true lover never find my grave
    To weep there!

*Shakespeare.*

## 358

Lay a garland on my hearse
    Of the dismal yew;
Maidens, willow branches bear;
    Say, I died true.

My love was false, but I was firm
    From my hour of birth.
Upon my buried body lie
    Lightly, gentle earth!

*Beaumont and Fletcher.*

## 359

Call for the robin-redbreast and the wren,
Since o'er shady groves they hover,
And with leaves and flowers do cover
The friendless bodies of unburied men.
Call unto his funeral dole
The ant, the field-mouse, and the mole,
To rear him hillocks that shall keep him warm,
And (when gay tombs are robbed) sustain no harm;
But keep the wolf far thence, that 's foe to men,
For with his nails he'll dig them up again.

*Webster.*

## 360

Hark, now everything is still,
The screech-owl and the whistler shrill,
Call upon our dame aloud,
And bid her quickly don her shroud!
Much you had of land and rent;
Your length in clay 's now competent:
A long war disturbed your mind;
Here your perfect peace is signed.
Of what is 't fools make such vain keeping?
Sin their conception, their birth weeping,
Their life a general mist of error,
Their death a hideous storm of terror.
Strew your hair with powders sweet,
Don clean linen, bathe your feet,
And (the foul fiend more to check)
A crucifix let bless your neck:
'T is now full tide 'tween night and day;
End your groan, and come away.

*Webster.*

## 361

Fear no more the heat o' the sun,
Nor the furious winter's rages;
Thou thy worldly task hast done,
Home art gone, and ta'en thy wages:
Golden lads and girls all must,
As chimney-sweepers, come to dust.

Fear no more the frown o' the great;
Thou art past the tyrant's stroke;

Care no more to clothe and eat;
  To thee the reed is as the oak:
The sceptre, learning, physic, must
All follow this, and come to dust.

Fear no more the lightning-flash
  Nor the all-dreaded thunder-stone;
Fear not slander, censure rash;
  Thou hast finished joy and moan:
All lovers young, all lovers must
Consign to thee, and come to dust.

  No exorciser harm thee!
  Nor no witchcraft charm thee!
  Ghost unlaid forbear thee!
  Nothing ill come near thee!
  Quiet consummation have;
  And renowned be thy grave!

*Shakespeare.*

362

## Upon a Child

Here a pretty baby lies
Sung asleep with lullabies
Pray be silent, and not stir
The easy earth that covers her.

*Herrick.*

363

## An Epitaph upon a Virgin

Here a solemn fast we keep,
While all beauty lies asleep
Hushed be all things, no noise here,
But the toning of a tear:
Or the sigh of such as bring
Cowslips for her covering.

*Herrick.*

364

## Epitaph on S. P., a Child of Queen Elizabeth's Chapel

Weep with me all you that read
This little story;
And know, for whom a tear you shed,
Death's self is sorry.
'T was a child, that so did thrive
In grace and feature,
As Heaven and nature seemed to strive
Which owned the creature.
Years he numbered scarce thirteen
When fates turned cruel;
Yet three filled zodiacs had he been
The stage's jewel;
And did act, what now we moan,
Old men so duly;
As, sooth, the Parcae thought him one,
He played so truly.

So, by error, to his fate
    They all consented;
But viewing him since, alas, too late!
    They have repented;
And have sought, to give new birth,
    In baths to steep him;
But, being so much too good for earth,
    Heaven vows to keep him.

*Jonson.*

365

## Epitaph on Elizabeth L. H.

Wouldst thou hear what men can say
In a little? Reader, stay.
Underneath this stone doth lie
As much beauty as could die;
Which in life did harbour give
To more virtue than doth live.
If, at all, she had a fault
Leave it buried in this vault.
One name was Elizabeth,
The other let it sleep with death.
Fitter, where it died, to tell,
Than that it lived at all. Farewell.

*Jonson.*

366

## On the Countess Dowager of Pembroke

Underneath this sable herse
Lies the subject of all verse:
Sidney's sister, Pembroke's mother:
Death, ere thou hast slain another,
Fair, and learn'd, and good as she,
Time shall throw a dart at thee.

Marble piles let no man raise
To her name: for after days
Some kind woman born as she,
Reading this, like Niobe
Shall turn marble, and become
Both her mourner and her tomb.

*Browne or Jonson.*

367

Death, be not proud, though some have called thee
Mighty and dreadful, for thou art not so;
For those, whom thou think'st thou dost overthrow,
Die not, poor Death, nor yet canst thou kill me.
From rest and sleep, which but thy picture be,
Much pleasure, then from thee much more must flow,
And soonest our best men with thee do go,
Rest of their bones, and soul's delivery.
Thou 'rt slave to Fate, chance, kings, and desperate
men,
And dost with poison, war, and sickness dwell,

And poppy, or charms can make us sleep as well,
And better than thy stroke; why swell'st thou then?
One short sleep past, we wake eternally,
And Death shall be no more; Death, thou shalt die.

*Donne.*

368

# Verses found in his Bible in the Gate-house at Westminster

Even such is time, that takes in trust
  Our youth, our joys, our all we have,
And pays us but with earth and dust;
  Who, in the dark and silent grave,
When we have wandered all our ways,
Shuts up the story of our days;
But from this earth, this grave, this dust,
My God shall raise me up, I trust.

*Raleigh.*

369

# Divination by a Daffodil

When a daffodil I see,
Hanging down his head towards me
Guess I may what I must be:
First, I shall decline my head;
Secondly, I shall be dead;
Lastly, safely buried.

*Herrick.*

370

# Verses Written in the Tower the Night before he was Beheaded

My prime of youth is but a frost of cares;
  My feast of joy is but a dish of pain;
My crop of corn is but a field of tares;
  And all my good is but vain hope of gain;
The day is fled, and yet I saw no sun;
And now I live, and now my life is done!

The spring is past, and yet it hath not sprung;
  The fruit is dead, and yet the leaves are green;
My youth is gone, and yet I am but young;
  I saw the world, and yet I was not seen;
My thread is cut, and yet it is not spun;
And now I live, and now my life is done!

I sought my death, and found it in my womb;
  I looked for life, and saw it was a shade;
I trod the earth, and knew it was my tomb;
  And now I die, and now I am but made;
The glass is full, and now my glass is run;
And now I live, and now my life is done!

*Chidiock Tichborne.*

# His Winding-Sheet

Come thou, who art the wine and wit
Of all I 've writ:
The grace, the glory, and the best
Piece of the rest.
Thou art of what I did intend
The all and end;
And what was made, was made to meet
Thee, thee, my sheet.
Come then, and be to my chaste side
Both bed and bride.
We two, as reliques left, will have
One rest, one grave.
And, hugging close, we will not fear
Lust entering here:
Where all desires are dead or cold
As in the mould;
And all affections are forgot,
Or trouble not.
Here, here the slaves and prisoners be
From shackles free:
And weeping widows long oppressed
Do here find rest.
The wronged client ends his laws
Here, and his cause.
Here those long suits of chancery lie
Quiet, or die:
And all Star-Chamber bills do cease,
Or hold their peace.
Here needs no Court for our Request,
Where all are best,

All wise, all equal, and all just
Alike i' the dust.
Nor need we here to fear the frown
Of court or crown:
Where fortune bears no sway o'er things,
There all are kings.
In this securer place we 'll keep,
As lulled asleep;
Or for a little time we 'll lie
As robes laid by;
To be another day re-worn,
Turned, but not torn:
Or, like old testaments engrost,
Locked up, not lost:
And for a while lie here concealed,
To be revealed
Next at that great Platonic year,
And then meet here.

*Herrick.*

## 372

# The Funeral

Whoever comes to shroud me, do not harm,
Nor question much,
That subtle wreath of hair, which crowns my arm;
The mystery, the sign you must not touch;
For 't is my outward soul,
Viceroy to that, which unto heaven being gone
Will leave this to control
And keep these limbs, her provinces, from dissolution.

For if the sinewy thread my brain lets fall
Through every part
Can tie those parts, and make me one of all,
Those hairs which upward grew, and strength and art
Have from a better brain,
Can better do 't; except she meant that I
By this should know my pain,
As prisoners then are manacled, when they 're condemned to die.

Whate'er she meant by it, bury it with me,
For since I am
Love's martyr, it might breed idolatry,
If into other hands these relics came.
As 't was humility
To afford to it all that a soul can do,
So 't is some bravery,
That since you would have none of me, I bury some of you.

*Donne.*

373

# The Pilgrimage

Give me my scallop-shell of quiet,
My staff of faith to walk upon,
My scrip of joy, immortal diet,
My bottle of salvation,
My gown of glory, hope's true gage;
And thus I'll take my pilgrimage.

Blood must be my body's balmer;
  No other balm will there be given;
Whilst my soul, like quiet palmer,
  Travelleth towards the land of heaven
Over the silver mountains,
Where spring the nectar fountains:
  There will I kiss
  The bowl of bliss,
And drink mine everlasting fill
Upon every milken hill.
My soul will be a-dry before;
But after, it will thirst no more.

Then by that happy, blissful day,
  More peaceful pilgrims I shall see,
That have cast off their rags of clay,
  And walk apparelled fresh like me.
  I'll take them first
  To quench their thirst
And taste of nectar suckets,
  At those clear wells
  Where sweetness dwells,
Drawn up by saints in crystal buckets.

And when our bottles and all we
Are filled with immortality,
Then the blessed paths we'll travel,
Strowed with rubies thick as gravel;
Ceilings of diamonds, sapphire floors,
High walls of coral and pearly bowers,
From thence to heaven's bribeless hall,
Where no corrupted voices brawl;
No conscience molten into gold,
No forged accuser bought or sold,

No cause deferred, no vain-spent journey,
For there Christ is the king's Attorney,
Who pleads for all without degrees,
And he hath angels, but no fees.
And when the grand twelve-million jury
Of our sins, with direful fury,
Against our souls black verdicts give,
Christ pleads his death, and then we live.

Be thou my speaker, taintless pleader,
Unblotted lawyer, true proceeder!
Thou givest salvation even for alms;
Not with a bribed lawyer's palms.
And this is mine eternal plea
To him that made heaven, earth, and sea,
That, since my flesh must die so soon,
And want a head to dine next noon,
Just at the stroke, when my veins start and spread,
Set on my soul an everlasting head!
Then am I ready, like a palmer fit,
To tread those blest paths which before I writ.

Of death and judgment, heaven and hell,
Who oft doth think, must needs die well.

*Raleigh.*

## 374

Come, cheerful day, part of my life to me:
  For while thou view'st me with thy fading light,
Part of my life doth still depart with thee,
  And I still onward haste to my last night.
Time's fatal wings do ever forward fly:
So every day we live a day we die.

But, O ye nights, ordained for barren rest,
  How are my days deprived of life in you,
When heavy sleep my soul hath dispossest,
  By feigned death life sweetly to renew!
Part of my life in that, you life deny:
So every day we live a day we die.

*Campion.*

## 375

When I have seen by Time's fell hand defaced
The rich proud cost of outworn buried age;
When sometime lofty towers I see down-razed
And brass eternal slave to mortal rage;
When I have seen the hungry ocean gain
Advantage on the kingdom of the shore,
And the firm soil win of the watery main,
Increasing store with loss and loss with store;
When I have seen such interchange of state,
Or state itself confounded to decay;
Ruin hath taught me thus to ruminate,
That Time will come and take my love away.
  This thought is as a death, which cannot choose
  But weep to have that which it fears to lose.

*Shakespeare.*

## 376

No longer mourn for me when I am dead
Than you shall hear the surly sullen bell
Give warning to the world that I am fled
From this vile world, with vilest worms to dwell:

Nay, if you read this line, remember not
The hand that writ it; for I love you so
That I in your sweet thoughts would be forgot
If thinking on me then should make you woe.
O, if, I say, you look upon this verse
When I perhaps compounded am with clay,
Do not so much as my poor name rehearse,
But let your love even with my life decay,
  Lest the wise world should look into your moan
  And mock you with me after I am gone.

*Shakespeare.*

## 377

Tired with all these, for restful death I cry,
As, to behold desert a beggar born,
And needy nothing trimmed in jollity,
And purest faith unhappily forsworn,
And gilded honour shamefully misplaced,
And maiden virtue rudely strumpeted,
And right perfection wrongfully disgraced,
And strength by limping sway disabled,
And art made tongue-tied by authority,
And folly doctor-like controlling skill,
And simple truth miscalled simplicity,
And captive good attending captain ill:
  Tired with all these, from these would I be gone
  Save that, to die, I leave my love alone.

*Shakespeare.*

## 378

Poor soul, the centre of my sinful earth,
Foiled by these rebel powers that thee array,
Why dost thou pine within and suffer dearth,
Painting thy outward walls so costly gay?
Why so large cost, having so short a lease,
Dost thou upon thy fading mansion spend?
Shall worms, inheritors of this excess,
Eat up thy charge? is this thy body's end?
Then, soul, live thou upon thy servant's loss,
And let that pine to aggravate thy store;
Buy terms divine in selling hours of dross;
Within be fed, without be rich no more:
So shalt thou feed on Death, that feeds on men,
And Death once dead, there's no more dying then.

*Shakespeare.*

## 379

# Comfort to a Youth that had Lost his Love

What needs complaints,
When she a place
Has with the race
Of saints?
In endless mirth,
She thinks not on
What's said or done
In earth.

She sees no tears,
Or any tone
Of thy deep groan
    She hears:
Nor does she mind
Or think on 't now
That ever thou
    Wast kind;
But changed above,
She likes not there
As she did here,
    Thy love.
Forbear, therefore,
And lull asleep
Thy woes, and weep
    No more.

*Herrick.*

# Notes

A part of this selection has been published, in another form and differently arranged, as one of the volumes of Blackie's "Red Letter Poets", where, in order to fit into the limits of a "Sixteenth Century Anthology", and not to overlap the "Seventeenth Century Anthology", already published in the same series, all writers born later than 1570 had to be excluded. Thus I had to do without almost all the Elizabethan dramatists, those great lyrical poets, and without Herrick, Donne, Drummond of Hawthornden, and Browne of Tavistock. The book as now arranged, with the addition of some hundred and twenty or so more poems (four only having been omitted) comes nearer to my original idea of a selection of the best poems of that period which is conveniently known as Elizabethan; a period properly ending with Herrick, after whom come the Cavaliers and the mystics, and a new world. To begin with Spenser and to end with Herrick is to include, I think, everything characteristic of that period, and nothing outside it.

In making my choice among the almost endless anonymous lyrics of the period I have thankfully followed the best of guides, not only a guide but a pioneer, Mr. A. H. Bullen, to whom we owe the recognition of Campion among English poets, the discovery and printing of many songs still in manuscript, and the almost faultless choice among those songs which, until his time, were but little known and but rarely accessible. I have used, by his kind leave, his texts of Campion, of the "Lyrics from the Song-Books of the Elizabethan Age", and of the "Lyrics from the Elizabethan Dramatists". Apart from the anonymous song-writers, I have read, I think, almost everything in which I could expect to find poems worthy of being quoted, and not too long to quote, in the literature of the period; and I have gone to the best editions for my texts, and, when possible, corrected them by a reference to original editions. The spelling I have modernized, except in cases where the metre would suffer; such as "prease" when it rhymes with a word with which "press" would not rhyme, or "chapelet" when "chaplet" would spoil the rhythm. In one case, "The Bargain" of Sir Philip Sidney, I have given a poem as it was first printed; but in every other case I have tried to give the author's latest text; and I have given every poem in full. And I may repeat here what I said in issuing my first anthology, that I have made no attempt to be representative in my choice of poems, but only to choose, as far as I could, the best. I have weighed each poem on its own merits, as poetry, or as what I conceive poetry to be; and I have been absolutely indifferent to the subject, sentiment, or tendency of the poems which I have chosen. "Give beauty all her right", I have tried to say, with Campion; and my pageant has grouped itself together, almost unconsciously, in the following of that single aim.

3. p. 2.—In Campion the art of the song-writers seems to concentrate itself, become individual, become conscious. He sums up, in a single name, the many nameless writers of perfect words and airs. It is difficult to distinguish between many of his lyrics and the lyrics of different unknown writers. Only, we must suppose that what is really many-sided in him is in them the whole expression of a temperament or character, which he multiplies, so to speak, in himself, as the man of genius does who is also a versatile artist. Mr. Bullen's edition of Campion should be on every book-shelf which holds a Blake or a Bridges. It is a book to take down, linger over, and read for mere idle pleasure, as one might listen to music played softly on a clavichord.

The unrhymed poem, No. 4, is given in Campion's "Observations on the Art of English Poesy" ("declaring the unaptness of rhyme in poesy") as a specimen of English Sapphics.

5. p. 3.—"Sidney, the siren of this latter age", as he is called by Barnefield; "divine Sir Philip", as he is called by Drayton; "the godlike Sidney", as he is called by Ben Jonson; though realized in his own time to his full value, or beyond it, has never since, except from one here and there, received full recognition as a man of letters. As a person he has remained interesting, and in a book which I notice here because it is a model of learning and the work of one who rightly "speaks with authority", Mr. Sidney Lee's "Great Englishmen of the Seventeenth Century", we see just that unreasonable choice among the elements which make up the complete Sidney, and a singular injustice in consequence.

The account of Sidney's life is interesting; we see

him in all his parts, each played, for its brief space, as if there were no other part to play, and each with the same "lovely and familiar gravity". We see him on all his public and private errands over Europe, actually meeting Ronsard in France and Tasso in Italy, bringing back personal gifts from those two great influences in poetry. Three million acres of undiscovered land in America are granted to him; but he has written his "Arcadia", not founded it, and he is to come no nearer to that dream of a world. All this part of the romance of his life Mr. Lee sees and realizes for us; he writes well on the "Arcadia" and on the "Apology for Poetry". But his fixed idea comes in to hinder him from seeing what was most significant in Sidney's life and in his work: the sonnets of Astrophel to Stella, and the love of Sidney for Penelope Rich.

Mr. Lee's fixed idea is that poets are very prosaic people at heart, and that the Elizabethan poets in particular were persons rather lacking in emotion or imagination, who translated and adapted the poems of French and Italian writers with great ability. He has done good service to literary history by finding out the origins of many sonnets and lyrics, from Sidney to Barnes, which were sometimes translated and sometimes imitated by one after another of the Elizabethan lyrists and sonneteers. He has shown that some whole collections of sonnets (like Daniel's sonnets to Delia) can in no sense be taken as personal confessions. This is valuable, because there were many estimable critics and historians of our literature who could not see for themselves (what to an unbiassed reader seems self-evident) that there was nothing whatever personal in such sonnets, no genuine emotion, no thrill of literal reality. But where Mr.

Lee allows his theory to blind his sight is in seeing no lyrical merit in a song of Lodge because it has come into life out of the soil of some Desportes graveyard; and in seeing neither personal poetry nor personal feeling in the sonnets and lyrics of Sidney because he was often content to express himself in conventional or borrowed language.

Mr. Lee speaks very positively about Astrophel's feelings for Stella, is certain that "passion did not enslave him", as indeed it probably did not until those mourning bells had rung out for Stella's marriage. "Genuine affairs of the heart", he considers, "the uncontrollable fever of passion, could have only remote and shadowy concern with the misty idealism and hyperbolical fancies of which the sonnet had to be woven." But where are we to find anything "remote and shadowy" in almost all of the lyrics and in all the best of the sonnets? Has Lamb, after all, written in vain? Lamb has said, with all his emphasis and all his unerring instinct: "They are full, material, and circumstantiated. Time and place appropriates every one of them. It is not a fever of passion wasting itself upon a thin diet of dainty words, but a transcendent passion pervading and illuminating action, pursuits, studies, feats of arms, the opinions of contemporaries, and his judgment of them." There we have a simple statement of fact, if plain words have their meaning and poetical sincerity is distinguishable from "hyperbolical fancies". Like most writers, with the incomparable exception of Lamb, Mr. Lee has not grasped the extraordinary value and importance of Sidney as a poet, nor did even Lamb pause to remember that it is in Sidney that we find the true beginning in England of the novel, of literary criticism, of the sonnet, and of the lyric. What Sidney brought into English lyric poetry was an absolute directness of speech, coupled with a perfected beauty of phrase. Who had there been before him since Chaucer? We find in one or two pieces of Wyatt a certain blunt straightforwardness of speech which, at its best, becomes poetical speech, though never of a rare or subtly passionate quality. Surrey did something more with metre, but had less to say; and Sackville added dignity; but it was for Sidney to create a language of the passions for the daily use of English poetry. The best parts of the best sonnets of Sidney have a plain homely rapture which was a new thing in English, and which has remained permanent in the language ever since; the best parts of his best lyrics are not to be matched for force and nobility of passion by any love-songs from that time to the time of Browning. He is the complete lover, the perfect youth and knight, the absolute Englishman.

29. p. 19.—In spite of Lamb, who did not happen to praise his best work, Michael Drayton has never had his due as a poet. Mr. Bullen made a privately printed "Selection" in 1883, and Mr. Oliver Elton wrote a valuable introduction to some reprints of the Spenser Society, reprinted as a pamphlet in 1895, and now enlarged into a book in 1905. But there is still no complete edition of his poems, and I have been obliged to buy an immense folio of the eighteenth century in order to read, not indeed the whole, but the greater part of them, in comfort. I am glad to know that a variorum edition, by a most accurate scholar, is now in preparation. Such an edition will be of unique value, for no English poet ever altered his work so much as Drayton. One long poem,

originally called "Mortemeriados", he rewrote in a different stanza, under the name "The Barons' War", in order to obey a metrical scruple which had assailed his too scrupulous conscience. Drayton comes nearer to being a great poet than any other not quite great poet of his period. He has done great work: the greatest sonnet, perhaps, in English, "Since there's no help, come, let us kiss and part"; the greatest fighting ballad, the "Ballad of Agincourt"; the best fairy poetry outside Shakespeare. He tried to do things which cannot be done in verse; what Lamb praised him for doing, in words that lend a generous beauty to the thing they praise: "that Panegyrist of my native Earth; who has gone over her soil (in his Polyolbion) with the fidelity of a herald, and the painful love of a son; who has not left a rivulet (so narrow that it may be stept over) without honourable mention; and has animated Hills and Streams with life and passion above the dreams of old mythology".

The "Polyolbion" needs a Lamb for its reader; who will ever again read through, and read with delight, a topographical epic? But I can imagine no more delightful reading, for any lover of poetry, than "The Muses' Elysium", a work of old age which has all the happy vagabond fancy of youth; or that splendid "Nymphidia", which I print in full, long as it is; or the best of the odes and sonnets, so original, so full of personal feeling, so vigorous and I might almost say piquant. One of Drayton's sonnets is so much finer than the others that professional critics are apt to assure us that the others are divided from this one by an impassable gulf. There are a dozen others only less fine than this one, and identical with it in manner and temperament. Drayton is never, in any part of his work, at his best for long together;

even the great sonnet is flawed by an inversion, and no long poem is strictly grammatical throughout. He improvises, and, if he tries to revise, must rewrite. But he has at once honest passion and delicate fancy, with a music of his own, pliant and nimble, though not notably sure-footed. To read Drayton is to enter a homely pastoral province of English poetry, where he is the only shepherd.

In my text of Drayton, I have followed the folio of 1619, the last collected edition during his lifetime, for such poems as are in it; for "Nymphidia", the "Battaile of Agincourt" volume of 1627; and for the poems from "The Muses Elizium", the volume of 1630.

32. p. 20.—Coleridge and Wordsworth were great admirers of Daniel, and I am sure that Wordsworth learnt much from him, in his graver and weightier manner. "The Character of the Happy Warrior" reads to me like Daniel, and hardly reaches to his level. Another poet in whom I hear a kind of echo of Daniel is FitzGerald. Is there not something of that curious poetically prosaic cadence of Omar Khayyám in these lines from "Musophilus"?

"And for the few that only lend their Ear,
That few is all the World; which with a few
Do ever live, and move, and work, and stir.
This is the Heart doth feel, and only know;
The rest of all that only Bodies bear,
Roll up and down, and fill up but the Row.

. . . . . . . . . . .

And if some worthy Spirits be pleased too,
It shall more Comfort breed, but not more Will.
But what if none? It cannot yet undo
The Love I bear unto this Holy Skill.

This is the Thing that I was born to do:
This is my Scene; this Part must I fulfil."

All this meditative work is fine, serious, really "well-languaged", and not always quite so essentially prosaic as Coleridge thought it to be. But when Daniel affects to be in love, as in the sonnets to "Delia" (only two of which, purely abstract ones, I have admitted), he is so obviously writing for writing's sake that I cannot understand why it has required Mr. Sidney Lee's documentary criticism, his proof of the foreign origin of most of them, to convince most people that there never was a Delia and that Daniel did not know what it was to be in love.

33. p. 21.—In the text of this song from "Valentinian" I have adopted Mr. Bullen's emendation, "light" for "sweet", in the rhyme-word of the fifth line.

35. p. 22.—Barnabe Barnes, a wretched rhymer, among whose "sonnets, madrigals, elegies, and odes" I could only find this one charming piece of verse, is conjectured by Mr. Sidney Lee to be the rival poet of Shakespeare's Sonnets. For his arguments see "Life of Shakespeare", 1899, pp. 131–136.

39. p. 24.—Lodge, a pamphleteer of measureless facility, one of our earliest novelists, from whom Shakespeare took two plots, was a lyric poet of quite original singing quality, though for the substance of his work he was ready to pillage whatever poet was fashionable in France or in Italy. The plagiarism, as it has been solemnly called, was of little consequence; he made his own verses sing better than Ronsard's, and taught a new music to English poets. No one before him had been so soft or so sweet, or

had put so rapturous a colour into song. His praise of beauty gushes out with an intoxication like the nightingale's.

43. p. 28.—I must quote here, as I could not give it in the text as a separate poem, the third "turn" of Ben Jonson's ode "To the immortal memory and friendship of that noble pair, Sir Lucius Cary and Sir Henry Morison":

"It is not growing like a tree,
In bulk, doth make men better be;
Or standing long an oak, three hundred year,
To fall at last a log, dry, bald, and sere:
A lily of a day
Is fairer far in May,
Although it fall and die that night;
It was the plant and flower of light.
In small proportions we just beauties see;
And in short measures life may perfect be."

57. p. 39.—Four of the six stanzas of this radiant pastoral were printed, anonymously, and incorrectly, in "The Passionate Pilgrim" of 1599, which has Shakespeare's name on the title-page. A stanza headed "Love's Answer" follows. In 1600 the whole poem, with Marlowe's name, was printed in "England's Helicon", with the six stanzas of the "Reply" (where "I walked along a stream" also appeared), signed Ignoto, which we know from Walton's "Complete Angler" to mean Sir Walter Raleigh: "it was that smooth song which was made by Kit Marlowe, now at least fifty years ago: and the milkmaid's mother sung an answer to it, which was made by Sir Walter Raleigh in his younger days."

59. p. 42.—This is the song of the River-God to Amoret in "The Faithful Shepherdess".

119. p. 139.—Lamb has defined with precision the quality of Lord Brooke's singular genius, "frozen and made rigid with intellect". But among his love-poems there are one or two really simple pieces, as beautiful as the two I have given, besides the exquisite genre picture of "Myra" (No. 212). If I had allowed myself the licence of cutting anything, in the poems which I have chosen, this is the poem which I would most gladly have cut. The first three stanzas make a poem which seems to me perfect of its kind, and unlike any other poem. They are curiously modern, but in the last two stanzas the conceits of the period step in; and the poem, to modern senses, is spoilt.

135. p. 150.—The sestet of this sonnet reads as follows in the two editions of "Delia" of 1592, and in the edition of 1594:

"When thou, surcharged with burden of thy years,
Shalt bend thy wrinkles homeward to the earth,
When Time hath made a passport for thy fears,
Dated in age, the Kalends of our death;
But ah, no more. This hath been often told,
And women grieve to think they must be old."

I give the later and better text of the collected quarto of Daniel's poems of 1623.

180. p. 182.—To understand Donne, we must read not only Walton's incomparable life but the careful analysis of Mr. Gosse, in his "Life and Letters". This morbid, nervous, hesitating, intellectually dispassionate creature is indeed almost an unknown

person whom Mr. Gosse has discovered for us; and now at last we are able to understand the poems, with their complexities of passion, their monstrous agility of mind, their pedantic modernity, their ferocities and ecstasies and entanglements of sentiment. Donne is one of the worst and greatest poets in English literature, a poet unlike any other. He has written some of the most splendid single lines that were ever written, and hardly a stanza without a flaw. He has influenced at once Browning in "Sordello" and Swinburne in "Anactoria". His metrical experiments have never even yet done all they might for the loosening of metre. Such a line as:

"Drown my world with my weeping earnestly",

a line so beautiful, so expressive, so clear in scansion if one will only be content to read for the sense, has scarcely yet been recognized as a perfectly legitimate English verse. More than almost anyone, this "metaphysical" poet has written really direct love-poetry, and in every mood. He "can love both fair and brown", is "Love's martyr", "must love her that loves not me", realizes of love that "This no to-morrow hath, nor yesterday", scorns

"Whoever loves, if he do not propose
The right true end of love",

and, on occasion, "can forget the He and She" in an ecstasy no longer of the senses. And this poetry is full of "masculine persuasive force"; it has not, as the greater part of love-poetry has, a feminine pathos, but the passion of a man. The subtlety of a great brain waits upon a "naked thinking heart"; the result is a new kind of poetry, which Donne invented for himself and in which he has had no successor.

181. p. 183.—In the five sonnets which I have put after one another Spenser paints the complete mental portrait of a woman and the full spiritual likeness of his love for her. The "self-pleasing pride" of the one, her "scorn of base things", her innocent and dismaying "art of eyes", are not expressed by "a greater craftsman's hand", with more fidelity to "the life of things indeed", than the noble and lofty humbleness of the other. There is in this love-poetry none of the rapturous familiarity of the "Epithalamium", none of its certain and possessive delight; but there is a kind of piety which I find nowhere else.

The text follows the tiny and exquisite first edition of "Amoretti and Epithalamion", printed in 1595, one of the daintiest volumes of poetry ever printed in England.

201. p. 200.—It is often forgotten that Raleigh is a considerable English poet. His rough verse, which seems always so intent on saying a given thing with emphasis, is really poetry. It is a knotted and gnarled kind of poetry, and in the poem which is almost certainly his,

> "As you came from the Holy Land
> Of Walsinghame",

he has played remarkable variations on a kind of folk-tune; the kind of folk-tune which we get in Shakespeare's "How should I your true-love know?" Later on, Blake is to do a not wholly dissimilar kind of transposition, putting wild meanings into ballad-stanzas. In some other poems Raleigh has the same hard, tight, intellectual pathos. His personal humour speaks always with disconcerting directness; his character, crotchety and self-reliant.

214. p. 212.—The first and second stanzas of this song are quoted by Sir Toby and the clown in "Twelfth Night", ii. 3.

241. p. 240.—In this poem, for once, I have allowed myself to print the first, briefer, and better version, as it appeared in Puttenham's "Art of English Poesy" in 1589. In the "Arcadia" of 1590 there is a second stanza:

"His heart his wound received from my sight;
My heart was wounded with his wounded heart;
For as from me on him his hurt did light,
So still methought in me his hurt did smart:
Both, equal hurt, in this change sought our bliss:
My true-love hath my heart, and I have his."

242. p. 240.—This song is found in a MS. in the Bodleian, with the signature "Sir W. R." Raleigh's authorship cannot be considered certain, on external evidence; but can, I think, on internal.

246. p. 245.—This poem, intensely characteristic of Donne, and of Donne at his best, does not appear among his poems in any old edition. It was printed anonymously in Davison's "Poetical Rhapsody" (1602) and in "Wit Restored" (1658), and, under his name, in "The Grove" (1721), from a MS. belonging to Sir John Cotton in Huntingdonshire. I have followed this text (given by Mr. Chambers in the Muses' Library) except in the last line, where it seems to me that the reading of the "Poetical Rhapsody", "And so I both enjoy and miss her", is infinitely preferable to the reading, "And so enjoy her, and none miss her".

249. p. 247.—For the reading of "ripe" instead of "rich", in the third line of the second stanza of

this incomparable lyric from Captain Tobias Hume's "First Part of Airs" (1605), with which Mr. Bullen begins his "Lyrics from Elizabethan Song-Books", I am indebted to Mr. Bullen, who has not yet been able to make the correction in his own edition.

260. p. 257.—The eighth line of this song, from "The Sun's Darling", 1656, reads "There all but books of fancy's writing". Mr. Bullen queries the "but", and I have ventured to replace it by "the", which at least makes sense.

294. p. 300.—Many readings have been suggested for the opening lines of the second stanza of this song from "The Two Noble Kinsmen", a song whose beauty is not beyond the reach of Fletcher, though certainly not outside the manner of Shakespeare. The commonly accepted emendation is "harebells" instead of "her bells"; but, as Mr. Quiller Couch points out in the notes to his "Golden Pomp", all that is needed is to restore the semicolon of the original edition after "Ver", which allows "merry springtime's harbinger" to refer to the snowdrop, and not, as it would seem to do if only a comma were used, to the primrose.

305. p. 307.—I have followed Prof. Arber in printing in full, and restoring to its author, a poem usually printed as it stands, anonymously, in Martin Peerson's "Private Music" of 1620. As there printed, it contains only the first four stanzas, with no suggestion of its religious character. The poem is contained in Richard Verstegen's "Odes in imitation of the Seaven Penitential Psalmes, with sundry other Poemes and ditties tending to devotion and pietie . . . Imprinted Anno Domini M.D.C.I.", at Antwerp. It follows other poems to the Virgin, among which

are "The Fifteen Mysteries of the Rosarie, of Our Blessed Lady". There is no name on the title-page, but the dedication "To the Vertuous Ladies and Gentlewomen Readers of these Ditties" is signed "Yours in his best endeavours, R. V."

311. p. 316.—This splendid fragment (as it probably is, though it can well stand as a poem complete in itself) was found by Mr. Bullen in one of those Christ Church MSS. from which he has printed other lovely things, such as the intoxicating song "Hey nonny no!" (No. 12).

321. p. 325.—I found this grave epigram in Mr. Quiller Couch's anthology, who had it from Grosart's "Unique and Rare Books", 1879. It is from "Newe Sonets, and Pretie Pamphlets written by Thomas Howell, Gentleman", 1567.

359. p. 364.—Only Lamb may be allowed to praise the dirge in "The White Devil": "I never saw anything like this Dirge, except the Ditty which reminds Ferdinand of his drowned father in the Tempest. As that is of the water, watery; so this is of the earth, earthy. Both have that intenseness of feeling, which seems to resolve itself into the elements which it contemplates."

366. p. 369.—It is not certain whether this epitaph belongs in whole or part to Ben Jonson (as has generally been supposed) or to Browne of Tavistock (who seems to have more claim to it). Mr. Gordon Goodwin, in his edition of Browne in the Muses' Library, claims it for Browne on the authority of a MS. in the Library of Trinity College, Dublin, dating from the middle of the seventeenth century, where it is signed "William Browne", and of Aubrey

(" Natural History of Wiltshire", of about the same date), who quotes the first six lines as "made by Mr. Browne, who wrote the 'Pastorals'". They were not attributed to Jonson before Whalley's edition in 1756, where they are quoted incorrectly, and are inserted for the reason that they were "universally assigned" to him.

370. p. 371.—This poem is found in many MSS., including the "Reliquiae Wottonianae", where it is said to be by "Chidick Tychborn, being young and then in the Tower, the night before his execution". He was executed in 1586, together with Antony Babington, for participation in the plot on behalf of Mary Queen of Scots. He is one of the characters in Swinburne's "Mary Stuart".

378. p. 379.—In the original Quarto of Shakespeare's Sonnets the words "my sinful earth", which end the first line, are repeated by mistake at the beginning of the second line. Two words are thus evidently missing, and they have been supplied in many ways, none of which can ever be satisfactory or final. I have accepted Palgrave's improvement of the conjecture of Malone, "Fooled by those rebel powers", and printed, though with hesitation, "Foiled by these rebel powers".

# Index of Authors

# Index of First Lines

Nos. 34, 51, 55, 810,